# Return to Peterloo

Manchester Region History Review
Volume 23
2012

The 1989 Peterloo edition
of the Manchester Region History Review
is available online at:
http://www.hssr.mmu.ac.uk/mcrh/mrhr/back-issues-index/

ISSN 0952-4320

ISBN 978-1-85936-225-9

© Manchester Centre for Regional History, 2014

Typeset by Carnegie Book Production, Lancaster.
Printed and bound by Jellyfish Solutions.

# Contents

# Editorial

Robert
Poole

'The single most important event in the region's history' was how the editors of the *Manchester Region History Review* described the Peterloo massacre in the 1989 special edition, marking its one hundred and seventieth anniversary. 1989 was a special year in other ways not yet apparent when the *Review* came out in the late spring. The summer of picnics and wire-cutters on the Hungarian-Austrian border that set in train the events that would lead to the fall of the Berlin wall was getting underway, while in Britain the phenomenon that was later dubbed the 'second summer of love' was brewing in Manchester. The events of 1819 and 1989 were brought together earlier this year in the Library Theatre Company's striking production *Manchester Sound: the Massacre* in a former warehouse in the city's northern quarter, which contrasted the reform culture of 1819 with the rave culture of 1989.

1819 and 1989 came together in another way, for the historian E.P. Thompson, author of *The making of the English working class* with its gripping account of Peterloo, was in 1989 enjoying a year's research fellowship at the University of Manchester's History department, having spent much of the 1980s campaigning in both east and west for nuclear disarmament in Europe. It was however the established university's younger neighbour Manchester Polytechnic (now Manchester Metropolitan University) which had taken up the cause of regional and social history with its own recently launched *Manchester Region History Review*.

The 1989 Peterloo special issue of the *Review* (available at http://www.hssr.mmu.ac.uk/mcrh/mrhr/back-issues-index/) is now itself an historical artefact. Thompson's own 1969 essay, in the form of a destructive extended review of Robert Walmsley's *Peterloo: the case reopened*, was among the articles. Among the many contributors were the future professors John Belchem, Diana Donald and Neville Kirk, while among the editorial team were Terry Wyke, a contributor to this issue, Melanie Tebbutt, now Director of the Manchester Centre for Regional History, and John Pickstone, moving force behind the Manchester Histories Festival. The newly relocated Working Class Movement Library in Salford was profiled, while the Mechanics Institute Museum, later to develop into the People's History Museum, advertised a 170th-anniversary Peterloo exhibition at its premises on Princess Street. A full-page advert for Robert Reid's book *The Peterloo Massacre* quoted admiring reviews from (improbably) both Enoch Powell and Paul Foot.

As the bicentenary of Peterloo approaches this latest edition of the *Manchester Region History Review* is again devoted to Peterloo, keeping up the public history tradition of commissioning high-quality work for a wide readership. As in 1989 we cover history, literature, verse, images, artefacts, and institutions, as well as presenting some important new sources. The contributors are once again a range of established and up-and-coming scholars and people from outside academia, including volunteers at the 2012 Manchester Histories Festival. There is more emphasis than last time on literature (Alison Morgan and John Gardner), on gender (Alison Morgan and Ruth Mather), and on the afterlife of Peterloo as political commemoration (Matthew Roberts, Terry Wyke and Paul Fitzgerald).

Perhaps the biggest change since 1989 is the inclusion of essays on loyalism (Frank O'Gorman) and patriotism (Katrina Navickas). Manchester in the 1790s was as notable for loyalism and patriotism as for radicalism, a situation later reinforced by a generation of war against revolutionary and Napoleonic France. As war-weariness and then the post-war slump set in, the case for reform gained traction but the reformers had a lot of ground to win back. They had not only to reclaim a version of patriotism but to assert the right to be recognized as citizens, to occupy public space, and indeed to be in the political game at all. The sharpness of the authorities' response in 1819 showed how little scope there yet was for both loyalists and radicals to inhabit the public spaces of Manchester. The reform movement cannot be understood in isolation from the rest of the political landscape for its significance lay in the clash between loyalism and radicalism. Peterloo was an event not just in labour history but in British history.

Peterloo has been in the news with increasing regularity in the twenty-first century. On TV, Simon Schama's BBC *History of Britain* (2002), the Channel 4 series *Georgian Underworld* (2003) and the BBC Series *Elegance and Decadence: the Age of the Regency* (2011) have all made a feature of Peterloo. The Peterloo Memorial Campaign has been launched and a new plaque fixed to the former Free Trade Hall; annual marches and commemorations around 16 August have become one of Manchester's summer cultural fixtures; the Peterloo Relief Fund book at the John Rylands Library has been entered into the UNESCO 'Memory of the World' register; the extended People's History Museum has reopened with a feature on Peterloo at the entrance to its permanent galleries; the Peterloo Witness Project has gathered all 300-plus eye-witness accounts of the events of 1819; and this year the drama *Manchester Sound: the Massacre* and the electric reading of Shelley's Peterloo rap *The Masque of Anarchy* by Maxine Peake at the Manchester International Festival have attracted national attention. In 2014 the massive Central Library/Town Hall/St Peter's Square redevelopment is set to provide Manchester with a superb regional studies centre and archive on the site of St Peter's Field.

On the day of the 2013 anniversary Manchester City Council restated its commitment to a major memorial to Peterloo in the city centre, designed by a yet-unnamed but eminent artist with a record of public collaboration, to mark (in the Lord Mayor's words) 'sacrifices that were made by brave men and women in the fight for a free and fair society, not just at St Peter's Field but around the world.' Peterloo is back.

Robert Poole
August 2013

# What don't we know about Peterloo?

Robert
Poole

The Peterloo massacre of 1819 is one of the landmarks of British history. Notwithstanding the weeks of partisan legal argument and the decades of noisy disputes about who was responsible, the sheer quantity of evidence is exceptional and the basic facts have never been in serious doubt. The question as we approach its bicentenary is not 'what do we know about Peterloo?' but rather 'what don't we know?'

The massacre itself began shortly after 1 pm on Monday 16 August 1819, when troops under the authority of the Lancashire and Cheshire magistrates dispersed a rally of some 50–60,000 reformers on St Peter's Field, Manchester. It lasted just twenty minutes. When it was over some 650 people had been injured, many of them by sabres, and fifteen people lay dead or mortally wounded. Most independent witnesses were horrified, for there had not been any disturbance to provoke such an attack, but the authorities were convinced that a rebellion had been averted. The battle of Waterloo, the final victory of the allies over Napoleon, had been fought four years earlier; now, British troops were turned against their own people. It later turned out that all the Waterloo veterans present were among the reformers. First known as 'The Manchester massacre', within days the event had also been dubbed 'Peter-loo' and the name stuck. There could have been no clearer demonstration that the mass of the people were still regarded as subjects, not citizens.

The Manchester meeting was the acknowledged climax of a high-profile national series of mass rallies for parliamentary reform. The aim was to confront government with the irresistible physical presence of vast communities of reformers assembled to claim the status of citizens – to demonstrate, as Shelley afterwards put it, that 'Ye are many, they are few'. Nothing could have been more frightening to Manchester's high-Tory local government: what legitimate reason could non-electors have for assembling mob-handed? More than this, the rally took place in the capital of the new factory system, itself (ironically) neither incorporated nor represented in parliament – whatever its industrial reputation, there was nothing modern about Manchester's local government. Middle-class

and working-class reformers united in outrage, while for several months afterwards the state appeared to be threatened by armed rebellion from below. Peterloo was the bloodiest political event of the nineteenth century on English soil, but it could have been a great deal worse. Although the number of deaths was modest by the standards of other historical massacres (hundreds in Egypt in 2013, 8,000 at Srebenica in 1995, 200,000 or more at Nanking in 1937), the violence was deliberate, prolonged and exceptional by the standards of its day. Peterloo can be ranked alongside other large-scale protests which have preceded major reforms by a generation or so, such as Amritsar (1919), Sharpeville (1960), Soweto (1976), and (although it is too early to tell) Tiananmen Square (1988).

The significance of what happened in Manchester that day has been argued over ever since. It has been called a battle, a massacre, a tragedy, an incident, a blunder, and a misjudgement. The responsibility has been variously laid on the government, the Manchester authorities, the military (whether volunteers or regulars), the reform leadership, militant elements among the reformers, and on nobody at all. Peterloo has been claimed both as a catastrophic setback for the cause of reform and as a heroic first step on the long road to democracy. It has been the subject of numerous anniversary commemorations over the years, and of books, scholarly articles, exhibitions, novels, plays, paintings, songs and verses,

Figure 1: The yeomanry attack the hustings. Detail from a commemorative print by John Slack of Manchester. Manchester Libraries, Information and Archives, Manchester City Council. For the full print, see Fig. 1, p. 69

including perhaps the most powerful of all political poems, Shelley's 'Masque of Anarchy'. In some books on British history in the industrial revolution period it occupies a central place; in others, a passing mention. On our interpretation of Peterloo depends our whole view of the British state in this period: a ramshackle conglomerate of 'old corruption' and political reaction at loggerheads with its subjects, or a modernizing fiscal-military state commanding widespread loyalty. Historians of the labour movement have also differed widely over Peterloo. For E.P. Thompson in *The making of the English working class* – a classic account whose fiftieth anniversary was celebrated this year – it was the climax of a 'heroic age of popular radicalism' led by handloom weavers and other artisans. It has also been seen as an early example of class-conscious industrial militancy, or alternatively as an immature political convulsion beneath the notice of the connoisseur of true class struggle.[1] The only interpretation which has found very few serious supporters has been that of the authorities themselves: that it was a well-judged and proportionate response to a genuine threat of armed rebellion.[2]

It is strange that there should have been so much to dispute about Peterloo since some 300 eye-witness accounts survive, making it one of the best-documented events of the nineteenth century. The problem is perhaps that there is too much evidence, rather than too little, allowing some grounds to be found for practically any interpretation. So much of it has been available either in Manchester or in print that there has been no need for authors to foray into the correspondence between the Home Office and the local magistrates in The National Archives. In this essay I will try to short-circuit the traditional comparison of claim and counter-claim in order to look at the evidential landscape as a whole. First I will summarize the eye-witness evidence, then analyze it (for not all 'evidence' is equal) and look at roughly how it stacks up, before going on to suggest what we still don't know about Peterloo.

Eye-witness accounts of the St Peter's Field meeting are scattered far and wide in national and local archives.[3] Ten press reports appear to contain substantial eye-witness material. Then there are fifteen written eye-witness accounts, fourteen by individuals and one collective effort by the Manchester yeomanry, scattered across various archives and printed works. There are another 243 eye-witness testimonies printed in the published transcripts of proceedings at the three Peterloo-related trials: the inquest into the death of John Lees (1819), the trial of Henry Hunt and other radicals (1820), and the civil action of *Redford vs Birley* (1822). As some people gave evidence at more than one trial, these represent 212 individuals. Finally, the Home Office correspondence for 1819 contains another forty-two sworn testimonies of events on St Peter's Field collected by local magistrates and their associates in support of the authorities' case at these trials. Thirteen of these also gave testimonies to one of the trials, so we have twenty-nine new individuals in all. (There are also four accounts of the riots later that evening in the New Cross area, now the northern quarter, and fifty-three accounts of allegedly threatening radical activity in the weeks before and the days after Peterloo). All this is not counting reports collected second hand, or accounts of the sufferings of the hundreds of casualties, or the summaries of evidence in the Treasury Solicitors' papers which include reference to a number of witnesses who were not in the event called.[4] Excluding the peripheral and second-hand reports, there are (at the latest count) 310 eye-witness accounts of the march and massacre by 266 individuals. There can be few events of any kind in the nineteenth century recorded in so many eye-witness testimonies.

To take the original press accounts first, ten is a lot for a period when it was unusual for the national and regional newspapers to send reporters to distant events. *The Times* of London had John Tyas on the platform, while Edward Baines junior of the *Leeds Mercury* and John Smith of the *Liverpool Mercury* also provided extended on-the-spot accounts.[5] Several Manchester papers observed the rally, but their accounts were as polarized as Manchester politics. The radical *Manchester Observer* and the reform-minded *Manchester Gazette* provided good eye-witness accounts while the loyalist *Manchester Herald* and *Manchester Mercury* carried shorter, hostile reports, drawing largely on information from the magistrates. The *Manchester Courier* refused to print the account of its reporter Jeremiah Garnett and substituted part of the *Mercury*'s. Garnett was sacked, and went on to join John Taylor in founding the *Manchester Guardian.* Peterloo was thus a key event in the history of journalism as well as of politics. The *Manchester Observer* printed Garnett's account in a special series of publications entitled *Peterloo Massacre.*[6] Elsewhere the campaigning journalist Richard Carlile, an eye-witness, furnished a brief account in *Sherwin's Weekly Political Register*, which promptly changed its title to *The Republican*, but in general the radical press outside Manchester offered summary and commentary rather than direct reportage of the day's events; full evidence and analysis only came with the trials.[7]

Of the fifteen individual written accounts the best known is that of the Middleton radical leader Samuel Bamford, in his autobiography *Passages in the Life of a Radical.* Bamford is the principal source for several later accounts, such as Archibald Prentice's *Historical Sketches of Manchester* (1851) and Charles Dickens's piece in *All the Year Round* (1867). Other radicals present who left accounts included the orator Henry Hunt and Bamford's co-defendants George Swift and Joseph Healey, and Bamford's wife Jemima whose account Bamford included in his own memoir.[8] Three agents of the authorities offered written accounts: the mounted special constable Robert Mutrie,[9] Major Dyneley of the Royal Artillery,[10] and William Jolliffe, a lieutenant in the

Figure 2: 'The people cannot get away!' Another detail from the print by John Slack of Manchester, from a version printed on a fine calico handkerchief.
© Trustees of the British Museum

Hussars.[11] To these we should add the account of the loyalist cotton manufacturer Francis Phillips, who patrolled the area on horseback and published a polemical defence of the authorities.[12] Several independent observers wrote up accounts: the manufacturer Joseph Barrett, the middle-class reformer John Benjamin Smith, the Revd William Stanley, the Manchester bookseller James Weatherley, and (many years later) the Manchester engineer John Galloway.[13] Those by George Swift and Joseph Barrett are printed for the first time in this volume.

Among these witnesses-in-writing, the neutral observers such as Barrett and Stanley in general corroborate the accounts of the reformers, stressing the peaceful and even festive nature of the marches into Manchester, the lack of provocation offered by the crowd, and the aggressive behaviour of the yeomanry. The accounts by those close to the authorities generally have a different feel, insisting on the intimidatory character of the mass large rally and picking out instances of individuals carrying sticks, throwing stones, or offering threatening language, much of it after the troops moved in. The exception here is the hussar William Jolliffe, who, while defensive, is critical of the yeomanry and careful to describe only what he saw:

> The Hussars drove the people forward with the flats of their swords, but sometimes, as is almost inevitably the case when men are placed in such situations, the edge was used, both by the Hussars, and, as I have heard, by the yeomen also; but of this last part I was not cognizant, and believing though I do that nine out of ten of the sabre wounds were caused by the Hussars, I must still consider that it redounds to the humane forbearance of the men of the 15th that more wounds were not received.[14]

Jolliffe's fair-mindedness stands out among the overwhelmingly self-justifying accounts of other agents of the authorities.

The same polarization can be seen in the 243 eye-witness accounts contained in the printed accounts of the three trials – or rather, one inquest, one trial, and one civil action. The first of these, the inquest into the death of John Lees of Middleton, took place in the autumn of 1819 while feelings were high and before the authorities had managed to organize themselves for a legal battle. The reformers seized on the chance to demonstrate in public what had happened and mobilized a large number of witnesses from among the crowd and the immediate spectators. Of the sixty-five witnesses, nearly all testified to violence by the troops and even the special constables. Several saw the yeomanry attacking the hustings and cutting indiscriminately at the crowd: Elizabeth Farren described how she was deliberately cut on the head by a yeoman as she begged him to help her protect her child; Ann and Elizabeth Rayborn told how troops had smashed their way into their lodging house looking for people throwing stones, and had fired out of the window the pistol shots which were later blamed on the protestors; and the Manchester cutler Daniel Kennedy told how he had sharpened dozens of swords for members of the yeomanry in the weeks before Peterloo.[15] Robert Lancashire of Middleton declared:

> I came here to indemnify [i.e. testify], that I saw EDWARD MEAGHER cut a woman's breast open, who had a child in her arms; and she fell down with the child, and I picked her up. ... EDWARD MEAGHER was the man that did it; and I spoke to him while he did do it.[16]

Meagher, identified by several witnesses, stayed away from the hearing. Most poignantly of all, William Harrison, a friend of John Lees, told how he saw him five days before he died of his sabre wounds:

> I found him in the kitchen on a couch, with a face ... as white as a cap; and he then told me he was at the battle of Waterloo, but he never was in such danger there as he was at the meeting; for at Waterloo there was man to man, but at Manchester it was downright murder.[17]

The inquest had a negative result but this was against the run of the evidence, which was damning. Only six witnesses supported the authorities: three constables, two attorneys and an innkeeper, all effectively in positions of dependence for their livelihoods. They produced little of any force or relevance. The coroner, Thomas Ferrand of Rochdale, clearly uncomfortable with public scrutiny, consistently used procedural devices to exclude evidence, prevent the naming of suspects, stop the jury from viewing the body, and generally restrict the scope of the investigation. The inquest collapsed in chaos without a verdict when the proceedings were declared void by the court of King's Bench. This outcome, while embarrassing, suited the authorities. A majority of the jurors afterwards declared that if allowed they would have returned a verdict of wilful murder.[18]

The next courtroom test was the trial of Henry Hunt, Samuel Bamford and eight other radical leaders in York in March 1820. Two of the six witnesses for the authorities at the Lees inquest – an attorney and a head constable – gave evidence at York, but only one of the witnesses for the reformers, the Manchester merchant John Shuttleworth. Travel to York for several days was beyond the means of any of the humble witnesses to the death of John Lees, but Samuel Bamford managed to organize a convoy of other witnesses on foot across the Pennines. Eighty-five witnesses appeared in all, with the defence outnumbering the prosecution in both quantity and quality of evidence. The guilty verdict at the York trial has left an impression of wrong-doing by the defendants, but in fact half were acquitted and the other five were found guilty on the only one of the six charges that did not require evidence of actual disorder: that of intention to foster sedition.[19]

We do not need to rehearse the evidence in detail in order to come to a conclusion, for we have the private conclusions of the government solicitor George Maule who followed every minute of the proceedings. A key moment was the psychological collapse of Joseph Nadin, Manchester's deputy constable, who was a key witness for the claim that the constables had been forcibly prevented from serving a warrant on Hunt at the hustings, making military assistance necessary to support the law.[20] Arrogant and unused to being challenged, Nadin, wrote Maule, 'was in such a state of mind as to make it impossible with any degree of prudence to venture upon his testimony'. After hearing the witnesses for the defence Maule despaired of securing any convictions at all:

> I must confess that upon the evidence as it stands unless the assembly was in its original formation unlawful there are no circumstances of insult or violence on the part of the people to make it so. The evidence uniformly agrees that the people assembled were peaceable in their demeanour, save as to shouting ... Our case will no doubt go to the Jury on the question of the unlawfulness of the assembly originally, or its tendency to create a rational alarm, but upon this latter point there is a great body of evidence for the defendants negativing the existence of reasonableness of any such apprehension.[21]

This was quite an admission for it conceded the heart of the authorities' case: the rally at St Peter's Field was not in itself seditious, nor did the behaviour of the demonstrators make it so. This is not to say that there was no case for any intervention but that it should have taken the form of individual arrests rather than an assault on the reformers as a body. It follows that it was not the reformers but the authorities who had breached the King's peace. When the chairman of the magistrates, the over-promoted and inexperienced William Hulton, sought to save his reputation by arguing that he had only ordered in the troops once the yeomanry had come under sustained and unprovoked armed attack from demonstrators armed with stones and pistols, his evidence was torn apart in cross-examination by Henry Hunt.[22]

The reformers' third opportunity in court came with an action for damages pursued by the injured Thomas Redford of Middleton against Hugh Hornby Birley, captain of the Manchester yeomanry, and three of its members.[23] These included the trumpeter Edward Meagher, who in the meantime had been in court accused of taking pot-shots with his rifle at the angry crowd gathered outside his windows in Deansgate. The case of *Redford vs Birley* was heard at Lancaster in April 1822, with ninety-five witnesses in all. By a great effort the reformers – who were this time the plaintiffs rather than the defendants – mustered fourteen witnesses who had testified at either the Lees inquest or the Hunt trial, matching the fourteen who were reappearing for the authorities. Sixty-seven new voices gave evidence in this determined push on behalf of the victims to bring their uniformed assailants to justice. The magistrates mounted their own push in defence of their yeomanry colleagues.

Once again, the verdict in favour of the authorities went against the run of the evidence. The defence lawyers spent much of the time arguing that the meeting was seditious in purpose, and that the magistrates had acted reasonably in calling in the military. That being so, explained the official report, 'The question for the jury was … whether the defendants were properly acting in aid of the magistrates; and if, in so acting without excess, they committed the acts complained of no action for trespass would lie.'[24] The reformers' lawyers argued that the yeomanry had acted with excess and (according to a count by E.P. Thompson) brought forward twenty-nine independent witnesses, including three journalists and three ministers of religion, who had seen no evidence of resistance by the crowd before the yeomanry attacked. The defence produced seventeen who did claim to have seen stones and sticks thrown from the crowd before the yeomanry attack, twelve of whom were magistrates, police, special constables and lawyers.[25] The overwhelming impression of the independent witnesses at *Redford vs Birley*, as at the John Lees inquest, is of a partisan Yeomanry who had run out of control.

*Redford vs Birley* took place three years after Peterloo, and the magistrates had been able to orchestrate dependent witnesses in a way which they had not managed at the Lees inquest and even the York trial. The evidence for this is to be found in the Home Office disturbances papers in The National Archives at Kew, where many of the original witness statements survive. Many of these statements were gathered in October and November 1819 in preparation for the York trial, but the failure of much of the prosecution case to stick at York prompted another round of evidence-gathering in the spring of 1820.[26] As the government solicitor George Maule privately conceded at the York trial: 'The fact is our opponents are not only too numerous but also too much of partizans to allow us to cope with them. If we had called twenty more witnesses they would without difficulty have doubled our number, and our testimony would have been met in all parts with contrary evidence.'[27] There are twenty-seven further accounts by magistrates, constables and other official witnesses and a further fifteen accounts by independent witnesses.[28] All were gathered months after the event and all conveniently focused on the same few points required by the authorities: alleged threats and intimidation by marchers coming to the meeting and stone-throwing at the meeting, with one or two unspecific claims of pistol shots heard. Eleven of these official witnesses went to either the York trial or

*Redford vs Birley* in Lancaster, but only two of the independent ones. This suggests that the authorities felt that independent witnesses might waver under cross-examination; they preferred to construct a well-rehearsed block of evidence from figures of authority and to challenge the jury to disbelieve them.

Of course, numbers alone cannot decide truth. Nor is a trial simply a process arbitrating upon evidence. Fair-minded modern educators tend to set up historical issues as an argument with two sides, assuming a rough equality of entitlement, and then to seek rational ways of arbitrating between them. If there is violence it is assumed to have been unintended, and (rather as in dealing with children's quarrels) emphasis is placed on the question of who cast the first stone. Those present at the time may not have shared these comfortable assumptions. A court case is more like a series of manoeuvres between combatants than a dispute between philosophers. To assess the contest of evidence that was going on at the three trials we need to ask: what exactly was each side setting out to prove?

For the reformers, the answer was simple: each trial was a stage upon which to broadcast publicly the violent conduct of the magistrates and the troops, especially the yeomanry, and so to vindicate the cause of reform. In the first of these aims they largely succeeded, for the tales of injury and abuse were numerous, moving, and hard to contradict. This strategy did not require any systematic selection and packaging of evidence, merely a lot of it from plainspoken and (in the old sense) disinterested witnesses. The authorities, although always ready to play down the number of casualties, spent relatively little time arguing over the human consequences of Peterloo. At the Lees inquest they simply tried to obstruct inquiries and in this they succeeded, though at the cost of incurring some odium. At *Redford vs Birley* by contrast those defending the yeomanry spent quite a lot of effort trying to show that they were responding to volleys of stones, making enough headway to give the jury enough grounds for doubt to avoid a verdict for the plaintiffs. But this was because one of the legal points at issue was whether the yeomanry had been 'acting without excess', and provocation was therefore a useful defence. The main argument of the authorities was always that the meeting itself had been unlawful, and that both the troops and magistrates had therefore been acting lawfully in dispersing it, whatever the consequences. Prosecution and defence were not testing out matching arguments but rather manoeuvring over the grounds for decision.

Behind this strategy was the legal advice supplied by the government. This is how the Home Office had summed up the law on unlawful assembly in 1818:

> Any meeting whatsoever of great numbers of people with such Circumstances of Terror as cannot but endanger the public peace and raise

fears and jealousies among the Kings subjects, seems properly to be called an unlawful assembly, as where great numbers complaining of a common grievance meet together <u>armed in a warlike manner</u> in order to consult together concerning the most proper means of recovering their Interests for no one can foresee what may be the Event of such an assembly.

The actual test for an unlawful assembly was that it should be conducted 'in such a manner as is apt to raise a terror in the people'. (Emphasis in the original.) The test for the more serious offence of riot was either actual violence, or 'if a number of men assemble <u>with arms in terrorem populi</u> tho' no act is done it is a riot'.[29] Before the Manchester meeting the magistrates accordingly collected numerous sworn statements of respectable people who declared themselves alarmed at the preparations of the reformers, and on the day rounded up by arrangement dozens of gentlemen who signed a prepared statement of alarm. Many more such statements, all in similar wording, were gathered afterwards.[30]

In the run-up to the meeting the authorities found another way of declaring the meeting illegal, for its original intention was to repeat the action of the Birmingham meeting and elect two 'legislatorial attorneys' – unofficial MPs – to represent the interests of Manchester to the House of Commons. The magistrates issued a notice declaring the meeting illegal and warning people that they would attend 'at their peril'.[31]

Such a meeting would have been illegal and the radicals backed down, rewording the notices to declare that they would merely *'consider the* PROPRIETY *of adopting the most* LEGAL *and effectual means of obtaining a reform'* and putting back the date so that the new meeting could not be equated with the old one.[32] The Home Secretary, Lord Sidmouth, then advised the magistrates to back down:

> His Lordship thinks that it would be imprudent to act up to the Spirit of the Advertisement ... But even if they should utter Sedition or proceed to the election of a Representative Lord Sidmouth is of opinion that it will be the wisest course to abstain from any endeavour to disperse the Mob, unless they should proceed to Acts of Felony or Riot. We have the strongest Reason to believe that Hunt means to preside & to deprecate disorder.[33]

The next day, however, Sidmouth wrote again to the magistrates. 'There seems no reason to doubt that the ultimate object of the disaffected is treasonable', he agreed, but warned that this would be difficult to prove in court:

New Bailey Court-House,
SATURDAY, 31st JULY, 1819

WHEREAS

It appears by an Advertisement in the "Manchester Observer" Paper. OF THIS DAY, THAT A PUBLIC AND

## Illegal MEETING,

IS CONVENED

FOR MONDAY,

THE 9th DAY OF AUGUST NEXT, TO BE HELD ON THE AREA. Near St. PETERS CHURCH, in Manchester,

WE, the undersigned Magistrates acting for the Counties Palatine of Lancaster and Chester, do hereby Caution all Persons to abstain,

At their Peril

FROM ATTENDING SUCH

## ILLEGAL MEETING.

| William Hulton | J. Holme. |
| James Norris, | H. Marsh, |
| John Entwisle | Trafford Trafford, |
| William Marriott, | Ralph Fletcher. |
| Thomas William Tatton. | |

WARDLE, PRINTER, 94 PALL PLACE, MANCHESTER.

Figure 3: The 'abstain at their peril' notice. In seeking to deter people from joining the rally the magistrates inadvertently conveyed the opposite message, but the threat was clear enough. John Ryland's Library special collections, Manchester

If the meeting is not convened for the unlawful purpose, the Illegality will not commence until the purpose is developed, and of course after the Crowd has been collected; when it must be a Question of Prudence and Expediency, to be decided by the Magistrates on the spot, whether they should proceed to disperse the persons assembled. Lord Sidmouth has no doubt that the Question will be judiciously decided by the Magistrates of Manchester.[34]

In making their decision, the magistrates would have been emboldened by Sidmouth's previously stated belief that 'your Country [i.e. county] will not be tranquillized, until Blood shall have been shed either by the Law or the sword', and by his private hint that they could always 'rely on Parliament for an indemnity'.[35]

All this explains why the magistrates' principal strategy, both in preparing for the meeting and in justifying their conduct afterwards, was to argue that the St Peter's Field meeting was unlawful, and to offer a long parade of loyal citizens declaring their own alarm and terror in order to prove the point. Further evidence of actual riot was not essential, and it was not forthcoming. In any case, to prove riot it was not necessary to demonstrate actual violence but only that demonstrators were carrying stones or weapons, implying a riotous disposition. As the ground had been cleared of stones before the meeting it was argued that any stones thrown must have been carried there. In short, the evidence collected by the authorities was dictated by what they needed to collect in order to demonstrate that the meeting was unlawful as defined by the Home Office.

How did this evidence hold up in court? Claims by loyalist witnesses that many demonstrators had carried large sticks and clubs were, as we have seen, discredited at the York trial. Although some marchers seem to have brought sticks to walk with, and a few to have waved them, far more impressive was the evidence of the many who had left their sticks behind in order to avoid offering provocation. The authorities were belatedly able to elicit testimony of stones having been thrown at the yeomanry in time for *Redford vs Birley*, but by this time it was easy for memories about the timing to become blurred; no-one bothered denying that some stones had been thrown at the yeomanry after their attack, but the significant question was whether the stone-throwing had come first.

The magistrates initially suggested that deputy constable Nadin and the special constables had been assailed with stones before the troops moved in, and the chairman of the magistrates William Hulton maintained so for the rest of his life. The key witness, Nadin himself, made no such claim. He baulked at giving evidence in York, and at *Redford vs Birley* counsel for the authorities acknowledged that his account of being attacked with stones referred to a different incident several days before.[36] The yeomanry themselves, in a lengthy apologia probably drafted by Hay, claimed this:

They struck no blow at any individual 'till they were assailed by the Mob. Before the rear of the Column had actually reached the Hustings Stones and other Missiles were thrown at them and this mode of attack was afterwards increased to such a degree that it became necessary in self defence to resist it.[37]

The stones however had come from a distance whereas those sabred were close at hand, which perhaps explains why the point was not pressed in court. Independent witnesses were convinced that the yeomanry had begun using their swords on their way towards the hustings and had rioted once they reached them. The yeomanry themselves emphasized that the main justification for their action was not direct self-defence but rather fear: 'The fact of the Magistrates having given at this point of time orders to Colonel L'Estrange to disperse the Mob not only shews that the yeomanry did not stand alone in their apprehension of the danger but furnishes a complete justification of their conduct.'[38] As with riot, it was *fear* of violence rather than actual violence that the authorities used to justify their actions.

A key figure here is the special constable Robert Mutrie. His testimony was cited by the historian Philip Lawson as evidence that 'Everyone and his dog carried some sort of weapon at Peterloo ... Armed radicals in the crowd stood around the hustings, and as soon as the yeomanry charged and attempted to snatch Hunt, they were met with swinging clubs and a barrage of stones.' Mutrie, insisted Lawson, although a special constable, was a dispassionate witness with 'no axe to grind.'[39] But on Mutrie's own account he had placed himself at the head of the yeomanry as they advanced on the hustings, and taken a central part in the violent confrontation with rioters at New Cross later that evening (which Lawson mistook for a 'mopping up operation in the streets surrounding St Peter's Field'). He was known and reviled by the radicals for his evidence at the John Lees inquest, and pistols were fired into his house one night. He supported the yeomanry's claim that they had not used their sabres until they were attacked by stones, but during a grinding cross-examination was forced to back down on one of his principal claims.

> Q. The people were not armed?
> A. I think not.
> Q. Have you any doubt about it?
> A. I think they were not.
> Q. Do you mean to say you saw any weapon in the hands of any of them?
> A. No, I do not think they had any weapons.
> Q. Don't you know they had not?
> A. Very well, Sir; then I admit it.

Mutrie also admitted that he was among the special constables blindly attacked by the yeomanry near the hustings: hit with flat of a sword he shouted, 'damn you, Sir, can you not see?' Mutrie was not called to either of the subsequent trials, for his evidence was hardly helpful to the prosecution case.[40]

Both sides gathered evidence to a brief. Samuel Bamford's 25-point instructions from the defence solicitors included the following specifications:

> To prove the peaceful demeanour of the different parties from the various townships, in the approach to Manchester. – To prove the proportion of those who carried sticks, – the description of such sticks as were carried, and the absence of all weapons of offence or defence. ... To shew the peaceable and quiet conduct of the persons at the meeting, before the military arrived. ... To shew the violence and inhuman conduct of the magistrates in directing, and the yeomanry in effecting the dispersion of the meeting.[41]

There was some amusement at the York trial when it became apparent that Bamford had drilled his neighbour James Dyson in his evidence over the peaceful demeanour of the march as it moved off from Middleton.[42] All that said, however, the reformers outgunned the authorities in both the quality and quantity of eye-witness evidence, as was privately acknowledged by the government, and their failure to carry legal points and verdicts was no measure of the overall balance of the debate.

In mid-November 1819, the home secretary remained as dissatisfied as anybody about the strength of the magistrates' case and wrote confidentially to Hay:

> I wish to know with more precision than is stated in any Document, which is at present in my possession, the manner in which the Manchester Yeomanry formed near the House where the Magistrates were assembled on the 16th of August, and whether they advanced in <u>Files</u>, and at what rate; the exact time when, and the circumstances under which, they began to use force, and how long the use of force was continued by them and the other Troops. I am also anxious to know whether any, and which of the Magistrates, besides Mr Hulton, observed the danger to which the Manchester Yeomanry were exposed at the time when, under the impression of that danger and the disorder and rioting which appeared, he called upon Colonel L'Estrange to employ the Military in dispersing the Meeting. I should also be obliged to you, if you would let me know, as far as you can ascertain it, the number of Persons who were maimed or considerably hurt on that day, distinguishing those who suffered from the Weapons of the Troops. The Number of those who lost their Lives, including these, was I think four.[43]

It seems extraordinary that, having received so much evidence from the magistrates, Sidmouth himself should have had so weak a grasp of the basics about Peterloo.

Whether in press reports, individual written accounts, or courtroom testimony, the body of evidence put forward by the authorities was recognizably distinct. The trial evidence was dominated by uniformed witnesses, special constables, lawyers, publicans, and others with links to the local establishment. It tended to home in repetitively on points of evidence dictated by legal advice from the Home Office; it was often gathered late and carefully selected, with the witnesses' links to the magistrates discreetly concealed; and it tended to be either exposed in cross-examination or outweighed by contrary evidence from more independent witnesses. Neutral witnesses from the middle classes, such as journalists and clergymen, generally corroborated the reformers rather than the authorities.

We can go further. The collection, in advance of the Manchester rally, of evidence designed to demonstrate that the gathering was illegal is itself evidence that the authorities anticipated sending in the troops. The authorities were genuinely fearful about the drilling practised in advance on local moors, but the collection of dozens of expressions of preconceived alarm before the start of the meeting were part of the authorities' preparations for the use of force against a meeting which they had already decided was a stage in a planned rising. The question of who started the violence on the day was a propaganda sideshow. The core of the magistrates' case was not that they had responded to actual violence but that they had acted to pre-empt expected violence. Military intervention was principally justified not by what had happened on the field but by the claim that the meeting itself was unlawful – that it was already riotous in character (albeit without any actual disturbance) before the speeches began. This enabled the organisers to be indicted for intending to provoke riot, an intention demonstrated (in the magistrates' view) by their insistence on delivering inflammatory speeches to an excitable mass of non-electors.

There is, then, no need for argument about the broad outlines of Peterloo: whether or not the magistrates were responsible for it, whether the government was implicated, whether there was a massacre or a battle, and so on. These questions, past staples of school essays and textbook exercises, are among the things that we do know, more or less. The evidence of the three hundred eye-witnesses and the six hundred or more casualties tells heavily against the authorities, at least as far as the events of the day are concerned. So: what *don't* we know about Peterloo?

Since any explanation for a massacre must lie principally with the perpetrators, we have to admit that it remains hard to explain why the magistrates were apparently so set upon confrontation, and why they failed to respond to the Home Office's late change of stance against forceful intervention. It was a high-risk strategy, in some ways out of character for a somewhat jittery and alarmist group of men. In 1817 they had relied upon police work, informers and the experienced regular troops stationed in the north to frustrate the march of the Blanketeers on London and to entrap the most militant radicals in a plan for an armed rising.[44] Some of the leading magistrates had a background

Figure 4: 'A view of St Peter's Plain, Manchester...' Engraved by J. Sudlow from a drawing by T. Whaite; published Manchester, October 1819. Manchester Archives and Local Studies image no. M07592

in the suppression of the 1798 Irish rebellion and its aftermath, as Katrina Navickas has shown, so tended to think in military rather than political terms.[45] As well as dominating Manchester's ramshackle institutions of local government they associated in a secretive network of orange and masonic lodges, and some had a high-Tory and even Jacobite political background that encouraged them to see themselves as an inner governing elite responsible to no-one. William Hay and his colleagues seem to have been genuinely convinced that the outwardly peaceful character of the Peterloo rally was merely a cloak for a deep-laid rebellion in the near future, and that as in 1817 serious political disorder had been averted by prompt and forceful action. Even so, to send in amateur local troops against the largest mass gathering Manchester had ever seen, and before any of the expected trouble had materialized, was quite a thing, and we still need a full explanation for it.

It is also difficult to know how to fit the Peterloo rally, and indeed the whole mass platform movement, into the social history of the period.[46] Activists on the left, who have (with justification) embraced Peterloo as part of the 'making of the English working class', often think in terms of a continuing 'progressive' movement for social and political change starting (as the People's History Museum mural has it) with the two-shot 'big bang' of the French and industrial revolutions. But in what ways was the radical movement actually a product of the industrial revolution or an accessory of 'progress'? Taking place as it did in the capital of the factory system, Peterloo has naturally been incorporated into narratives about the effects of the industrial revolution and the rise of the modern industrial city. The authorities however saw the march to

St Peter's Field very much as an invasion of 'strangers' from the 'country districts' an hour or two away from Manchester itself, and the evidence of the casualty lists for once bears them out. It was carried principally by handloom weavers from the surrounding towns, villages and folds rather than by factory workers from Manchester, although Mancunians from the inner industrial districts, particularly Ancoats, were also well represented among the casualties.[47] Handloom weavers could extend their weekend to a Monday but factory workers could not; in Joseph Barrett's account, it was the troops who broke into a factory with a radical reputation to force the workers out to face the music. Radicals had sought to turn the Manchester region's spinners and weavers' strikes of 1818 into political channels, but had had only limited success as the strikes began to collapse.[48]

The involvement of women in the radical movement of 1819 also resists simple characterization. The presence of women on the march and of activists such as Mary Fildes and Elizabeth Gaunt in the thick of the action, the role played by organisations of female reformers in Stockport and Blackburn, the poisonous satires directed at them, the disproportionate violence meted out to the women at Peterloo, the moral force of the images of female suffering that it generated, and the astonishing speech of the female figure of Hope in Shelley's 'Masque of Anarchy', all suggest that something unusual was happening in the radical movement. Historians such as Dorothy Thompson, Anna Clark, Linda Colley and Paul A. Custer have shown how any kind of female involvement in politics carried great significance in this conservative period, and how the culture of the handloom weaving districts in particular fostered new and creative forms of female political engagement.[49] At the same time, the tacit decision of the radical movement to avoid the controversial demand for women to vote relegated women to a role as cheerleaders for the franchise to be exercised by their menfolk on behalf of their families, just as it seemed that the movement could aim for more. How far did the presence of women at St Peter's Field, and their brutal treatment by the troops, influence the direction of the female reform movement?

Finally, it may seem odd but we do not we really know what the radicals thought they were doing at Peterloo. They could not possibly have anticipated the actual outcome: a heroic failure that would in time become seen as one of many incremental steps towards modern democracy. The nearest available models in 1819 were all revolutionary: the American revolutions of the generation of 1776; the initially hopeful French revolution of 1789, with its bloody and chaotic aftermath; and the dramatic English 'Glorious Revolution' of 1688–9 (and its Scottish and Irish counterparts) that had forged the ingenious constitutional settlement which radicals now saw as mutating into 'old corruption'. The hope of the Blanketeers of 1817 seems to have been for a mass march on London which would snowball until it climaxed in a decisive confrontation; the crown would give way and the lost rights of the people would be restored, rather on the model of 1688. Quite how the 'mass platform' gatherings of 1819 were intended to translate into political change is unclear, for there were as yet no democratic mechanisms by which mass pressure could be made effective. The established consensus was that turning up mob-handed was not legitimate politics. How were boots on the ground expected to translate into political change?

The Manchester massacre effectively channelled a powerful mass movement for radical reform into a crusade for justice for the victims and liberty for the prisoners. Government meanwhile had (happily enough) boxed itself into a corner where it had to justify its claims of widespread sedition by bringing in emergency legislation to limit the public right to meet, march, organize and write about politics – the notorious Six Acts. Had the Manchester meeting demonstrated, to the amazement of high Tories, that large numbers of working people could rally peacefully for a political purpose without erupting into riot, what would the reformers' next step have been, and how would the authorities have countered it? How far could the radicals have gone in their bold campaign to reclaim the cultural paraphernalia of patriotism, constitutionalism and liberty for the cause of reform?[50] Would there have been a Great Reform Act of 1820 rather than 1832, or a second Glorious Revolution, or decades of self-renewing conservative hegemony, or just more repression? One thing that we don't know about Peterloo is what would have happened if it hadn't happened, for we are still living in its aftermath.

# Manchester loyalism in the 1790s

Frank
O'Gorman

Manchester rose to greatness during the period of the industrial revolution, and, as a consequence, has attracted the attention of historians of all persuasions. This is entirely unsurprising in view of its size and rapidly expanding population, its geographic situation at the centre of a circle of numerous textile and other industrial towns, and, not least, because of its dominance by a commercial middle class. Manchester was the central hub of the economy, and increasingly, the politics, of the north west of England. And by the end of the eighteenth century, it was certainly beginning to write its own political agenda. That political agenda has usually been taken to be progressive and reformist. In particular, the clubs, the ideologies and individuals demanding the reform of parliament and a wide range of social and economic reforms have not been without their chroniclers.[1] Yet there were few places in Britain which opposed that progressive agenda as strongly as Manchester and for so long. Quite simply, Manchester became the pre-eminent centre of patriotism and, more specifically, of what historians have come to term 'loyalism' in the north west of England. It will be the purpose of this essay to consider the experiences of these loyalist anti-reformers who invoked the spirit of patriotism with which to oppose those who wished to change the status quo both in Manchester and, more broadly, across the country.

Historians have traditionally been hostile to loyalism. Given the liberal and, until recently, leftist bias of many historians, loyalism was traditionally dismissed as either reactionary bigotry, constitutional platitude or the consequence of some kind of intimidatory 'hegemony'. Indeed, until the 1960s it was scarcely considered a suitable subject for discussion or even for research. On the basis of a handful of examples, E.P. Thompson dismissed the loyalists as upper class reactionaries who pushed Pitt into a 'white terror' of social and legal intimidation.[2] Most writers have followed Thompson's lead. Eugene Black and Donald Ginter agreed that it was essentially a panic-stricken upper-class response to fears for the security of property.[3] Even more balanced treatments of loyalism, such as those of Harry Dickinson and Robert Dozier, which rest on respectable mountains of research, still accept that the dynamic of loyalism was to be found in its elite motivations.[4] And even the most recent, and in many respects, most impressive treatment of the subject, by Nicholas Rogers, finds it difficult to avoid the conclusion that loyalism played largely on the politics of fear.[5] And while other writers have pointed to other qualities, such as patriotism, civic loyalty and religion, perhaps the most balanced view of loyalism is that pronounced by David Eastwood as 'an accommodation between an elitist state struggling for survival and the broad mass of the people'.[6] In any case, practically all historians recognize that loyalism is a respectable, indeed, central subject in any discussion of public opinion, reform, national identity and a number of other issues.

One can now go much further. The great effusion of loyalist sentiment in the 1790s was far from being a novel and totally spontaneous phenomenon. The loyalism of that period had been carefully rehearsed on several occasions in earlier decades, indeed, in rallying their counties and towns in times of emergency. The propertied classes of Hanoverian England were simply doing what they had done in times of crisis ever since the sixteenth century. In 1688–9, 1714–16, 1744–6, 1779–84 and now in the 1790s the Hanoverian political system had been plunged into thoroughgoing crises of legitimacy and security, generating on all these occasions some kind of loyalist reaction. For example, the '45 had seen Loyal Associations adopting civilian as well as political functions, spawning a nationwide pro-Hanoverian Association which as well as protecting the monarch and defending the security of the country, even encouraged the manufacture and purchase of British products and discouraged the purchase of French products and, in addition, provided financial and other resources with which to confront the rebellion. Nor did they neglect the ritual element, celebrating the birthday of George II with unusual vigour on 30 October 1745 while effigies of the Pope and the Pretender were burned throughout England. The loyalism of the 1790s, then, was merely the most recent, and arguably the most spectacular, incidence of an almost cyclical pattern of political and social self-preservation.

What happened in Manchester in the 1790s, then, was a provincial element in an almost cyclical national experience. At first, it may seem strange that Manchester should have experienced loyalism with such intensity given its own political backwardness. Its political institutions were in serious need of reform. Manchester was not represented in parliament and those who enjoyed the vote used it in other boroughs or, more frequently, in the (rarely contested) county constituencies of Lancashire and Cheshire. The town lacked corporate status and thus had no oligarchical corporation that protected and regulated its trade. In default of a municipal corporation the town's government consisted of a Court Leet which was presided over by the steward of the lord of the

Figure 1: 'The Contrast' (1792), by Thomas Rowlandson. Loyalism deployed novel images of the French Revolution, but also drew on a longstanding, all-party tradition of British patriotism. Britannia still carries a cap of liberty on a pole, the Roman symbol of the freed slave; this was adopted by the revolutionaries in France and was shortly afterwards replaced on the British penny by the trident, symbol of seapower. © Trustees of the British Museum

THE CONTRAST
1792

BRITISH LIBERTY.

FRENCH LIBERTY

| RELIGION.             MORALITY. | ATHEISM             PERJURY |
| LOYALTY OBEDIENCE TO THE LAWS | REBELLION TREASON ANARCHY MURDER |
| INDEPENDANCE PERSONAL SECURITY | EQUALITY MADNESS CRUELTY INJUSTICE |
| JUSTICE INHERITANCE PROTECTION | TREACHERY INGRATITUDE IDLENESS |
| PROPERTY INDUSTRY NATIONAL PROSPERITY | FAMINE NATIONAL & PRIVATE RUIN. |
| HAPPINESS | MISERY |

WHICH IS BEST

manor. It met only twice yearly and devolved power over the markets and highways to a 'jury' of twelve individuals. The chief officer in Manchester was the boroughreeve whose functions were largely honorific. This leisurely regime did not exclude outsiders and a wide variety of people, such as English and Scottish Dissenters, Irish Catholics, Jews and other European immigrants were able to ply their trades in the town. It was inevitable that discontent with this administrative inertia would sooner or later become evident.

Nevertheless, there was before 1789 little to suggest that Manchester was to become the scene of an epic struggle between the forces of reform and those of loyalism. There was, for example, little popular interest in the city in the great issues and interests which were evinced by the American War of Independence (1775–83). The first signs of strongly and consistently organized public opinion occur over the issue of the reform of the slave trade. In the later 1780s political opinion in Manchester was dominated by an anti-slavery society, formed in 1787 and led by Thomas Walker, a cotton merchant and later reformer. This combined a wide range of opinion, which joined together to submit a petition to parliament, signed by over 10,000 signatures in 1788. However, these divisions were revealed when over 4,000 signatures were attached to a counter-petition. Such stirrings of public participation were underlined by the celebrations on the occasion of the centenary of the Glorious

Revolution (1788–9) which aroused much excitement in Manchester. This was quickly followed by the reaction in Manchester to the illness of King George III in the winter of 1788–9 and the celebrations which greeted his recovery in March 1789. This so-called 'Regency Crisis' marked a significant alignment, when Manchester's Tories and Whigs divided along party lines, to some extent anticipating the future conflict between reformers and conservative loyalists. Yet, for the moment, these were purely political disagreements among the town's leading families. They did not cause permanent divisions amongst the townspeople at large. There seemed nothing paradoxical in the Lancashire and Cheshire dissenters celebrating King George's recovery while continuing to press for the repeal of the Test and Corporation Acts, which imposed a sacramental, Anglican test upon every holder of any office in church and state and imposed the oaths of supremacy and allegiance.[7] And indeed it was the campaigns for repeal in 1787 and, more importantly, 1790 which were to cause deep and long-lasting divisions. This provoked an ugly Anglican backlash throughout the country and, in Manchester, the establishment of a Church and King Club in March 1790.

The emergence of a Church and King Club marks the first signs of an organized loyalist movement in Manchester.[8] The ancient rallying cry of 'Church and King' had been heard ever since the Reformation of the sixteenth century when political and social stability were threatened and it was now to be heard with some intensity during the coming years in Manchester and throughout the country. Yet old Church and King loyalism was to be transformed into something more dramatic, more comprehensive and sharper. It was seen in the early hostility displayed to the words and actions of reformers who advocated not only the repeal of the Test and Corporation Acts but the reform of parliament and the ending of corruption. This was next evident in the almost morbid interest that attached to the sufferings of the king of France after the flight to Varennes in June 1791 when he was captured and subsequently put on trial, to be executed in early 1793. Furthermore, Manchester shared in the general fears that what had happened in France might be imitated in England unless men and women rallied to the defence of the monarchy, the church and, indeed, the entire political system. In Manchester this meant the defence of local structures of power and office which were dominated by a high Tory oligarchy and which would need some defending. From an early date predictions of anarchy, war and poverty and accounts of anarchic and bloodthirsty chaos in France began to appear in the newspapers. As loyalism developed its formal institutions in 1792, it revelled in anti-French and anti-revolutionary propaganda. Furthermore, and adding a further edge to panic and hysteria, the figure of Thomas Paine, the famous revolutionary, became something of a lightning rod for many of these fears. Paine and his adherents were suspected of the most subversionary and atheistical activities. In the winter of 1792–3, indeed, he became something of a diabolical object. After the French declared war on Britain on 1 March 1793 predictions of an easy, early military victory in Europe were soon overtaken by more fearful and less optimistic expectations.

It would be unwise to dismiss as farfetched the sincerely held fears of large sections of the population of Manchester. There was much for them to be concerned about, not least the casual belief that even moderate and well-intentioned reform might run to extremes, as they certainly had in France. Already in November 1790 Edmund Burke had articulated in *Reflections on the Revolution in France* the essentials of what later generations have come to see as Conservative social theory, that society was a complex and delicate organism that matures over centuries, that reformers might endanger institutions and manners that had been serviceable to past generations, and which possessed the capacity to adapt and change and that the French, through their attachment to atheistical Jacobinism and natural rights were endangering the very fabric of European society. At first, Burke was regarded as a fanatic but his ideas, focussing reactionary fears into a reasonably coherent shape, gradually won acceptance. Indeed, the Manchester newspapers were full of alarming news from France as the Revolution deepened. Reformers in Manchester argued that such extremes might best be avoided by extensive reform undertaken immediately. In Manchester, at least, their schemes were quite radical. George Philips, for example, argued for male and female suffrage, annual parliaments, secret ballot and payment for MPs.[9] Such proposals worried many people in the town. If this was what moderate reform might lead to then there was no place for it in Britain. Consequently, there was a warm welcome in Manchester for the government's Proclamation of May 1792, bidding magistrates to be on their guard against seditious writings. The reaction to the Proclamation in Manchester was to be significant.

It came on 4 June 1792, when a town meeting was held at the Exchange at which 'the most Loyal testations were heard from every individual' and support expressed for the Proclamation.[10] The reformers were denounced and their evil purposes condemned. At the same time, the supporters of Church and King were quick to take advantage of the fact that the same meeting could conveniently be utilized to celebrate the date of the King's birthday on 4 June. The borough officials and the officers of the Royal Northern British Dragoons met and feasted at the Bull's Head Inn. After the firing of cannon in St Ann's Square to capture the attention of the townspeople, a further feast was held at the Bull's Head, this time attended by 200 gentlemen 'to testify their loyalty to their King and their approbation of our happy Government'.[11] They were not finished yet. In the evening a crowd gathered in St Ann's Square to admire the illuminations of some shops and houses. Violence erupted and was turned on the dissenters. The doors of the Unitarian chapels in Mosley Street and

*Promis'd Horrors of the French INVASION, — or — Forcible Reasons for negociating a Regicide PEACE.* Vide. The Authority of Edmund Burke.

Cross Street were attacked.[12] Such rowdiness was reminiscent of the Church and King agitation against the repeal of the Test and Corporation Acts in 1790 rather than hostility to reform of parliament and opposition to the French Revolution. That, however, was shortly to change.

There was a European crisis as the armies of the French Revolution occupied the Low Countries and the Church and King Club realized that its instinctive hostility to Protestant Dissenters must now be turned against the reformers. Meeting at the Weavers Arms a few weeks later, they condemned 'Plots and Associations' designed to subvert our system of government and they called on good citizens to 'step forward and express their Abhorrence' of the reformers and their schemes.[13] This the local innkeepers did on 13 September, when they publicly resolved to refuse the use of their premises to reformers and their meetings. Well they might. A Regiment of Scots Greys had been billeted on the town and was now showing signs of infiltration by local reformers. Some of the soldiers, in fact, had formed a club to read Paine's works. After considerable lobbying it was agreed that the Regiment had to leave the town. On 14 December they marched away from Manchester, much to the relief of the loyalists.[14] During this period, the Church and King Club had been directing its attention at the Manchester reformers themselves amidst an atmosphere of growing concern at the prospect of a French invasion and deepening fear of reform and where it might lead. A meeting on 12

November acknowledged the need to retain the Test Acts but now the Club explicitly committed itself to the defence of the constitution and the rooting out of reformers and their deadly theories.[15]

On 13 December 1792 against a darkening European scene as the armies of the French Revolution swept into the Low Countries and as the reform movement at home appeared to be reaching menacing proportions, Pitt's government issued a second Proclamation, this time embodying the militia, a matter which could only be justified on the pretext of a domestic insurrection. Throughout the country, organized local loyalist Associations began to spring up, notably in Manchester. One was established in late November at the Fleece Inn, in the Old Shambles, and in early December another at the Black Swan, at Smithy Door.[16] In mid-December two more appeared, one at the Blackmoor's Head and one at the York Minster.[17] Two town meetings in Salford led to the formation of two more.[18] A fervent wave of loyalist patriotism swept over Manchester. It only took a town meeting in Manchester on 11 December and the provision of food and drink for an angry crowd to produce a violent attack on the home of the Manchester reformer, Thomas Walker. For three successive nights loyalists paraded up and down the streets shouting slogans and holding aloft a board proclaiming 'Church and King'. Although this shameful instance of violence was scarcely compatible with the constitutional protestations of which the loyalists were so fond, the magistrates turned a blind eye. The riot only served to encourage the momentum with which loyalism spread over the next few weeks. More and more Associations were formed: three more in the second half of December, one in January, two in February and two in March.[19]

The formal organisation of loyalism in Manchester came with the Bull's Head Association, unquestionably the most important and most extensive loyalist body in the town.[20] A town meeting on 11 December 1792 was demanded by no fewer than eighty individuals. Details of the meeting on 11 December suggest a considerable degree of prior planning. There seems to have been a unanimous decision to establish an Association and to vote an Address to the King. The Association met on the following day and proceeded to establish a committee of executive officers.[21] Its eight members were all well known and highly regarded Mancunians, most of them public officers or merchants. No fewer than 148 original members served on the general committee of the Bull's Head Association, twenty-four more being added at a later date. The executive committee met daily for the first ten days, organizing its procedure, sponsoring and distributing propaganda and establishing contacts with other loyalist bodies. After 24 December it met twice weekly but then in mid-February its regular meetings were suspended. Its initial work, of quashing seditious activity in the area, had apparently been accomplished. The executive committee did not meet again until

15 October 1794. Thereafter its meetings were irregular and took place usually in response to a specific demand. In 1795 it attempted to resist radical demands for peace with France and proceeded to defend the Two Acts. In 1794, 1796 and 1797 its meetings considered the formation of a volunteer force in Manchester. By 1798 its days were numbered. In 1798 and 1799 its meetings failed to reach their quorum.[22] Nevertheless, it would be something of an error to accept the commonly held view that the loyalist impulse was exhausted, in Manchester, as elsewhere, by the spring of 1793.[23] There were no fewer than seventeen loyalist associations in the Manchester area. In 1794 twelve were still in existence, in 1795 ten. New Associations were still being formed, the last in 1798.

As the town settled down to the arduous exertions required in the long and dangerous war against revolutionary France, the loyalists set about their business. The primary justification for their existence had been from the first, as the Bull's Head minutes make crystal clear, the need 'to discover and bring to justice, the Authors, Publishers, Distributors of all Seditious and Treasonable Writings'. The threat of prosecution sent the reformers underground. Although acquitted after his trial for conspiracy in April 1794 Thomas Walker had acquired enormous legal expenses and by mid-1794 was a broken man. The other leaders of the reform movement in Manchester fled to America in the face of this legal onslaught. Meanwhile, several of the sub-committees of the Bull's Head Association began to adopt specialized functions. Three of the Associations formed in 1793–4 concentrated on fund raising. Others concentrated on the practicalities of resisting a French invasion, especially in 1797–8. One of the Bull's Head sub-committees in fact specialized in propaganda, rebutting the claims and demands of the reformers, deciding on which newspapers it ought to support, and, finally, preparing petitions to present to Parliament. The scale of such work should not be underestimated. Between 1792 and 1795 it issued a staggering 50,000 handbills and placed a steady stream of notices and advertisements in the local press. This was a startling output for a provincial Loyal Association. Utilizing local newspapers, its own financial and personal resources and its control of outlets within Manchester, the Bull's Head Association could reach a wide audience both within the town and beyond. Surviving evidence indicates that it reached not only Oldham and Bolton but Saddleworth, Liverpool, Chester, Macclesfield and even North Wales. There can be little doubt that the Bull's Head Association was the pre-eminent Loyal Association in the North West.

Who were the loyalists? Thanks to the happy survival of the minutes of some of the Loyal Associations in the Manchester and Salford areas we can at last begin to approach this question on the basis of reasonable solid evidence. Almost all writers have assumed that the loyalists were composed largely of elite, wealthy and propertied elements.[24] There is some truth in this traditional view but it needs considerable refinement. Members of the highest classes tended to fill ornamental roles, the practical functions of loyalism being the work of men from the middling orders. But of the 172 individuals concerned, no fewer than 60 per cent were involved in the textile trade, men clearly from the middling orders. The clergy, gentry and senior professions are indeed represented but only as small minorities of the committee men. For example, only 8 per cent of the Bull's Head Association committee men were described as gentlemen, in Salford only 12 per cent. Two thirds of them were merchants or manufacturers. But the men who actually dominated Manchester loyalism were those from the middling orders of the town, and principally from the ranks of the trading, manufacturing and official elements, some of the from quite humble backgrounds.[25] Furthermore, there was a powerful popular element in Manchester loyalism. The committee and sub-committee lists include working people, shopkeepers, innkeepers, artisans and tradesmen. Consequently, we should not assume that Manchester loyalism was simply the result of upper-class bullying; nor should we imagine that adherents of Church and King were a mindless rabble. Both assumptions dominate the literature on this subject. Of course, their assumption that the mass of the people were loyal but liable to be seduced from their loyalty by scheming reformers, was condescending and paternalistic but not necessarily erroneous for that. An important element in Church and King loyalism was the experience of Anglicanism where 'on the parish level at least, the church played a positive role and was respected'.[26] Such genuine Anglicanism, if not expressed in constant church attendance, was a powerful element in maintaining popular loyalty behind the existing regime in church and state. Consequently, it is hardly unrealistic to imagine that conscious political choices were being made by many people from a humble background, who were prepared to contribute in one way or another to the success of the war. It is perhaps at the very lowest levels of society than an unthinking patriotism and an instinctive attachment to the country's institutions and practices may be found.

Indeed, from its earliest days, Manchester loyalism had been proud, assertive and militant. Loyalists had stoutly opposed the pleas of Protestant dissenters and domestic reformers. Now they condemned the reformers as allies of the French and accused them of wishing to import a similar revolution into Britain. The Manchester civil authorities were determined that this should not happen. The Manchester magistrates and constables were almost all members of anti-reform groups. Between 1792 and 1797 all but two were members of the Bull's Head committee. In Manchester and Salford over one half of the committee men held positions as town officials. The link between loyalism and the governing institutions of the two towns is obvious. Town officials could be relied upon to defend and protect their town – to expect anything else is to deny human nature. The loyalists believed that it was their duty to come forward, to denounce the spread of sedition, to root out reform and to resist it with firm statements of what they took to be correct, political opinion. These included loyalty to the king, country and the much vaunted balanced constitution (between king, Lords and Commons), the supremacy of parliament and the rule of law. Reform was thus unnecessary. Even the smallest innovation might open the door to anarchy. Loyalist opinion in Manchester was thus profoundly conservative. In spite of attempts to depict loyalist ideology as little more than common eighteenth-century constitutional platitudes[27] an analysis of the loyalist declarations, handbills, and newspaper editorials in Manchester leave the impression of a somewhat harsher stance. Only one out of the twenty-four recorded loyalist declarations in Manchester in fact conformed to a conventional and traditional view of the constitution. The remainder delivered the somewhat harsher message that strong measures were urgently needed to root out sedition and save the constitution. Loyalist resolutions invariably condemned the reformers for peddling innovation and sedition and for subverting the constitution. Their version of the French Revolution may be summarized as Burkean; they regard it as a subversive threat to the peace and security of both Britain and Europe, a threat which had to be stoutly resisted.

Indeed, although loyalist elites needed to be careful, they were anxious to deploy popular elements of society in their public capacity, notably in their parades, processions, demonstrations and in other forms of ritual. Although they were not prepared to concede theoretical political power to the masses (neither were the reformers) they were prepared to enlist them in the patriotic cause and to display what they took to be mass, popular approval for their proceedings. And of all the loyalists' techniques of popular display, unquestionably the most sensational were the burnings in effigy of Thomas Paine, in which Paine was substituted for the traditional Guy Fawkes ritual.[28]

The effigy was dragged around the town over a lengthy period, like a common criminal, enduring a form of popular trial. The effigy was then normally hung on a gibbet for some hours before being burned on a bonfire, usually at night time.

Figure 3: 'The End of Pain[e]' (1793) by T. Ovenden. Loyalist organizations in Manchester and elsewhere carried out a wave of ritual executions of the radical writer Thomas Paine in 1792–3. © Trustees of the British Museum

There were no fewer than twenty-six burnings within a twenty-mile radius of Manchester, three burnings in Manchester itself. We have only one recorded account of a Manchester burning, that on 17 December 1792:

> The inhabitants at top of Deansgate, hanged the effigy of Tom Paine, dressed in a Maroon coloured Coat, Striped Waistcoat, and a greasy Pair of Breeches, a Barber's Block with a Wig on supplied the Place of a Head, from his Coat Pockets hung shreds of Paper and on his shoulder a Quantity of Thread, emblemmatical of his ci devant Trade, with 'The Rights of Man' stitched on his Breast; thus he hung an Hour, amidst the Acclamations of Hundreds of Spectators; he was afterwards dragged through the Streets, and then committed to the flames the Populace singing 'God Save the King'.[29]

This was magnificent street theatre at its most compelling: humorous, entertaining and not a little frightening, designed to captivate and to deliver powerful social and political messages. The size of the crowds and the (largely) unanimous confirmation of the sentence on Paine was unmistakable. The verdict of the community as a whole was being delivered, not merely that of a small elite. What is not clear is how far such activities contributed to some sort of social domination. It is certainly difficult to follow Mark Harrison's view that late-eighteenth century towns had become 'a controlled set of enclosed spheres' in which unofficial crowd activity was becoming 'incomprehensible and alarming'.[30] The whole point of the Paine burnings is that they amounted to a consensual verdict on the great radical. Similarly, Nicholas Rogers has argued that the burnings illustrate the volatility of local opinion. It is hard to see how this can be so in view of the outstanding success of almost every single one of the burning rituals which occurred in many hundreds of places in the winter of 1792–3.[31]

Indeed, burnings of Paine were by no means the only type of street theatre in which the Manchester loyalists indulged. Loyalists were ready to carry their message on to the streets and squares of Manchester and to express it in specific acts of ritual. Loyalty to their King was absolutely essential to the ideas, sentiments and rituals of loyalism. Consequently, the Manchester Loyal Associations took great pains to celebrate the king's birthday every 4 June. Here is an account of the scene on 4 June 1795:

> The Boroughreeve and Constables, accompanied by a number of Gentlemen, and the different Loyal Associations, preceded by a band of Music, went in procession from the Star Inn, at noon, into St. Ann's Square, where a detachment of soldiers were drawn up. Wine as usual being placed on tables, the health of the King, Queen and Royal Family, was drunk with loud acclamations, 'God Save the King' was repeatedly played and the soldiers fired three volleys. The ceremony ended, the Gentlemen returned to the Inn.

> At three in the afternoon, an elegant public dinner was prepared at the Star, and a large company attended. The evening passed with the most cordial hilarity, and a general sentiment of loyal attachment.[32]

This was clearly a very different kind of event than the burning of Paine in effigy. This was an expression not only of the loyalty of the town and its inhabitants but a celebration and – in a very real sense – an exhibition of the elite of Manchester. Local pride is the order of the day as the town celebrates its people, its prestige, its wealth and its loyalty, as it parades before itself and allows its citizens to watch themselves, each in their orders, trades and churches. This identification of loyalism with the social elite goes far towards affirming its power and legitimacy.

In addition to these public performances, there were four further occasions on which the town formally and loyally celebrated the nation's military and naval victories. The victory at Valciennes (28 July 1793) and Howe's victory of 1 June 1794 were celebrated with informal street parties and the continuous pealing of bells. These were popular and relatively spontaneous occasions but by the time of the celebration of Admiral Duncan's victory over the Dutch fleet in 1797 such celebrations had acquired a rather more formal and pre-organized character. Long and winding processions made their way around the town and houses were illuminated to attest to the loyalty and enthusiasm of their inhabitants. The same pattern was followed following Nelson's triumph at the Nile a year later with a procession highlighting the officials and gentlemen of the town, accompanied by a volunteer regiment. Since an orderly and opulent procession was thought to reflect well on the town, it is difficult to avoid the connection between the ideals of loyalism and sentiments of civic pride.[33]

Manchester loyalists were thus anxious to take positive and practical action to defend their country and to prosecute the war against France. To do so they threw their energies into the opening of subscriptions to aid the war effort and, later, to finance the establishment of volunteer regiments in the town. They launched no fewer than seven subscription drives between 1793 and 1798. It was a mark of local pride that the citizens of a great town like Manchester should outshine others by the generosity of their actions. Such subscription appeals and advertisements usually led to the publication of lists of individual donors and of their individual subscriptions, a convenient opportunity for citizens to register publicly their loyal support for the war. The most remarkable subscription in Manchester in these years came in 1794 when it was suggested that the town raise a local marine regiment of 1,000 men by offering a bounty of three guineas. Between February and October 1793 over £5,300 was raised and around 1,000 men recruited. Furthermore, in the winter of 1793–4 over £500 was subscribed to supply the troops in Flanders with warm clothing. In 1795 a yet further subscription raised £1,400 to subsidize food for the poor of Manchester. Two further subscriptions produced around £8,500 towards the raising of local volunteer regiments in 1797–8.

The establishment of volunteer regiments had been only a partial success in 1794 but similar efforts in 1797–8 met with much greater success. By then, the voluntary principle was more firmly established. In 1798 Manchester raised a magnificent £26,000 in response to Pitt's call for a national contribution and most of the money thus raised was devoted to the establishment of volunteer regiments.[34] John Cookson has sought to disconnect these activities from the narrative of loyalism as such and to label them as a distinctive form of what he terms 'national defence patriotism' (in 1798, 1801 and 1803–5) from the loyalism of the earlier 1790s.[35] Clearly, the situation with which the volunteer regiments were confronted in 1798 was different from those of 1792–3 but they were by no means wholly different. And there are clear and obvious distinctions between the two. Yet the volunteer regiments were used to suppress disorder. As Navickas notes, 'Many Church-and-King magistrates and manufacturers saw the potential for using the institution both as an extension to the loyal associations and as a means of inculcating loyalism among the rank and file'. Furthermore, there remain significant continuities between the two, of leadership, ideology, language and ritual. The fact that the volunteer regiments included a very small number of men who had in the past supported reform makes little difference.[36] It is worth adding that the Manchester volunteer regiments were involved in no fewer than eight civic or public ceremonies in 1797–8, notably on the king's birthday when the civic procession was combined with a military review.

Towards the end of the decade loyalism in Manchester tended to abandon the militant, reactionary, associational loyalism of the Paine burning mobs of 1792–3. Already by 1795 there were signs that the hysteria of 'Church and King' was coming to an end and within a couple of years the earlier ideological fears of the French Revolution were beginning to abate. The urgent need for Loyal Associations began to disappear after the Two Acts and the palpable decline in the activities of reformers. Loyalism was now coming to be integrated into the civic routine of celebration and display, procedures and institutions and, by the end of the decade, sustained by the power and influence of the volunteer regiments. As Katrina Navickas notes: 'Loyalist clubs and anti-Jacobin pamphleteering were replaced by Volunteer reviews and patriotic sermons'.[37]

Yet the story of Manchester loyalism does not end in 1798, nor was it subsumed in the 'national defence patriotism' of the volunteers. Although the days of Church-and-King mobs had gone, Church-and-King magistrates were in secure control of the town. The loyalist elite distanced themselves from what one historian has termed the 'vulgar conservatism' of the lower classes.[38]

Yet there is little doubt that loyalists succeeded in maintaining their popular following and that they were able to mobilize it whenever they felt the need to do so. Manchester Loyalism continued its independent path, requiring little or no prompting from outside. It had gone its own way and largely ignored the central body of the Loyal Associations, the Association for Preserving Constitutional Order and Liberty, in 1792–3, just as by the end of the decade it was asserting its own independence in the support which it chose to give to the war effort against the French. It professed its own objectives and manifested its own, independent dynamic.

The war against Napoleon was a much less ideological enterprise than had been the case in the earlier years of the war against the French. Manchester loyalists, at least, were unquestionably conscious that they were not fighting in isolation but as part of a national, and even international, conflict. By the later years of the Napoleonic wars loyalism had become part of a generalized patriotism, even accessible to many sections of opinion that may earlier have been marked out as reformist. Thus, the incessant patriotic effusions not only of loyalists but reformers alike may have done something to reinforce the patriotic identity of many people in the town.

# Lancashire Britishness: Patriotism in the Manchester region during the Napoleonic Wars

Katrina Navickas

On 25 October 1809 Britain celebrated George III's fiftieth year on the throne. The golden jubilee occurred during the middle of the Napoleonic Wars, although Britons at the time were obviously unaware how many years of wartime hardship still lay ahead. According to Linda Colley and other historians of British patriotism, the wars against revolutionary and Napoleonic France between 1792 and 1815 marked the 'apotheosis' of George III. The monarch was lauded as the paternal head of the United Kingdom, four nations that were recently united by constitutional union and a shared determination to resist the threat of French invasion. This was the era of 'Rule Britannia' and 'God Save the King', of Trafalgar and Waterloo, of John Bull and Britannia pitted against the diminutive character of Napoleon 'Boney' in the caricatures and songs of wartime propaganda. This was the era in which 'Britons' were made.[1]

In some senses, this national ebullience was indeed centred around the monarch and national events such as the Jubilee and the king's birthday. The wealth of satirical cartoons and broadside ballads in this period pitted John Bull against Napoleon 'Boney', and as Colley and other historians have shown, did much to shape the imagery of Britishness in this period. The development of patriotism, however, was not a top-down process originating from the central state and diffusing out to the periphery. On the contrary, enthusiasm for defence of the country was shaped and defined by local and regional priorities. William Wordsworth recognized that 'local attachment … is the tap-root of the tree of Patriotism', echoing a theme common to other Romantic poets and to Edmund Burke.[2] Caricaturist James Gillray portrayed John Bull in his cartoons as the archetypal Briton, but he appeared as the southern English country bumpkin.

The character did not and could not solely represent the industrious working classes of the Pennines. National elements of British identity were accepted by inhabitants of the region, but these only formed part of the overall fabric, through which existing allegiances shone through from below.

This article examines how patriotism in Manchester and its surrounding towns and 'neighbourhood' had a distinctive character, reflecting its sense of regional as much as its national identity. The region's inhabitants responded to Napoleon's threat of invasion with gusto, and were keen to demonstrate their loyalty to the Hanoverian crown. Yet patriotism in the region was not unthinking. South Lancashire patriotism did not produce a carbon-copy of the images, songs and forms of organization that Colley and other historians have assumed to have been a mark of Britishness in this era. The region did feel 'British', but only after its population had filtered the elements of patriotism through their own local identities and socio-economic structures. Civic patriotism in particular, in the form of volunteer regiments and celebratory processions, reflected the desire of Manchester and its surrounding towns to demonstrate their increasing respectability, wealth, and importance to the nation. The inhabitants of Lancashire adapted national propaganda about the importance of Britishness through the filter of local and regional structures of social authority and economy. The result was 'Lancastrian Britishness'.

## The response to the Napoelonic invasion scares

> When the Demons of Faction hung over our realm
> And threat'n'd our law rolls and charters to burn;
> Our throne to demolish, our Altars o'erturn,
> Then a Patriot Band
> The True Sons of the Land
> In Armour stept forth at Britannia's command,

The Standards of Loyalty eager to rear
Each proud of his birth right, a firm Volunteer.

'The Standards of Loyalty' was composed and sung for the presentation of colours to the Ashton-under-Lyne volunteer regiment on 10 July 1799. With a characteristic combination of female patriotism and local aristocratic paternalism, the colours were donated to the volunteers by Lady Stamford, the wife of the district's lord of the manor and main landowner the Earl of Stamford and Warrington. The 'demons of faction' referred to the revolutionary French, but loyalists could also interpret them to mean local radicals. Ireland had rebelled in the year before, and from 1799 to 1802 magistrates feared that the district around the Tame was swarming with United Irish emissaries and secret republican United English cells. Major Gore, commander of the regular military troops in the Ashton area, was informed that men were 'regularly sworn in' by oaths to the revolutionary movement 'at Hurst near Ashton ... every Thursday night'.[3] The volunteer regiments enabled loyalist local elites to regroup, infuse patriotic propaganda with loyalist sentiments, and keep an eye on the working classes within their rank-and-file.

The invasion scares of 1797–8 and 1803–5 stimulated a collective determination of defence among the inhabitants of Manchester and its region. The government's *levée en masse* called upon all Britons to serve in defence of the nation. This ranged from forming and signing up to volunteer corps to support from women by raising money and sewing uniforms. Inhabitants employed in transport had to be prepared to use their carts and other vehicles to drive supplies and livestock away from invading forces. The government had usually relied on county-based and aristocratically-controlled militia regiments and fencible units raised by large landowners and financed by the Treasury. Unpaid volunteer corps had been raised during the American war of independence, and again during the first French invasion scare of 1797–9, as at Ashton-under-Lyne. By contrast, the scale of the *levée en masse* from 1803 was novel. The raising of volunteer regiments involved almost a fifth of adult males. By December 1803, Lancashire had raised a total of fifty-three volunteer regiments, with sixty-one officers commanding 14,278 rank-and-file. The Home Office did not accept all the regiments that the towns offered: this was partly because of restricted funds, and partly out of fear of the consequences of arming so large a number of the industrial working classes. Manchester was allowed nine regiments, composed of over 4,000 rank-and-file.[4]

The wars gave the merchants, manufacturers, and other members of the increasingly wealthy middle classes an ideal opportunity to display their largesse and become involved in the running of civic institutions. The volunteer regiments in particular raised the profile of the urban bourgeoisie, making them firmly part of the loyalist establishment. The accounts of the committee for General Defence for Manchester totalled over £21,500 in 1803. It involved over 1,300 subscribers, including the major manufacturers and merchants the Gould brothers, who gave £315; Lawrence Peel, £300; the lord of the manor, Sir Oswald Mosley, £200; James Ackers, the Philips family, the Unitarians Samuel Greg and Benjamin Heywood, who all donated £100 each.[5] Being a volunteer officer meant that merchants and manufacturers could flaunt the trappings of military prowess without having to participate in a full-time military career. In December 1803, for example, the *Blackburn Mail* reported how 'Thomas Cooper Esq, Lieut of the Preston and Chorley Light Horse and commander of the Chorley Division, gave a most sumptuous Entertainment to them and the gentlemen of the Neighbourhood; everything the season could possibly produce was given on the occasion'.[6] Volunteers were reviewed in public squares, racecourses or outside commanders' mansion-houses, all symbols of the 'urban renaissance' that had brought northern towns to the fore in the latter part of the eighteenth century.

The urban bourgeois and gentry officers sought social order through the observance of hierarchy. But the ideal could also involve community and independence. The 'Fourth class' was composed of men too old or with too many family responsibilities to belong to the other types of volunteers. The father of the bookseller James Weatherley belonged to the Manchester Fourth Class volunteers, who were nicknamed 'Old Fogeys' because of their age. The 'Dad's Army' connotations of the volunteer corps were apparent at the time. Weatherley noted in his autobiography:

> I recollect on the Parade days when they were turning out they would send out their wives to see if Mr so and so was ready as they could not forshame to go to Parade singly but would wait until they could muster 7 or 8 to go together in the Group. There would perhaps be one as fat as Falstaff and another as fat as the living Skeleton that was once exhibited in Manchester, one five feet five another six feet one another bow legged and another inkneed.[7]

A portrait of 'A private of the first battalion of the Independent Manchester and Salford Volunteer Infantry' from 1805 shows a proud volunteer standing ready for muster on Kersal Moor. The painting, published by the Italian craftsman, Vittore Zanetti of Market Street Lane, shows how Manchester, and the nature of patriotism, has changed by the Napoleonic Wars. There is a picturesque background common to military portraits, but the landscape is also industrial. McConnel and Kennedy's large factory complex in Ancoats, and chimneys across the Manchester townscape are proudly on show. This was a world away from the southern country bumpkin of John Bull of the London-made caricatures.

Some volunteer corps reflected the personalities and paternalism of their commanders. A broadside ballad about the Warrington volunteers for example praised each officer at length. Many of the officers were

factory owners employing the ninety-eight weavers and other artisans and mechanics who were the privates of the corps. Volunteer corps expressed the geographical extent of their identity and the reach of their commanders. John Trafford Esq of Trafford House raised a regiment of 350 from the tenants and workers on his estates. When they assembled in Trafford Park in August 1803, he made a speech proclaiming that Napoleon pledged to deprive Englishmen of their right to England as a nation. Therefore, he asserted, 'the towns of Barton, Stretford and Eccles have sent Heroes to the field, and victory has crowned their zeal'.[8] This was a localized patriotism, filtered through and firmly centred around the identity of the local area and its resident landowner. By contrast, the regular militia and army lacked this immediacy of contact, with their

Figure 2: Vittore Zanetti, 'A private of the first battalion of the Independent Manchester and Salford Volunteer Infantry', 1805. Courtesy of Manchester Libraries, Information and Archives, Manchester City Council

aristocratic commanders and soldiers who rarely resided in the region and usually served outside it. The volunteers were a brief but significant movement enabling local notables to display their status through civic patriotism. Outside the big urban centres like Manchester and Liverpool, the North West had lower rates of recruitment relative to other areas of the country.[9] In inland areas, where the threat of invasion was less immediate, this social motivation proved stronger than national defence patriotism.

## Local patriotisms

The French Wars had an emotional and cultural, as well as military and political, impact upon the British populace. Victorian patriotism harked back to the memory of Trafalgar and repeated the mantra of 'Rule Britannia' as the empire expanded. Underneath the rhetoric of the songs and civic celebrations, however, these events and patriotic activity had a more complex and contested history.

Civic patriotism focused on naval battles as the real indicators of national success and vindication of Britain's (or more often England's) providential mission against the French. Again this was an example of local elites appropriating and ritualizing popular patriotism. To celebrate Nelson's victory at the Battle of the Nile, the boroughreeves and constables of Manchester and Salford arranged with the officers of the volunteer regiments to have a military procession through the two towns in October 1798.[10] Naval admirals were regarded as the greatest type of war heroes. They were disassociated from both the hated press gangs and the idea of a standing army, both of which dogged the reputation of military generals in the eighteenth century. Naval victories were regarded as separate from the failures of Pittite foreign policy and the lengthening war. Local notables seized on the cult of Nelson to enhance their own civic patriotism. Nelson's career was read in some circles as a commentary on the establishment's ingratitude for spectacular victories and on the ways in which political and social influence affected the distribution of national honours. Many perhaps preferred a somewhat maverick hero to a royal family and government that was beginning to be revealed as corrupt as soon as Nelson had been interred.[11] This 'cult of Nelson' filtered down into popular patriotism. In January 1806, Oldham diarist William Rowbottom bemoaned the 'late disasterous events upon the Continent' and the 'unparalleled victories of Buonaparte', which had 'thrown Europe into the greatest consternation' and 'had a visable effect upon Trade and Commerce'. Yet this was followed by a statement that could almost have been lifted out of patriotic propaganda: 'but the glorious victory of Trafalgar, has been of great utility to the Commerce and Credit of this nation, and has placed us at present triumphant over our enemies, which may ever be the case, is the wish of every honest Englishman'. Rowbottom certainly hoped for a successful end to the war, achieved quickly in order to save the burgeoning textile industry of south Lancashire. Perhaps he was more comfortable using the generic language of public patriotism to express hope than bitter negativity over the government's economic and foreign policies.

National patriotism was often expressed and understood through the filter of localism. A common theme of ballads, sermons and tracts was to portray Napoleon and his troops raiding each individual town and family of their property and liberty.[12] News of local events and national print distribution were dependent upon local means of transmission. Both radical and loyalist views of national events used analogies of local places to explain them. Dialect writer and self-proclaimed 'Tim Bobbin the Second', Robert Walker of Rochdale, wrote a radical diatribe *Plebeian Politics* during the brief peace of 1801–3. Initially published in instalments by the radical newspaper printer William Cowdroy, the text was later published as a whole and remains as one of the only surviving radical dialect pamphlets from this 'patriotic' period. Using the comedic literary device of a conversation between two protagonists, 'Tum' and 'Whistlepig', Walker attacked local loyalists for what he regarded as their hypocritical triumphalist support for the war against France. Discussing the British acquisition of Trinidad and Tobago in 1802–3, the character of 'Tum' retorted using a fusion of local and international analogies:

Figure 3: Robert Walker of Rochdale, radical and dialect writer from his *Plebeian Politics* (1798)

> Dun they think ot too ilonds ar' a recompense for o th' blud an tresure ot has bin spilt an spent? Beh th'wuns I'd oz leef a had Duck'nfilt Ho,

and Shepy Ho; gan meh; beside theese ilonds ne'er belung'nt to France; Bonnipeeter wud naw let us ha nout ot belungt to France.

[Do they think that two islands are a recompense for the blood and treasure that has been spilled and spent? But you know I'd rather have had Dukinfield Hall and Shepley Hall given to me; besides, these islands never belonged to France; Buonaparte would not have let us have anything that belonged to France].

By referring to specific landmarks, Walker thus appealed to a Tame audience, giving both their radical sympathies and geographical identity a local distinctiveness. During a time when many writers regarded the use of dialect as vulgar and backward, Walker attempted to foster an alternative language for patriotism that expressed pride in locality and heritage as much as in the new 'modern' nation.[13]

## Varieties of patriotism

Despite their efforts, however, Walker and Cowdroy were among few radical 'patriots' during the Napoleonic Wars. Loyalism colonized the definition and forms of patriotism in reaction to the French Revolution. Yet as with patriotism, loyalism was not a homogeneous concept and descended from a range of different lineages, several of which were distinctive to Lancashire. Three elements distinguished south Lancashire Britishness from other regions: an identification with the industrializing economy; a Jacobite heritage; 'Church-and-King' loyalism; and in some cases, Orangeism. All of these were product of the socio-economic changes that made Manchester and its surrounding towns into the centre of the industrial revolution, as well as a response to the political ideologies emerging from the French Revolution.

South Lancashire was the heart of popular radicalism and industrial unrest throughout the French wars. Inspired by the French Jacobins and the writings of Thomas Paine, the middle and working classes formed radical societies for the first time, calling for parliamentary reform and universal suffrage. Patriotism maintained its original association with reform; indeed the working-class Manchester Patriotic Society laid claim to the meaning of the term in their title as they campaigned for universal manhood suffrage. Anti-radical legislation passed by William Pitt the Younger's government and repression by local 'Church-and-King' loyalists, however, dampened the fervour of radical agitation from 1795 onwards. What Mark Philp has termed the 'vulgar conservatism' of the populace ensured that during the Napoleonic Wars, loyalism elided with patriotism. The French invasion scares of 1798–9 and 1803–5 fostered what J.E. Cookson has termed 'national defence patriotism'. A solid commitment to defend the nation came over and above internal dissent, and calls for reform were muted in the lead up to Trafalgar.[14]

Yet by 1809, reformers were trying to regain the meaning of patriotism that they had had to subdue during the years of invasion threat. The joy of the jubilee was tempered by bad harvests and economic depression. Loyalty was the watchword, but popular discontent with the government and mistrust of the monarchy were rising. This was the year of a major scandal involving the Duke of York and venal corruption in the military. The furore in parliament and in the newspaper press over the Duke of York affair opened the gateway for a revival of petitions for parliamentary reform. Philip Harling has argued that 1809 marked a flash point for the opposition to government during the Napoleonic Wars.[15] The magistrates, clergy, and other 'Church-and-King' local elites were anxious about the resurgence of popular collective action. Their fears were further heightened by renewed strikes and other illegal trades union action among the textile workers. George III's jubilee therefore provided loyalists with an opportunity to reassert their control over the meaning of patriotism.

Although Linda Colley acknowledges that radicals criticized the planned jubilee festivities, she generally portrays the event as a successful marshalling of public sentiment for loyalism. Stuart Semmel by contrast argues that the jubilee was 'constructed by contention as much as it was by consensus'. The meaning of patriotism in 1809 was shaped by a loyalist reaction against radical criticisms, particularly by William Cobbett and reformers in the City of London. Nevertheless, he also points out the significance of localism and regionalism. The jubilee allowed 'far-flung towns and villages … to knit themselves … into an encompassing narrative'.[16] This was patriotism from the bottom-up.

In Manchester, the 1809 jubilee celebrations centred on a procession of the 'principal inhabitants' from the Exchange to the Collegiate Church and, after divine service, a further procession to St Ann's Square, where the military fired a *feu de joie*. By following this route in the view of thousands of spectators, the local elites enacted a perambulation of power. They connected physical representations of their source of wealth, the established church and the state, and thereby confirmed their authority as guardians of the economic and moral as well as political order. This was not unusual and indeed was an expected element of civic patriotism. But the patriotism of the event was layered with a further loyalist reaction against popular radicalism. Petitions for peace and reform had revived in 1808, and the popular reaction to the Duke of York affair earlier in 1809 provoked the local authorities to use the jubilee celebrations to reaffirm their loyalist rule. In his sermon during the service at the Collegiate Church, Revd Charles Wicksted Ethelston preached on the verse, 'My son fear thou the Lord and the King and meddle not with them that are given to change'. Ethelston (1767–1830) was an active magistrate, and later gained notoriety when he read out the riot act at what became the Peterloo massacre in 1819.[17]

## Industrial civic patriotism

The celebrations in the Manchester region differed from those elsewhere in the country in that local elites made sure to emphasize the manufacturing identity of the region and its distinctive contribution to the national economy. In Manchester, 'the warehouses and shops were closed, business was suspended'. In some senses, merchants and manufacturers, increasingly members of civic bodies who organized the events, were keen to show their role at the forefront of progress and new technologies of 'improvement'. The most spectacular scene was provided by the major cotton manufacturers Philips and Lee. The roof of their large twist mill in Salford 'exhibited a splendid Crown, formed of gas lights, which, from the pure flame emitted by that curious preparation, looked beautifully luminous'. Manchester and Salford merchants and manufacturers already had form in displaying their own identity and economy through patriotism. During the most serious invasion scare of the autumn of 1803, Prince William, Duke of Gloucester and Commander General of the North West military district, travelled round Lancashire to survey the extent of defence preparations. He was given a tour of Philips and Lee's factory, where he was shown the machinery and the unique iron structure of the building, which he observed 'might afford a useful hint for a deposit of military stores'. At Greenwood and Bateman's factory, the prince was given a demonstration of 'the operation of weaving the Imperial Arms of the United Kingdom'. The manufacturers therefore shaped royal symbols physically as well as symbolically through the produce of their wealth, using innovative technology in gas and textiles. Philips and Lee's factory was the first in the world to be lit by gas.[18]

Another element of Lancashire patriotism at the jubilee involved overt shows of paternalism, reflecting the socio-economic changes that had taken place during the eighteenth century. The older type of paternalism of lords of the manor towards their tenants persisted in the more rural areas of the county, but by this time it was paralleled by merchants and manufacturers bestowing their largesse upon their employees. The *Manchester Mercury* reported how Bolton celebrated George III's jubilee on 25 October 1809 in distinctive style: 'The roast beef of old England, with its usual national accompaniments of plum pudding and ale, were plentifully distributed to many thousands of the labouring classes at the cotton factories, bleaching grounds, foundries and other places by the truly patriotic spirit of their employers, Messrs Brand, T. Ainsworth, Carlile, Jones, Bollings, Slater, Bolton, Rothwells'. Similarly, attorney's clerk John Holden noted in his diary:

> A great number of different Sorts of work people went in procession to the Church, Mr James Carlisle's [sic] work people to the number of 300 or upwards ... Mr Rich'd Ainsworth of Halliwell gave meat and drink to all his

men 500 and upwards and paid every man his day's wage, Mr Jones gave his work people a meal and drinks.

Another account marvelled at how Richard Ainsworth's workers assembled in the quadrangle of Smithills Old Hall, their employer's residence, sang 'God Save the King', before proceeding to a field. They were there addressed by Ainsworth 'in very impressive and appropriate terms', before sitting down to dinner. Ainsworth also presided over giving soup, meat, and potatoes to the 'poor of the neighbourhood', and subscribed 100 guineas towards the establishment of a new school.[19]

The major Bolton manufacturers shared a similar economic and social vision. These were ambitious local men who looked towards the future in trade and industry. Katrina Honeyman identified how most were 'hereditary leaders', former workshop owners who had previously worked in the fustian trade. The later part of the Napoleonic Wars was the crucial period for such entrepreneurs to expand their businesses into the cotton industry. The Carlisle brothers were instrumental in Bolton's rise to prominence as a cotton manufacturing centre, and their Bradshawgate mill was the second largest in the town in terms of mule spindlage in 1811. Richard Ainsworth ran an extensive bleaching works in Halliwell. Nevertheless, the actions of these entrepreneurs at the jubilee harked back to the paternalism of the old gentry. Economists, antiquarians, and compilers of trade directories, all lamented how the old gentry and yeomanry lineages were dying and how landownership was fragmenting in the region. For example, Dr John Aikin noted in his *Description of the Country from Thirty to Forty Miles Round Manchester* of 1795 that Mottram-in-Longdendale 'was formerly famous of the number of halls occupied by their owners, who resided on their own estates'. South-east Lancashire was no longer a land of established gentry, but rather a mix of socially-aspirant 'squirearchy'. Richard Ainsworth had bought the medieval Smithills Hall in the 1790s from the Byrom family for the princely sum of £21,000.[20]

Significantly, some of the new manufacturers organized their own jubilee events separately from the Bolton civic celebrations. Situated out of the urban centres, somewhat isolated in their 'neighbourhood' townships, their actions echoed if not deliberately imitated the gentry holding their own events on their estates for their tenants. Spinning and bleaching works became the new demesnes. At Thomas Ridgway and Sons's bleachworks at Wallsuches near Horwich, three large flags were displayed on the highest rood early in the morning. The workers assembled and 'the heads of the different departments in the Works selected their men, and after calling over their names, the whole formed in one line, amounting to upwards of 500'. Echoing the military arrangement of volunteer regiments, the workers sang 'God Save the King' 'in a very impressive manner' before being led by their overlookers in procession to church. Money was distributed to the women and children, and the 'men returned to two Public Houses in the village, where excellent dinners were provided'. The account of the event noted approvingly, 'after dinner, every man was allowed to drink as much as he pleased, so long as he remained peaceable, and from the report of the men, who were overlookers on the occasion, never was there so large an assembly of people that conducted themselves with more harmony and good humour'.[21] Of course we cannot take this report as a completely accurate representation of the attitudes of Ridgway's workers, but it is clear that the intention of the employers was a paternalism of control and social order. Potential trouble was anticipated, not just because of working-class drinking culture, but also considering the industrial disputes that had troubled the district the year previously.

Similar tales of manufacturer paternalism featured at Ardwick, Denton, Ramsbottom, and other industrial villages and townships in the region. In the more aristocratically-dominated district around the river Tame, lords of the manor did likewise. The Earl of Stamford and Warrington 'aided liberally' a subscription for linen and blankets given to 500 poor families in Ashton-under-Lyne and its neighbourhood. Local elites nevertheless kept their distance from the plebeian entertainments. In Ashton, after parading the town (the rest of the population carefully segregated as spectators), and hearing divine service at the church, sixty gentlemen dined at the Globe Tavern, where 'a number of appropriate toasts were given, the first of which was 'The King, and may the present Jubilee form a lasting impression on the hearts of his faithful subjects'.[22]

Malcolm Chase argues that the idea of jubilee had altered. Before 1809, 'jubilee' had held radical or millenarian connotations as a period of revolution. George III's jubilee, by contrast, was firmly loyalist in character, the effect of two decades of reaction against the French Revolution. Bolton in particular was 'long famed for its loyalty and adherence to the royal cause'. What was ostensibly an embracing and inclusive patriotic event, therefore served to entrench loyalist and elite control over the concept of patriotism.[23] Paternalism became a process of looking backwards not forwards. Local notables used the jubilee to display an explicitly Christian paternalism, with such biblical actions as setting debtors free from prison and feeding the deserving poor of the parish. Stuart Semmel has also suggested that these actions became the dominant narrative of the national celebrations after radicals in London put pressure on the authorities not to waste money on luxurious displays of elite wealth such as illuminations and excessive feasting. Following the lead of the Common Council of the City of London, therefore, provincial authorities soon realized the utility of shifting from 'jollity' towards philanthropy during the period of economic distress.[24]

The efforts of local elites were nevertheless still a show of power as much as an expression of humanitarian concern. Paternalistic patriotism was an attempt to prevent popular disorder at a time of extreme hardship.

War had become a fight of attrition with both the British and the French engaged in economic blockade. Indeed, many of these merchants and manufacturers petitioned the government to repeal the Orders in Council that were harming their trade and imports as well as severely affecting the livelihoods of their workers. Brian Lewis has noted with regard to Richard Ainsworth's efforts at the Jubilee: 'this largesse was little more than tokenism at a time when gentry and gentlemen-capitalists between them were dismantling a more extensive paternalism and undermining the moral economy in Parliament'.[25] The Combination Acts of 1799 and 1800 prohibited workers from combining to raise wages. Handloom weavers petitioned parliament in spring 1808 for legislation to enforce a minimum wage and piece prices. Upon the failure of the bill in May 1808, weavers and other textile workers held mass meetings in St George's Fields in the Newtown district of Manchester and strikes broke out across the region. A major part of the demands, as with the cotton spinners' strike in 1810 and the Luddite outbreaks of 1812, involved the maintenance of statutory regulation of prices and working conditions, established by custom and by the Elizabethan Statute of Artificers. From the point of the view of the textile workers, government had bowed under pressure from manufacturers who had drunk deep from the new political economy of *laissez-faire* free trade preached by Adam Smith.[26] The jubilee paternalism of the manufacturers therefore proved little more than a sticking-plaster over these divisive tensions about class and the future shape of the Manchester region's industrial economy.

## Jacobite loyalism

Another distinctive element of the patriotism of Manchester and its region involved a less obvious and more diffuse political heritage, that of Jacobitism, support of the old Stuart monarchy displaced by the Glorious Revolution of 1688. Jacobitism is usually portrayed as dead, both ideologically and as a physical presence, soon after the end of the 1745 rebellion. In Lancashire, a majority of those gentry involved in the rebellion were arrested, executed, or had their estates confiscated. Yet Paul Monod and several other historians have suggested that Jacobitism maintained a cultural legacy well into the late eighteenth century. This heritage was particularly strong in the Manchester region, and centred on a small non-juring community associated with the Collegiate Church (that became the Cathedral in 1847). A grocer, 'Bishop Garnett', was still administering to a congregation of thirty in 1804. He distributed non-juring litany and prayers to five fellows of the Collegiate Church in 1798. Although mock corporations, another feature of Jacobitism, had died out in Preston, Walton and Sefton, the Ardwick Ancient and Loyal Corporation still functioned, if somewhat benignly. It still adhered to the Jacobite ritual of drinking Charles's health over the water and reserving an empty chair at the dinner table for many years after the 'Prince of Wales' had died in 1788. The members included respectable merchants and manufacturers who settled in the new development of bourgeois villas away from the smoke and noise of Manchester centre: Thomas Tipping, James Potter, and James Bateman consecutively held the post of 'mayor'. Many of its officials would see each other regularly again at John Shaw's punch house, formerly a Jacobite club near the Collegiate Church. They also became members of loyalist societies in the 1790s and the Tory Pitt Club in the 1810s.[27]

There is some evidence that Jacobite culture persisted in the region. Samuel Curwen, an American loyalist visiting England during the American revolution, passed through Manchester on Restoration Day, 29 May 1777. He claimed that his landlady was a Jacobite who informed him that all those 'in the abdicated family's interest, which is here openly professed', were in the habit of 'putting up large Oak boughs over their doors on 29 May to express Joy at the Glorious Event of the restoration of the Stuart family to the English throne'. He saw oak branches on houses that had reputedly harboured Bonnie Prince Charlie and members of his court in 1745, including Mr Dixon's residence on Market Street and at Mr Bower's on Leigh Street. In 1780, he again noted oak branches in Manchester on Restoration Day. During the American Revolution, the dominant sentiments among Manchester elites were Tory and loyalist, in favour of coercion of the American rebels. This was a position that contrasted greatly with the pro-American reform movement that consumed the efforts of Yorkshire elites.[28]

The Lancashire loyalist calendar reinterpreted the past in a new context. Whereas the Restoration Day had been neutralized into a politically benign 'Oak Apple Day' in many parts of the country, in the Manchester region it maintained its Jacobite cultural heritage. Vestry accounts show that 29 May was celebrated annually in Didsbury and Bolton with bell ringing and dinners. The 'martyrdom' of Charles I on 30 January was commemorated with church sermons on 30 January. In the Manchester region, these commemorations, according to Peter Nockles, served to 'keep alive a distinctly High Church political identity', distinguishing the local elites against Whiggery and theological heterodoxy.[29] Here is where the surviving threads of Jacobitism were appropriated by the 'Church-and-King' loyalism of the 1790s. In Blackburn, Oak Apple Day was combined with popular loyalism; the number of oak boughs on show in May 1794 was noted as conspicuously high and 'the sight at this time was truly pleasing, as it evinced the detestation entertained of French Tyranny etc by the loyal inhabitants of the town'. There is some evidence that 10 June, the birthday of 'James III', was still remembered. William Rowbottom remarked on 9 June 1799 that Oldham church steeple was to be adorned with oak branches but the unseasonably cold weather meant that 'some of the most loyal Burning enthusiasts of the day made diligent search to have found a sprig but in vain to the joy and triumph of the Jacobin party'.[30] The taints of Jacobitism therefore pervaded the new anti-radical loyalism, if somewhat inchoately. High Church High Tory strongholds in previously Jacobite centres were more susceptible to principles of divine right and passive obedience to the monarchy.

## Orange loyalism

The final feature of the processions and church services of the jubilee celebrations that made south Lancashire patriotism distinctive if not unique compared to the rest of England was the participation of Orange lodges and societies. In Bury, 'the Orangemen marched in procession to St John's Chapel, where the Rev H. Unsworth preached an appropriate sermon'. At Oldham, 'that loyal body of men, the Orange Society, was drawn up with the Staff [of the local militia], and went in procession to the church'. Oldham diarist William Rowbottom noted how they 'made a fine show'. The Manchester procession of the rifle regiment, musicians and freemasons to the Collegiate Church was joined by 'the Orangemen ... in their orange scarves'. These bodies were clearly respected as part of the associational local elites. Working-class Irish Protestants were also represented. John Holden recorded in his diary how in Bolton the factory workers marched to the church 'with the Orange Men from John Baron's, Church Bank, and the Freemasons from two Lodges'.[31]

The rapidity and apparent ease with which the Orange societies had been accepted into local elite culture is testimony to the strength of the particular type of loyalism in the Manchester region. The Pennine areas of Lancashire and the West Riding of Yorkshire had been more strongly Protestant than the rest of the region. Bolton was dubbed 'the Geneva of the North'. Orangeism is usually associated with social clubs of immigrant Irish Protestant labourers, as it became in the Victorian era in Liverpool and Glasgow. In this first decade, however, the Orange movement was not just a working-class social phenomenon. The first lodges were formed by gentry, magistrates and clergy. Orangeism facilitated and shaped their ideas of loyalism and their enforcement of law and order. Some of the acting magistrates who sent in the yeomanry at the Peterloo Massacre had been officers of militia regiments that had been sent over to Ireland in 1798–9 to quell the rebellion there.[32]

In 1793, the number of Irish residents in Manchester and Salford were estimated at 5,000 or about 8 per cent of the population. Irish immigration increased on a large scale from the 1798 Irish Rebellion onwards. The first record of Orange societies in Manchester, Salford and Stockport appeared around 1802. 12 July parades were prohibited by the boroughreeve of Manchester after a disturbance in 1803. The more respectable 12 July parades were by contrast encouraged in Oldham,

Mottram and Bolton, where the vicars gave 'appropriate sermons' in the parish churches.[33] The Grand Lodge of Great Britain had been formed only two years prior to the jubilee, during a period of heightened sectarian tension. Lord Howick's Roman Catholics Army and Navy Service Bill of 1807 would have allowed Catholics to become military officers. The anti-Catholic feeling roused by the bill echoed the reaction to the Catholic Relief Act of 1778, which had sparked the Gordon Riots in 1780. Local loyalist elites held meetings to compose addresses to the King congratulating him on the defeat of the bill in April 1807. The Manchester address was composed at the Bull's Head Inn, the headquarters of the loyalist societies. The loyal address was signed by, amongst others, three vicars (including Rev Ethelston) and the major manufacturers Charles Frederick Brandt, James Ackers, and John Leigh Philips. A riot broke out between Protestant and Catholic Irish in Newton Lane, Manchester, after an Orange parade on 12 July. In response to the disturbances, the English Grand Orange Institution was formed at the Star Inn. Colonel Ralph Fletcher, magistrate of Bolton, was Grand Master, with James Lever Esq, bleacher and joint lord of the manor of Bolton as Grand Treasurer. By 1830, there were 77 lodges in Lancashire (out of a Great Britain total of 230). A lodge (Irish warrant 1128) was formed in the Manchester and Salford rifle volunteers, commanded by Colonel James Silvester, magistrate and owner of mills in Atherton and Chorley. His regiment put down the 12 July 1807 riot in Manchester. 500 members of his militia regiment were called out by the magistrates to suppress the Luddite disturbances in the area in May 1812. His regiment were later involved in the Peterloo massacre of 1819.[34]

Orangeism therefore involved more than just gentry show and sociability and benefit societies for immigrant Irish Protestants. Underneath the civic patriotism lay more sinister aspects of local government. Magistrates' military connections and their determination to track down 'sedition' enabled the Orange movement to provide a useful network for the enforcement of law and order in the Manchester region. The most energetic employers of spies to track down radicals were Orangemen, including Colonel Ralph Fletcher of Bolton, Joseph Radcliffe of Ashton and Huddersfield, Rev Robert William Hay, head of the Salford bench, William Chippendale of Oldham, and Charles Prescott and John Lloyd of Stockport. These were the most active magistrates against Luddism in 1812 and the mass platform radicalism leading up to Peterloo in 1819. The Irish Grand Lodge issued a declaration to the English Grand Lodge on 12 July 1813, which rejoiced that 'following your loyal example, the British Orangemen have saved their country by suppressing the treasonable bands calling themselves Luddites'. At a dinner in the Spread Eagle in Manchester on 4 November 1814, the anniversary of the landing of William III in Britain, Colonel Ralph Fletcher proclaimed in a speech that he had 'witnessed the utility of the Orange Institution, in the cheerful co-operation of its members with the civil and military powers, at an alarming period, in maintaining the peace of the country, and he knew nothing better calculated for public good than a great diffusion of its principles'.[35]

## Conclusion

Patriotism in the Manchester region was distinguished by multiple meanings and political interpretations. However sincere attachment to the ideal of a common British identity was, the inhabitants of the Manchester region could only accept it when filtered through local particularities and identities. Lancashire Britishness shared something of the defiance and independence of the archetypal John Bull. But it was also accompanied by a good measure of northern grit, political and sectarian tension, and a sincere pride in the contribution of the region to the burgeoning industrial economy of the nation.

The contested nature of the Jubilee was a signpost for a changing politics, changing society and economy in the region. Just over two years later, Bolton and Middleton would be convulsed by Luddite machine-breaking. Following the end of the war, popular radicalism revived, culminating in the Peterloo massacre of 1819. The first two decades of the nineteenth century were therefore crucial in the development of the Manchester region's identity and politics.

# 'These Lancashire women are witches in politics': Female reform societies and the theatre of radicalism, 1819–1820

Ruth
Mather

In early July 1819, the *Morning Chronicle* reprinted reports from Manchester of a new and, to its conservative audience, unwelcome development in north-west radical politics. This was the establishment of the Blackburn Female Reform Society, 'from which', the reader was informed, 'a circular has been issued to other districts, inviting the wives and daughters of the workmen in the different branches of manufacture to form themselves into similar Societies. They are not only [to] co-operate with the different classes of workmen in seeking redress of their grievances but "to instil into the minds of their children a deep and rooted hatred of the Government and the Houses of Parliament" whom they are pleased to call "our tyrannical rulers".'[1] On 5 July, the Society appeared publicly at a meeting of Blackburn reformers, mounting the hustings to present an embroidered Cap of Liberty and an address to the chairman, which he proceeded to read to the assembled company. The *Morning Post* was horrified, declaring the women to have rejected all morality and religion, while *Trewman's Exeter Flying Post* assured its readers that 'the females are women well known to be the most abandoned of their sex'.[2] The societies which so shocked these observers spread across the region, assembling in public meeting rooms, making public presentations and speeches and offering their support for parliamentary reform.

Despite this public presence, women's speeches at meetings were overwhelmingly couched in terms of their roles as wives and mothers, rarely stepping beyond the acceptable boundaries of the domestic sphere. Historians have tended to see this simply as an attempt to deflect criticism. Anna Clark, for example, states that 'women had to use modest language because they faced vitriolic attacks for their activities', while Paul Custer describes the societies as 'equally famous for their novelty and their unoriginal rhetoric – the latter designed mainly as a tranquillizer against the former.'[3] Yet it is evident from the reports above that, if the intention was to neutralize criticism, the strategy was a spectacular failure. It is time to look again at the addresses of these early female reformers, and to see them instead in the context of the highly polarized politics in industrializing Lancashire. As Frank O'Gorman and Katrina Navickas demonstrate in this volume, Lancashire also had a strong loyalist tradition, which drew power from the presence of many local elites within its ranks. The divide between radical and loyal forces was particularly bitter in the region, and power was publicly contested in the use of local space. The female reform societies should be seen as part of this performance of power, acting within a tradition of theatrical subversion within Lancashire radical politics.

The female reformers of Blackburn began their address with an apology for their lack of experience in politics. Likewise, the chairwoman of the Stockport female reformers requested that the men present withdrew before she made her first speech, fearing that she might make embarrassing blunders, 'for it is something new for women to turn political orators'.[4] There were, however, precedents for women making public speeches. The industrializing north-west region had strong dissenting traditions, and many early Methodist sects allowed women as well as men to preach. Women also had experience of exclusively female organisation in charity groups and friendly societies, and in the campaign against the slave trade.[5] Nor was participation of working-class women in public demonstrations new. Women were known to be the main culprits in the initiation of food riots at the Lancashire markets; they were involved in Luddite violence and they suffered alongside men in the bitter strikes of 1818.[6] Following these strikes, one woman even published a pamphlet imploring local men and women to form unions for the sakes of their families.[7] As the movement for political reform became more organized after 1815, women were involved in a number of ways, sheltering fugitives and providing alibis as well as attending and voting at radical meetings.[8] One spy reported seeing 'about sixty Gorles and Women' leaving a radical meeting at Besses o' th' Barn near Manchester in April 1818.[9] Nonetheless, these meetings tended to be dominated by men. The novelty of the female reform societies was in the provision of an organized forum exclusively for women.

The female reform societies therefore offered women an opportunity to share their distinctly feminine reasons for seeking reform. Although women worked alongside men in the textile industries which dominated the district's economy, they tended to focus on their experiences as wives and mothers rather than as workers. While their male counterparts elaborated on abstract ideas of the ancient constitution and the rights of Englishmen, the women literally brought the cause home. The Manchester female reformers described themselves as 'compelled ... to associate together in aid of our suffering children, our dying parents, and the miserable partners of our woes.' They went on to describe their fear each day that 'the light of heaven should present to us the corpse of some of our famished offspring', and to lament that they could no longer even retain the sanctity of the sabbath, being 'compelled to employ in repairing the tattered garments, to cover the nakedness of our forlorn and destitute families.'[10] The Blackburn women complained that:

> our houses which once bore ample testimony of our industry and cleanliness, and were fit for the reception of a prince are now alas! robbed of all their ornaments, and our beds, that once afforded us cleanliness, health and sweet repose, are now torn from us by the relentless hand of the unfeeling tax gatherer.[11]

Likewise, the female reformers of Bolton-le-Moors informed William Cobbett:

> we would once have welcomed you by spreading before you a board of English hospitality, furnished by our industry. Once, we could have greeted you with the roseat countenances of English females. Once, we could have delighted you, with the appearance of our decent, and well-educated offspring: whilst we could have presented to your view, our Cottages, vieing for cleanliness and arrangement with the Palace of the King.[12]

The chairwoman of the Stockport society, Mrs Hallworth, made fewer allusions to home and family, but her references to religion and charity were also well within the bounds of a traditional female role. She declared the radical cause to be 'a good cause, it is the cause of God', and that the intention of the female society was to 'co-operate with other Unions for the general cause, and to give relief to incarcerated victims.'[13] None of these addresses made mention of female equality or the right of women to vote; the aim was 'to join the Male Union for constitutionally demanding a Reform in … The Commons House of Parliament.'[14] Rather than seeking to elevate women, the campaign for reform and the maintenance of family were presented as a joint enterprise between husband and wife. As Joanne Bailey notes in her study of pauper letters, the presentation of a respectable, loving family in distress was a key theme employed by Lancashire's poor to evoke the sympathy of the reader.[15] Some of the female reformers may have had experience of writing such letters, and at any rate they were likely to have been aware that their addresses would be published to a wide audience whose support they would hope to solicit. Their speeches fit within an established tradition of women addressing authority figures in the hope of some alleviation of their family's distress.

Nonetheless, conservative responses ranged from shocked outrage to amused ridicule. Commentators painted a picture of neglected men and children, whose wives and mothers favoured making speeches rather than meals, and who were too preoccupied with mending the constitution to notice their relatives' ragged clothes.[16] A handbill signed by 'An Englishwoman' warned the women of the irresponsibility of their actions, advising industry and frugality as an alternative and pointing out that the penny subscriptions of radical societies did little to feed their children.[17]

Others preferred to dismiss the women as drunks or nymphomaniacs. The *Morning Post* had the Stockport female reformers in an unseemly battle for a bottle of brandy, which they proceeded to swig throughout their speeches.[18] J.L. Marks (Fig. 1) caricatured the Blackburn ladies with their pikes and proclamations at suggestive angles, twisting their speech into crude *double-entendre*:

> I feel great pleasure, in holding this thing 'um-bob in my hand, as we see our Sweethearts, and Husbands, are such fumblers at the main thing, we

must of course take the thing, in our own hands ... a REFORM is very much wanted (among us) though we should not put on Armour, or carry Guns, (it is my opinion) Though we should be start [*sic*] naked, we could make the whole Army Stand! – It is our duty as Wives to assist our Husbands in every Push and Turn.

To the front of the image, one observer has clearly taken the ladies' plight to heart, covering the breast of his flushed female companion with the assurance, 'I feel for your sex'. Themes of drunkenness and promiscuity indicated a lack of proper femininity, and the *Manchester Comet* likewise highlighted these in their grotesque depiction of female reformers at the Union Rooms in 1822 (Fig. 2), in which the women seem far more interesting in the contents of their glasses than in the speech being read. While these images ridiculed the women's attempts to intervene in politics, George Cruikshank's 'Belle Alliance' (Fig. 3) is more threatening. Although there are still humorous depictions of Hogarthian gin-addled battleaxes and ribald references to poles and love tokens, the women in this print are armed with daggers, reminiscent of the viragos of the French revolution. One declares, 'If they von't grant us Libeties vhy d—me ve'll take 'em.' Their clear desire is to subvert the established hierarchies in both gender and social status, establishing a 'Petticoat government' instead.

As suggested by Cruikshank's cartoon, there is evidence that the modest femininity of the public addresses ran in tandem with a more militant reality, and that some women were indeed frustrated with the inadequacy of their male counterparts, growing impatient at the repeated thwarting of their efforts for reform.[19] In the same month as the female societies emerged, an article in the *Morning Post* claimed that one female reformer was training the inhabitants of Leigh to make pikes, and an anonymous spy reported from Middleton that:

> the Women are going about from House to House begging for Money ... to Make Caps of Liberty ... they say in public they will begin with the Branches and cut them all down till they come to the Ball, the Meaning of that is that they will murder all their Neighbours that are against their Purpose.[20]

The addresses themselves contained occasional threats of violence, which ranged in subtlety from the Blackburn women's reminders of historical precedents for female conquest to the Manchester females' impassioned refusal to 'bear the ponderous weight of our chains any longer, but to ... tear them asunder, and dash them in the face of our remorseless oppressors.'[21] The form of presentations to male radical leaders also had a threatening undertone. William Cobbett pointed out the key parallel in his justification of the female reformers' actions:

> it is notorious that the several *Volunteer Corps, Corps of Yeomanry*, and *Militia Regiments*, have had their *ensigns*, their *emblems*, their *banners*, presented to them by *titled women*, all over the country ... these women came, like you, out into the open air amongst crowds of men. They there, like you, made addresses to the men. They, like you, exhorted the men, to stand bravely by to the emblems they presented.

The difference was, Cobbett argued, in the righteousness of the cause being fought. The 'tame gentlemen' of the volunteer corps would go on 'to attack whole hosts of starving women and rebellious boys.'[22] His reference here is not only to the actions of the Manchester yeomanry at Peterloo, or the strikes of 1818, but to the numerous occasions during the French revolutionary and Napoleonic wars when troops ostensibly embodied to defend against French invasion were used for the military repression of dissent at home. This dual purpose was sometimes recognized, as at Ashton-Under-Lyne, where Lady Stamford and a Mrs Hays ceremonially presented the newly-formed volunteers with a banner and a song, which called for their protection not only against the French but also against the 'Regicide host' at home.[23] Such ceremonies were usually conducted very much in public, intended to be highly visible to local people, providing entertainment but also a warning for the opponents of government. They defined patriotism in terms which excluded reformers, characterizing them as anti-British. Lancashire radicals were therefore appropriating a ritual which had in the past been used against them, with the women designating radical societies as the force for patriotism. Furthermore, the militaristic references did not end with such ceremonies. Throughout the summer of 1819, large groups of radicals – including women – showed their strength as they drilled to march in military step on the moors around the industrial towns.[24] In this context, Michael Bush rightly asserts that 'the intervention of self-organized women in the cause of radical reform had evoked the prospect of a fight to the death'.[25] The

Blackburn women handed over their Cap of Liberty with the warning that 'we trust no ruffian banditti will be allowed to wrest [it] from your hands but with the forfeiture of your existence'; they were literally exhorting their men to victorious liberty or glorious death.[26]

It seems, therefore, that the female reformers were both parodying the rituals of their opponents and encouraging their menfolk to take action. Female persuasion was held to be a powerful tool: one radical orator encouraged women at a meeting to 'tease their Husbands till they promised to do their endeavours', while on another occasion a Middleton woman boasted that her sex were able to 'bias their Husband almost to anything.'[27] This, according to a correspondent of the *Literary Chronicle*, was the most troubling aspect of female involvement in the radical movement. 'In the present case, the men are stirred up by the women, who only look to rebellion, and not to industry, for relief', he worried. 'I own that I tremble when I think of men with starving families urged on by the double impulse of hunger and a mistaken sense of duty ... I consider the involvement of women to be the most dangerous feature in the aspect of the affair.'[28] For as long as their wives and daughters took part in the radical struggle, men could not for shame abandon it. Yet, although they may have been frustrated at the lack of progress made by the radical movement since the end of the French wars, the women chose to encourage, rather than embarrass, the men into action. The presentations by female reformers flattered the male leaders by imbuing them with chivalric qualities of honour and bravery, just as had been the case with wartime volunteers. Furthermore, by focusing on home and family, the women employed the same rhetoric which had been used to justify the creation of these loyalist forces during wartime.

The vast manpower and financial resources required to fight the French had meant that the British army had to draw support from all sections of the populace, and therefore a distant war needed to be made meaningful to the average Briton. What had the poorest farmer to fight for? The evangelical loyalist writer Hannah More offered the answer – he was to protect 'King, Church, babes, and wife.'[29] Wives, families and homes played a key role in creating and sustaining a sense of national pride. The treatment of women was, in Enlightenment thought, an indicator of a country's civilisation, and British men were portrayed as strong and chivalrous in contrast to the weak, effeminate and sexually incontinent French.[30] Furthermore, the family was, in the British political tradition, a 'little commonwealth', in which the paternal authority of even the lowliest husband and father mirrored that of the British king over his people. It followed, the propagandists argued, that those who had no respect for the hierarchy of state, be they French revolutionaries or British radicals, would have similar disrespect for the institution of family, and prominent radicals were discredited in these terms.[31] Thus one of the first resolutions of the Association for Preserving Liberty and

JOHN BULL in his GLORY.

CITIZEN. COUPE TÊTE in his MISERY.

Property Against Republicans and Levellers, famed for its intimidation of suspected radicals, was to:

> preserve and transmit to their Children that Constitution and domestic Happiness which they received from their Ancestors; which has always distinguished them above all the Nations of the Earth.[32]

Throughout the war, comparisons between the cosy British cottage and the destitution of the French family were standard in print culture. T. Ovenden's contrast between 'John Bull in his Glory' and 'Citizen Coupe Tête in his Misery' (Fig. 4) was typical. The latter print carries the caption:

> The Mother oe'r her Children moans,
> Hears their sad sighs and dying Groans,
> In vain to Heav'n she prays.
> Till overwhelmed with poignant Grief,
> In Death they only find Relief.

The French family in the image are starving to death, having foolishly put their trust in the revolutionary 'heroes' whose portraits adorn their walls. Yet in 1819, the image could have been an illustration for the Blackburn women's lament that 'language cannot paint the feelings of a mother, when she beholds her naked children, and hears their inoffensive cries of hunger and approaching death.' But it is not revolutionaries who have wrought *this* destruction; it arises 'entirely from the

Figure 4:
T. Ovenden,
'John Bull in His Glory'. Library of Congress; and 'Citizen Coupe Tête in his Misery' (London: J. Downs, 1793). Hand coloured etching. British Museum Satires 8293. © Trustees of the British Museum

misrule of a profligate system of government.'[33] The female reformers may not have seen the Ovenden prints, but their message would have been commonplace: the war against France and against reform was to protect against the destruction of the family. Yet as the female reformers demonstrated, their own families were suffering terribly and their homes in a wretched state. Their circumstances, they argued, were not their own fault but 'the consequences resulting from the mad career of the Boroughmongers' war ... The hypocrital [sic] hireling will blasphemously tell you that these things are of divine ordinance; but in vain does he publish this to reason and common sense'. They were aware of the real interests behind the 'unjust, unnecessary, and destructive war, against the liberties of France': it had 'tended to raise landed property threefold above its value, and to load our beloved country with an insurmountable burden of Taxation' which was driving them to destitution whilst funding extravagant aristocratic lifestyles.[34] The female reformers turned loyalist propaganda on its head to legitimize their own cause – it was the corruption of government which harmed *their* families, and if war for this purpose was justified, they were prepared to encourage their men to fight. As Ethelinda Wilson, writing in the *Republican,* put it, they hoped that 'the signature of a female would stamp the eloquence of a Burke with insignificance.'[35]

This is not necessarily to suggest that the radical movement was seeking a battle. Even if, as the conservative press supposed, they were arming themselves secretly with pikes, they must have been aware that the authorities had vastly superior military power at its disposal. Rather, I believe that both the interchangeability of militaristic and domestic imagery were part of what Paul Custer has, borrowing from the magistrate Ralph Fletcher, termed a 'mischievous pageant', in which true intentions were deliberately ambiguous.[36] Women in protest had long alternated between the characters of meek, delicate femininity and strong, determined Amazon. Charles Wrigley, reporting on a parade of the 'Ladies Union' at Leigh, complained that 'These Lancashire women are proverbially witches in politics (if not in beauty)'.[37] His reversal of the traditional Lancashire compliment on female beauty seems to be referring instead to the womens' fascinating ability to 'shape-shift', adopting different forms and positions as circumstance and audience demanded. The authorities were left in a frustrating state of uncertainty as to how much of the radical appropriation of loyalist ritual and discourse constituted genuine threat and how far they were being openly ridiculed, and this confusion gave power to the radicals by reducing the authorities' sense of control. Moreover, it allowed the movement to display this power, taking control of public space just as the forces of loyalism had done some years earlier. The reformers, both male and female, were probably aware that staunch conservatives would never view them as reasonable or respectable. However, by claiming for themselves the same legitimizing notions as were used by their opponents, they could hope to convince those on the fence while simultaneously putting two fingers up to the civil power.

While it is important to recognize the playful theatricality of radical discourse, my emphasis on subversion in the use of domesticated rhetoric is not to deny the reality of the affectionate working-class family. Rather, the female reformers were employing what Helen Rogers describes as 'melodramatic realism', an exaggerated version of what women genuinely experienced within the home.[38] Respectability was important, not just in the campaign for political representation but for one's own self-worth. Cleanliness was vital: even at times of severe hardship, Samuel Bamford's mother was described as 'cleanly to an excess' and his own home in later years was 'humble but cleanly', animated more by the people within than by material ornament.[39] For the respectable worker, a wife was seen as an asset, not just economically but because of moral influence women were believed to exert. Bamford, for example, made the decision to take a wife to curb his hard-drinking bachelor lifestyle, recognizing that the lure of the tavern could be replaced by that of the 'ever-welcome home'.[40] Yet genuine love and regard was important in the choice of a partner. Bamford chose to marry his childhood sweetheart, Jemima, a woman who had already borne him a daughter, and his love for both wife and child is evident throughout his written works. Likewise, the merchant David Whitehead of Rawtenstall sought a wife who would not only assist with the promotion of his business interests, but that the marriage would be one of 'sincere friends, faithful partners, and useful assistants to each other.'[41] Nor was it only men who had a say in the courtship process. While the freedoms of women should not be over-emphasized, it does seem that they did have considerable agency in deciding their marital prospects, possibly due to their ability to earn an independent living in the textile trades. The pace of David Whitehead's relationship with Betty Wood was firmly dictated by her, with her warning her enthusiastic suitor that 'hasty marriages often prove unhappy ones.'[42] Even with an illegitimate child, Jemima Bamford seems to have avoided becoming too great a burden on her family as a single woman. Such a combination of choice, practicality and passion seems likely to have been a strong basis for companionate marriage, and many working-class autobiographies from the period emphasize the importance of having a partner in one's struggles.[43]

There were, of course, many struggles for the working-class family, whose delicately-balanced economy was easily disrupted by price fluctuations or the loss of a family member. While workers could aspire to the domestic ideal, in reality it could be difficult to achieve despite their best efforts.[44] By 1819, families confronted with such difficulties were forced on to the defensive by Thomas Malthus, whose doctrines seemed to blame them for their own destitution.[45] For those who sought respectability, this was an insulting intrusion. Elizabeth Salt's distaste for the 'Reverend DIVINE Malthus' was palpable in her 1818 pamphlet, in which she lamented that 'the only happiness we have in prospect for our youths (that of joining them in marriage with those they love) is to be prevented, in all cases where they cannot show ... that they *are* able to maintain themselves and a family of children.'[46] Further interference came from the state, especially for the families of prominent radicals. Following the suspension of Habeas Corpus in 1817, a number of male reformers were arrested or fled to avoid the attentions of the authorities. Samuel Bamford recorded that 'Personal liberty not being now secure from one hour to another, many of the leading reformers were induced to quit their homes, and seek concealment'. He himself made illicit and perilous trips home, where 'his wife would rush into his arms, his little ones would be about his knees, looking silent pleasure – for they, poor things, like nestling birds, had learned to be mute in danger.'[47] Whole families were affected by the incursions of state surveillance as well as enduring the critical observations of outsiders. In such circumstances, the female reformers emerged to give their version of events. They distinguished themselves from their male counterparts by forming female-only groups because, as the sex most associated with home-making and caregiving, they could offer an authentic testimony of domestic conditions. The *Black Dwarf* defended their efforts, sneering at 'Parson Malthus, who would punish a poor female for bearing honest children' and 'Slop, who would destroy her for sharing and sympathising in the pure patriotic feelings of a father, brother or husband'.[48] If their homes were in disarray, their families starving and themselves forced to work even on the sabbath, it was through no fault of their own. It must have been satisfying to rebut accusations of their own irresponsibility by placing the blame on the shoulders of their accusers, neatly reversing their own propaganda.

Women, and the female reform societies in particular, therefore had an important part to play in 1819. As the radical movement recovered from a series of defeats and began to rejuvenate itself after the reinstatement of Habeas Corpus in 1818, women helped to build the confidence of their male comrades and to project an image of their power through public theatre. Radical theatricality was at its finest on 16 August 1819, as the members of radical societies from across the North West marched towards St Peter's Field in Manchester to listen to their hero, Henry Hunt. Again, this procession was highly ambiguous. The magistrates clearly saw it, or at least claimed to see it, as a military march, and later brought forward a number of witnesses to testify to their alarm at the meeting and the drilling which had preceded it. The reformers marched in step, with banners and with music, just like a military regiment. At their later trial, however, the radicals argued that the processions had been like those of the local wakes, and held up the presence of women as proof of their peaceful intentions.[49] Women themselves gave testimony.

The 65-year-old Nancy Prestwich, who out of respect for her age, headed a procession from Moseley, insisted at Hunt's trial that 'We went in peace ... I certainly would not have gone to the meeting if I expected any riot or tumult.' Lucy Morville pointed out that she not only took her two sons, aged nine and twelve, to the meeting, but she was sufficiently assured of their safety to let them walk on ahead of her in the procession. The servant of Mr Moorhouse, 'a good religious man' at whose home Hunt had been a guest, pointed out that her master had even taken his pregnant wife to the meeting.[50] As we have seen, the presence of women was not, in reality, a guarantee against violence, but the reformers were once again asserting their image of the protection of respectable and loving families. They would not have risked the wellbeing of their loved ones, they argued, had they anticipated the barbarity of the authorities.

Whatever the intentions of the crowd, the Manchester magistrates took no chances and sent in the cavalry as soon as Hunt mounted the hustings. The female reformers, dressed distinctively in white, intending to repeat their ritual presentations in offering emblems and addresses to Hunt, were clustered around the hustings, and therefore inevitably suffered in the panicked crush as the crowd sought to escape. But there is also evidence that they were deliberately targeted by the Manchester yeomanry, with a disproportionate number of the women in attendance receiving blows, many of which were savagely inflicted with the intention of disfiguring the victim. One ballad sheet, celebrating the actions of the soldiers, included the lines 'His [Hunt's] mistress sent to hospital, for her face to renew; For she got it closely shaven on the plains of Peterloo.'[51] Michael Bush suggests such brutality was the result of fears that sexual, as well as social, hierarchies were being dismantled by the prominence of women at the meeting.[52] It may also have been that the soldiers recognized and resented the part the women had played in parodying their own pompous proceedings. Either way, the treatment of women only encouraged the radical appropriation of patriotic chivalry. 'Your amiable wives and innocent children have been inhumanely butchered by the cowardly hands of those who ought to be their guardians,' Hunt declared, encouraging his followers to continue their struggle.[53] Women were placed in the foreground of prints of the event and they appeared prominently on commemorative memorabilia, such as the jug shown in Fig. 4 of Alison Morgan's article, p. 72. Cruikshank's 'Manchester Heroes' (Fig. 5) emphasized their maternal role, depicting a child pleading with the Yeomanry for his mother's life.[54]

The destruction wrought upon loving families was again highlighted in reports, such as the testimonies of Ann Scott and her husband published in the *Cap of Liberty*. The pair described their enforced separation, despite Ann's illness, during her nine-month incarceration, under an editorial which read:

MANCHESTER HEROES

Figure 5: George Cruikshank, 'Manchester Heroes' (London: S.W. Fores, Sep. 1819). Hand-coloured etching. British Museum Satires No. 13266.

The partisans of Government are ever holding up to public view the horrors of the French Revolution, and cautioning the People of England to beware such sanguinary scenes, and yet while they are penning these precepts of prudence and morality, which the other they are acting over again the Robespierrean part of universal massacre.[55]

Here the reversal of wartime propaganda was explicitly made. Perhaps aware that the reformers had gained the moral high ground, both local and national government moved quickly to shut down opportunities for public assertions of opposition. The leaders of the radical movement were rounded up and imprisoned, while strict new legislation explicitly prohibited the actions which had caused most alarm for the authorities. Marches with banners, emblems and music were forbidden, as were meetings of more than fifty people, without the permission of a magistrate, and further intrusions into privacy were sanctions by the granting of powers to search without a warrant. Harsh penalties were imposed for any transgression. The extent of the authorities' reaction shows just how troubled they were by the ambiguity of radical protest, and also by the tide of public opinion against their actions.

Manchester's loyalist civil authorities, and the government who sanctioned the use of military force, could no longer lay claim to a chivalrous patriotism. Reports of the violence of Peterloo, especially that committed against women, shocked people across Britain, and helped to forge new links between radical and more moderate reformers.[56]

Diana Donald has demonstrated that the portrayal of female reformers in particular changed drastically after Peterloo. The caricaturists, ever attuned to changes in public opinion, swiftly changed their depictions of harpies and floozies for tragic heroines.[57] If not quite respectable, the women were now portrayed as righteous by many of their former detractors. After Peterloo, the female reformers were willing to play up to this portrayal in open letters to Hunt and Cobbett in order to highlight the brutalities of the massacre. 'The days of chivalry are passed', the Manchester women lamented in their letter to Cobbett, 'but in you the Female Reformers feel they shall never want a sufficient advocate.'[58] Off the public stage, however, women were far less willing to quietly surrender their fate into male hands. On 17 August, groups of women were seen marching toward Manchester, declaring 'we sent our sweethearts to Manchester yesterday and we are going to look for them, damn it now the revolution is begun and we will never work again.'[59] There was little of the helpless heroine in those who took part in violent reprisals against loyalists, or in a woman like Ethelinda Wilson, who carried a pistol in her dress as she launched a campaign for a second mass meeting among London radical societies and in the press.[60]

The female reformers vowed to 'keep our course – still speak and even fight' after Peterloo,[61] and were again prominent as radical theatricality burst triumphantly back into the open in the summer of 1820. As the recently-crowned George IV sought to exclude his estranged wife, radicals nationwide attached their cause to that of Queen Caroline, who was accused of adultery by the famously philandering king. The case allowed the radical movement to sidestep the provisions of the Six Acts and publicize their grievances. As Henry Hunt gleefully pointed out, 'no seditious meeting act can apply to her, no multitude, however numerous, can be deemed sedition for its number' if it was a meeting in support of the monarchy.[62] Women from across the political spectrum showed support for Caroline, with a number of female-only addresses sympathizing with her treatment by a cruel husband and expressing their consternation that the king's action set a precedent for 'every careless and dissipated husband to rid himself of his wife ... and to render his family, however amiable, illegitimate, thereby destroying the sacred bond of matrimony, and rendering all domestic felicity very uncertain.'[63] Lancashire's radical women, however, were keen to take the opportunity to publicly complain at their own treatment by the king's servants. The chairwoman of the Manchester meeting to address the queen argued that 'when the character of a defenceless and injured woman was at stake, whether it was the Queen in the palace, or the peasant in the cottage, it ... ought to call forth the united effects of all her sex to shield her from harm'. The link between the treatment of the queen and the barbarity of Peterloo was explicitly drawn:

As the chiefs of a cruel and corrupt system have levelled their menaces at you, so have the drawn sabres and fixed bayonets of their armed satellites have been brandished at us ... Not even the infant at the mother's breast was spared by the swords.[64]

By tying their own cause to that of the queen, radical women were again able to publicly assert their own experiences as evidence against the government. Yet, like the queen, their respectability was ambiguous. Caroline and many of her supporters protested her innocence, but others were just as happy to celebrate her as a bold advocate for women's sexual freedoms.[65] As the queen triumphed against her persecutors with the abandonment of proceedings against her, the radicals felt renewed confidence to display their power in public, audaciously celebrating her victory in the face of the disapproving authorities. In numerous Lancashire towns, large numbers of people assembled to parade the streets with banners and music, often burning effigies of the queen's opponents in prominent public meeting spaces. Women played a prominent part, often dressed in white to represent the queen's – and their own – innocence. Most of these events resembled traditional holidays, but, in tracing the streets where radicals had previously suffered persecutions, radical forces were redrawing a map of political power. The involvement of women in the radical movement made their association with the queen a natural extension of the appropriation of a chivalric, patriotic ideal.

The female reform societies, then, should not be dismissed for their adoption of a seemingly traditional role. As we have seen, that role was much more subversive when set against a political contest over the idealized British home. Women made themselves distinctive in the radical movement as the authoritative experts on domesticity, giving testimonies based on their real-life experiences, and thereby enabling their male comrades to lay claim to a chivalrous patriotism that had previously been the preserve of their opponents. Still more threatening to the authorities than the women's words were the military associations of their actions in presenting tokens to male leaders, which seemed to call on the men to display their honour in battle. The contradictory effect created by the juxtaposition of domesticated language and militaristic behaviour was deliberate. It was part of a 'mischievous pageant' which had long been employed in the radical movement to confuse the authorities and thus assert their own power. In 1819 and 1820, women were important players in this 'pageant', capitalizing on the widespread political rhetoric which focused on their own preserve: the home. The intervention of the female reformers came at a key time, reviving confidence after a number of setbacks for the radicals, and despite their own sacrifices, women continued to participate in radical demonstration, maintaining their ability to shift between domesticated and militaristic personas. At dinners held to celebrate Henry Hunt's birthday in 1820, the toasts to 'Those Lancashire witches who use their spells to comfort and redress the wrongs of men'[66] may well, like Charles Wrigley's description of female radicals, have added a political dimension to the traditional compliment. We too should recognize the importance of the shape-shifting women of Lancashire in the public performances of radicalism during these crucial years.

*With thanks to the York University Centre for Eighteenth-Century Studies and to the British Society of Eighteenth Century Studies for opportunities to try out earlier versions of this paper, and to Robert Poole for assistance with source material.*

# Starving mothers and murdered children in cultural representations of Peterloo

Alison Morgan

Of the fifteen people killed at Peterloo, four were women and one was a child.[1] Margaret Downes was sabred, Mary Hays was trampled by the Manchester yeomanry, Sarah Jones was hit on the head with a truncheon, and Martha Pilkington was thrown into a cellar. Two-year-old William Fildes was the first victim on 16 August 1819 when he was trampled to death by the horses of the yeomanry whilst they were on their way to St Peter's Field.[2] Of the 654 recorded casualties, 168 were women. These statistics reveal that more than a quarter of all casualties at Peterloo were women, even though they comprised only 12 per cent of those present.[3] This apparent targeting of women by the yeomanry resulted in the widespread use of the motif of mother and child across a range of print media and other cultural artefacts produced in response to Peterloo.

One of the most enduring cultural representations of Peterloo is George Cruikshank's print, 'Massacre at St. Peter's, or "Britons strike home!!!"' (Fig. 2). Published by Thomas Tegg in 1819, it plays a pivotal role in the iconography of Peterloo. The corpulent middle-aged yeomanry dominate the image, yet central to the composition is a young woman holding a baby and pleading for her life with the puffing buffoon, who bears an uncanny resemblance to the portrayal of the prince regent in other satirical prints of the time, and who is poised to bring down a sabre on her head. The yeoman's raised sabre is set against the Union Jack, symbol of nation and empire, thereby explicitly linking the British state with violence perpetrated against its own, unarmed, people.

The cultural responses to Peterloo ranged from prints to poems, songs, ceramics and textiles, all of which sought to construct a framework in which the events of 16 August 1819 could be both discussed and remembered. Whilst the authorities voiced their support for the actions of the Manchester magistrates and yeomanry, radicals established their own discourse in opposition to that of the state. This contestation for ownership of a significant event was not new in 1819 but was part of a wider battle being waged between loyalists and radicals regarding the representation of such a turbulent era for both contemporaneous and future societies. As James Chandler so aptly observes, 1819 was a remarkable year and one in which there was a realization that cultural responses were both 'making and marking history'.[4]

This trope or motif of the mother and child pervades the cultural representations of Peterloo, its widespread use leading to a greater impact rather than a dilution of effect through repetition. Through the exploration of this significant trope, this essay demonstrates how a range of texts and artefacts including songs, poems and prints are inter-related. This connection between texts and artefacts creates a powerful discourse with the repeated use of the trope resulting in a sense of a collective response to these terrible events. This essay begins by outlining the scale and variety of responses to Peterloo that employ the trope of mother and child, firstly in newspaper articles followed by satirical prints and other cultural artefacts and, finally, poetry. It can be shown that this trope, shared across many genres, is crucial to the creation of a shared radical discourse following Peterloo.

As the only self-consciously literary poet to respond to the massacre, Shelley swiftly produced a number of poems that he intended to publish.[5] His use of women in these Peterloo poems is of interest. However it is his inclusion of mother and child in the neglected poem, 'The ballad of the starving mother' that is considered in this essay. Although Shelley was in self-imposed exile in Italy in August 1819, gaining news through letters and newspapers sent by his friend, Thomas Love Peacock, 'The ballad of the starving mother' has much in common with other responses to the massacre. John Gardner also notes the similarities between Shelley's Peterloo poems and the 'imagery and ideas' found in contemporaneous prints and pamphlets.[6] Even though it is unlikely that Shelley would have had access to the majority of the Peterloo representations discussed here, he was aware of the plight of women and children at St Peter's Field. [7] Shelley's use of the trope connects his poem with both the written and graphic satire of the time, thereby contributing to this very specific form of radical discourse, despite Shelley's geographical and social isolation from the public sphere in which these representations appeared. Through an exploration of 'The ballad of the starving mother', I show how Shelley developed the use of the trope of mother and child from a specific criticism of the state at Peterloo to a general condemnation of a society in which its most vulnerable citizens were viewed as expendable.

## Newspapers and periodicals

The battle to shape the representation of Peterloo in the public consciousness began before the blood had dried on St Peter's Field. News of the event spread quickly throughout the country, due in part to the publication of a lengthy article in *The Times* on 19 August by John Tyas, the only journalist employed by a national paper present at St. Peter's field and who was arrested alongside the radical leader, Henry 'Orator' Hunt. In his extensive article Tyas stressed the peaceful nature of the crowd, even when the yeomanry rode into their midst: 'Not a brick-bat was thrown at them – not a pistol was fired at them during this period – all was quiet and orderly'. Once arrests had been made, the yeomanry began to attack the banners carried by the marchers, 'cutting most indiscriminately to the right and the left in order to get at them'. When the crowd began to fight back, wrote Tyas, 'From that moment the Manchester Yeomanry Cavalry lost all command of temper'.

Following their arrest on the hustings, Hunt and Tyas were taken to the local magistrates. On his way Tyas saw 'a woman on the ground, insensible, to all outward appearance, and with two large gouts of blood on her left breast'.[8] Such reporting galvanized the radical press and, it could be argued, began the 'feminisation of suffering', to borrow Ian Haywood's phrase, in cultural responses to Peterloo.[9] Leigh Hunt reprinted Tyas's article in the *Examiner* on 22 August. It was subsequently read by Shelley in Italy when he received copies of the periodical from Peacock early in September.[10] Shelley would almost certainly later have read the testimony of Elizabeth Farren published in the *Examiner* on 19 September. Farren claimed she was attacked by a member of the yeomanry, whom she named, whilst standing at the edge of the crowd with her six-month-old baby. She sustained a head injury inflicted by a sword but managed to protect her child.[11] The treatment of women at Peterloo was also addressed on 21 August in the *Leeds Mercury* which stated: 'Sex itself could not secure protection; defenceless women and tender children shared in the common overthrow'. The newspaper also reported the death of two-year-old William Fildes.[12]

Despite widespread condemnation of the yeomanry, conservative periodicals such as the *Gentleman's Magazine* held a different opinion, writing of their 'strongest approbation of the conduct of unprincipled individuals, whose only object, under the specious names of patriotism, is to effect a Revolution, and aggrandize themselves on the ruins of their country'.[13] Both the *Quarterly Review* and *Gentleman's Magazine* focussed on the injuries sustained by the yeomanry, rather than those inflicted by it upon women and children. The *Gentleman's Magazine* dispassionately noted that 'four persons were killed' before detailing the injuries of one of the yeomanry, a 'Mr. Hume'.[14] An article in the *Quarterly Review* in January 1820 placed the blame firmly on the protestors: '[The yeomanry] were assailed not only with abuse, but with heavy stones and brickbats: several yeoman were felled from their horses; one was hurt mortally'.[15] In the eyes of the Tory press the actions of the yeomanry were justified for the protection of the state from a riotous mob. The government chose to ignore the protests of many of the newspapers and the outrage emanating from a large part of the British public by sealing their support of the magistrates with a letter from the prince regent thanking the Manchester authorities for their actions.[16]

Peterloo resulted in the proliferation of London-based radical weeklies, such as the *Medusa*, the *White Hat* and the *Cap of Liberty*, all of which had disappeared by January 1820, victim to the repressive Six Acts passed in the frantic aftermath of Peterloo when the government feared revolution. Along with the more established *Black Dwarf* (1817–24), edited by Thomas Wooler, Richard Carlile's *Republican* (1819–26) and Hunt's *Examiner* (1808–86), these weeklies contain not only editorial comment and letters but poems and songs written to eulogize the dead and rouse the living into action. On 25 August the *Black Dwarf* reported the plight of women and children at Peterloo, emphasizing the unnaturalness of the yeomanry's actions: 'They *have trampled* on and SABRED WOMEN – children have been bathed in their mother's blood'.[17] In the same issue, the paper printed an address by the radical MP Sir Francis Burdett, dated 22 August. Outraged that English soldiers could attack their compatriots, Burdett declares, rather flamboyantly: 'What! Kill men *unarmed*! *Unresisting*!, and, Gracious God! WOMEN too, *disfigured, maimed, cut down,* and *trampled upon* by DRAGOONS. Is this ENGLAND? THIS A CHRISTIAN LAND! A LAND OF FREEDOM!'[18] Such emotive language is testament to the outrage felt by radicals towards the actions of the state. The reporting of such brutality resulted, in the words of Ashley Cross, in the 'victimised woman' becoming a 'central sign in the struggle to control how Peterloo would be represented'.[19] The intense interest of London weeklies in events in Manchester demonstrates that Peterloo was regarded as an event of national significance. Such attacks on the mother indicated how corrupt the state had become, thus contributing to the portrayal of Peterloo as the epitome of a state at war with its people. By destroying the maternal, the state could also be seen to be destroying itself.

## Graphic satire and cultural artefacts

Among the cultural artefacts of Peterloo, printed handkerchiefs were sold to raise money for the injured. In Fig. 1, a cavalryman is depicted with sabre raised about to strike two fallen women while bystanders watch helplessly.[20] The title of the print declares itself: 'A representation of the Manchester reform meeting dispersed by the civil and military power. August 16, 1819'.[21] It appears that this self-awareness of artefact as 'representation' extends to the variety of genres and forms within the radical public sphere following Peterloo, as they all share a consciousness of their role in shaping public opinion about the events in Manchester. The feminization of suffering is also prevalent in graphic satire produced in

Figure 1: 'A representation of the Manchester reform meeting dispersed by the civil and military power. August 16, 1819' by John Slack, with detail. © Trustees of the British Museum

immediate response to Peterloo. Several of the Peterloo prints published in 1819 contain a central image of a woman.

Cruikshank's 'Britons strike home' (Fig. 2) bears a striking similarity to 'The Massacre of Peterloo', published by J.L. Marks (Fig. 3). Central to both images is the defenceless mother, protecting her baby from the onslaught of the yeomanry. As with 'Britons strike home', the yeoman's

sabre is raised and is covered in what appears to be blood. In Marks' image the pig-faced trumpeter decries: 'How Glorious our Ardour to Lay down the Lives of defenceless Children, Husbands and Wives', highlighting the state's destruction of its people.

Another Cruikshank caricature entitled 'Manchester Heroes' (depicted in Fig. 5 of Ruth Mather's article, p. 61) reverses the portrayal of mother protecting her child in another indictment on the unnatural relationship between the state and its people. Here we see the young boy pleading with the yeoman as his mother falls to the ground: 'Oh pray Sir don't kill Mammy, she only came to see Mr Hunt'. Both Julie Kipp and Stephen Behrendt argue that the portrayal of motherhood and the family in the romantic period often symbolized the nation, illustrating how, in the words of Behrendt, 'the devastation of the family parallels the inevitable destruction of the state'.[22] It is evident from these examples of graphic satire that the depiction of the brutalization of women and children is making a wider allusion to the future demise of the state, as once the state began attacking the nation at its maternal roots, revolution could not be far behind.

The powerful combination of image and text is a technique adopted successfully by William Hone, described by John Gardner as 'one of the best-known radical writers in the country'.[23] Hone's pamphlet, *The Political House that Jack Built*, illustrated by Cruikshank, sold more than 100,000 copies in the first few months of publication in 1819, making it the 'most notorious public satiric reaction to the Peterloo Massacre', according to Marcus Wood.[24] A satirical re-working of the children's nursery rhyme, 'The house that Jack built', Hone's house is the constitution, the mainstays of which, including the Magna Carta and the Bill

The Massacre of Peterloo! or a Specimen of English Liberty. August 16ᵗʰ 1819

of Rights, are plundered by politicians, lawyers and the monarchy. The illustration accompanying the text 'These are the people' directly alludes to Peterloo in its depiction of the slaughtering of a woman and child in the background, whilst in the foreground ragged men are depicted as powerless to defend their womenfolk. A child, who has presumably lost his mother, pleads with his father for food (see Fig. 1 of John Gardner's article, p. 84). Here the state is portrayed as both the violator of defenceless women and the emasculator of men.

Another of Cruikshank's images shows a woman and child about to be sabred by a soldier on horseback. Although this image was published by William Hone in his satirical pamphlet *A Slap at Slop* in 1821, it was originally a design for a Peterloo statue. Clearly for Cruikshank, the image of mother and child was the iconic representation of Peterloo. The base of the statue was to be decorated with skulls, alluding both to the dead of Peterloo but also victims of other occasions of state brutality. It is worth noting that there is still no memorial to the victims of Peterloo.

As well as Hone's pamphlets and countless caricatures, other cultural artefacts were produced in response to Peterloo, including commemorative pottery. Although commonly produced to celebrate military, royal or sporting events, it appears that Peterloo was the first time that radicals had used pottery to commemorate a political event.[25] This ceramic jug (Fig. 4), one of a collection housed in the Manchester City Art Gallery, bears the familiar image of a woman under attack from a cavalryman with sabre raised. The falling woman carries a flag declaring 'Liberty or Death'. It would seem that her slaughter suggests she sacrificed her life in the cause of liberty. The inscription on the jug states: 'Murdered on the Plains of Peterloo'. Similarly a ceramic plaque manufactured in Staffordshire by D.M. and P. Manheim bears the image of a woman being sabred by a gleeful yeoman with a second woman lying dead on the ground and a third fleeing. Whilst the jug depicts the threat of violence, this plaque chooses the point of death for its image, thereby rendering it even more shocking. Whereas the caricatures were designed for immediate impact, it appears that artefacts such as this jug and plaque were designed for longevity.

These cultural productions, united by both their sentiment and a shared iconography, had a collective role, binding not only audience and artist but also audience and audience. Although it is not known how many jugs, plaques and handkerchiefs were sold, Hone's pamphlets and Cruikshank's caricatures reached a wide audience. For those not wealthy enough to purchase one of Cruikshank's prints, they were able to view the images displayed in the windows of printsellers. According to Diana Donald, copies of such prints would have appeared alongside those printed in Manchester in the windows of the *Manchester Observer* office on Market Street and the shop of its editor James Wroe in Ancoats Street.[26] The repetition of the violation of the maternal in these artefacts strengthens the radical discourse, presenting a unified opposition to the state.[27] Donald notes the prevalence of women and children in the Peterloo caricatures produced in London, suggesting that they had more in common with the 'atrocity imagery' of the sixteenth and seventeenth centuries than with Georgian satire.[28] If indeed that is the case and paintings such as Albrecht Dürer's 'Four horsemen of the apocalypse' (Fig. 5) and François Dubois's 'St. Bartholomew's day Massacre' were inspirational to Cruikshank and others, it would suggest that their desire was to elevate Peterloo beyond satire to an event of historical significance.

Figure 4: Ceramic jug. Courtesy of Manchester City Art Gallery

Figure 5: 'Four horsemen of the apocalypse' by Albrecht Dürer

## Radical poetry

Alongside graphic satire, the poems of the radical press and broadsides contributed to the creation of maternal iconography. 'The Manchester yeoman' printed in the *Examiner* on 5 September, in parallel with Cruikshank's caricatures, satirizes the yeomanry:

> I am d'ye see, a Yeoman,
> All fine from top to toe, man;
> And make my mare to go, man;
> And draw my sword out so, man.[29]

Whilst the caricatures depict the yeomanry as fat, this poem focuses on their stupidity through the simplistic language and style of the poem, in which every line ends in 'man'. The final quatrain intensifies the satire:

> And ride to meet the foe, man,
> And prove that there is no man
> Such 'more than man' can show, man,
> By cutting down – a woman.[30]

The awkward metre in 'woman' where the stress falls on the first syllable highlights the yeoman's idiocy. His bravado is revealed as cowardice in his slaying of a woman, his stupidity expressed in his aggression.

The genre of satire is continued in the *Black Dwarf* on 15 September in a poem entitled 'From Mr. Batty, clerk to – Milne, esq., coroner, to his friend in London'.[31] This epistolary poem relates events at the inquest of one of the Peterloo fatalities, John Lees. Batty despises the reformers and is revealed as being more concerned with his dinner than justice. The poem ends with his championing of the yeomanry as more valiant than the regular soldiers due to their ability to attack women:

> But your soldiers – they vaunt of their pleasure to save,
> Say that 'mercy's the boast of the valiant and brave';
> And for women – they love, they adore the dear race,
> Could they wound their fair forms, if they looked in their face;
> No, our Manchester Yeomen alone could do this,
> For to cherish weak women they ne'er knew the bliss.[32]

The humorous satire of 'The Manchester yeoman' which aims to ridicule the yeomanry is contrasted by the satirical bitterness of this poem. Batty clearly differentiates between the bravery and honour of the regular soldiers and the cowardice of the yeomanry, which accords with the general view that it was the yeomanry rather than the 15th Hussars who were responsible for the deaths and injuries at Peterloo. The final line appears to suggest that, denied conventional relationships with women, the yeomanry lack human compassion and, as a consequence, their violence becomes a form of sexually charged revenge.

'A new song' written 'in commemoration of the invincible courage of the Manchester Yeomanry Cavalry' was published in the *Medusa* on 9 October.[33] The tone of biting satire, as seen in the previous poem is continued here. In the penultimate stanza, the poem appears to allude specifically to the death of William Fildes:

> A woman and child,
> In their way ran so wild;
> The woman cried – 'spare, spare my child, O'
> But these true sons of Mars,
> Exclaim'd 'now for the wars,
> Our glory must never be spoil'd, O'.[34]

Not courageous enough to battle the French at Waterloo, the yeomanry seek their own glory in the indiscriminate slaying of women and children.

In 'The sword king' by H. Morton the yeoman is no longer a comic character, mocked for his size or stupidity, but a hunter, pursuing his prey of mother and child away from the chaos of St. Peter's Field. Published in the *Black Dwarf* on 22 September this somewhat melodramatic ballad narrates the tale of a mother and child fleeing from the eponymous 'sword king with sabre so bloody and bright'.[35] The yeoman sees it as his mission to destroy the next generation of reformers:

> Base brat of reform, shall thy cries bar my way,
> To the laurells [sic] that bloom for the loyal today?
> Shalt thou live to rear banner, white, emerald, or blue?
> No! this is our yeomanry's own Waterloo.[36]

The corrupted morality of such actions is again illustrated by the comparison between the murder of a defenceless mother and child and the defeat of Napoleon. The quasi-gothic tone of the poem is evident in the final quatrain:

> The mother she trembled, she doubled her speed,
> But dark on her path swept the black yeoman's steed;
> And ere she arrived at her own cottage door,
> Life throbb'd in her poor baby's bosom no more.[37]

Although this ballad personalizes victim and aggressor, moving away from a generalized attack on women to a specific story, it nevertheless allegorizes the conflict between a masculine state and a feminine people. As with many of the other representations shown here, the yeoman, with his shining sabre, is seen as a sexually threatening presence, a potential violator of the mother. In a brief allusion to Peterloo in his 1819 satire, 'Peter Bell the third', Shelley writes:

> Let thy body-guard yeomen
> Hew down babes and women
> And laugh with bold triumph till Heaven be rent![38]

Spoken by Peter, a thinly disguised Wordsworth, Shelley exploits the emotive nature of the trope by pluralizing the victims with the word 'hew' implying the yeomen cut the women down as if they were trees to be felled. However it is in 'The ballad of the starving mother' that Shelley most fully explores the relationship between the mother and the state.

## 'The ballad of the starving mother'

In the many portrayals of women in his poems written in the aftermath of Peterloo, it is the figure of Hope in *The Mask of Anarchy* that is probably the best known. As with the woman in 'The ballad of the starving mother', in the figure of Hope, Shelley presents a woman who is both active and passive, a potential representation of nation. Ian Haywood asserts that Hope is 'a hybrid symbol of self-sacrifice and resistance, and a figure who is clearly based on the trampled women who were at the visual and moral centre of the popular iconography of Peterloo'.[39] Hope's act of passive resistance has specific resonances with events at St. Peter's Field; she challenges the embodiment of power in the figure of Anarchy through an act that is simultaneously sacrificial and defiant:

> Then she lay down in the street,
> Right before the horses' feet,
> Expecting, with a patient eye,
> Murder, Fraud and Anarchy.[40]

The understated language and clear syntax engender a feeling of calm. Hope's apparently suicidal act confronts notions of victimhood by transforming the sacrifice of the victims into a source of strength.

In many respects 'The ballad of the starving mother' is the least Shelleyan of his poems written in the aftermath of Peterloo. It was written in 1820 but remained unpublished until 1926. Carlene Adamson claims that the ballad was ignored by editors 'because they felt it was an embarrassment to Shelley'.[41] Within Shelley's group of Peterloo poems 'The ballad of the starving mother' can be seen as a companion piece to 'The Mask of Anarchy', in which the large-scale themes of freedom and slavery are condensed into the tale of one woman. The ballad genre, so rarely used by Shelley, and its underlying philosophy connect the two poems, displaying the range that can be achieved within the genre whilst simultaneously pushing its boundaries. Through the blending of ballad with masque and liturgy, 'The Mask of Anarchy' demonstrates how the genre can be transformed whilst still retaining its integrity and historical provenance. In 'The ballad of the starving mother' it is the content rather than the form of the poem that shows Shelley's desire to confound expectation.

The narrative of domestic tragedy has almost no precedent in Shelley's other work. However, it is part of a very strong balladic tradition of tales of wronged women and abandoned or murdered children, a sub-genre also used by Wordsworth and Southey, as well as being found in countless ballad collections and broadsides. 'The ballad of the starving mother' contains no references to Peterloo, nation or contemporary politicians and yet its employment of the trope of mother and child allies it to other cultural representations of Peterloo. Through this shared discourse, Shelley has written a poem that is both in tune with contemporaneous radical expression and rooted in a cultural tradition. Therefore, despite its domestic setting, it can be demonstrated that this ballad is one of Shelley's Peterloo poems and is suggestive of his desire to harness the appeal of the chapbook and broadside which were so often selected as the print medium for these tales of fallen women.

Like Morton's 'The sword king', Shelley's 'Ballad of the starving mother' uses a personal tale to evoke the moral bankruptcy of a repressive regime through the exploration of maternal iconography. 'The ballad of the starving mother' is largely narrated by a woman who seeks help from the parson to save both herself and her child from starvation. Her pleas are met with silence and both she and the child die. It is only in the penultimate stanza of the poem that the true extent of the parson's culpability is realized when it is revealed that he is the father of the child:

> The child lay stiff as a frozen straw
> In the woman's white cold breast –
> And the parson in its dead features saw
> His own to the truth expressed.[42]

The unnamed woman is initially described as 'with a babe at her breast', which signifies her role as a mother.[43] However, instead of the maternal bond symbolizing 'social connectedness', the subsequent death of the baby evokes a fragmented society.[44] Shelley's portrayal of motherhood accords with the many representations of Peterloo where the mother-and-child relationship is moved from the private and into the public sphere to become victims of state-sanctioned violence. However, in contrast with the passive women depicted in other Peterloo images and poems, in Shelley's ballad, the mother is not a passive, nurturing presence but an active force, questioning both the individual and the society that are responsible for the downfall of both her class and gender. Her voice appears in the seventh line and continues for the following sixteen stanzas. The use of the first-person places the reader in the position of Parson Richards and therefore complicit in her suffering.

Shelley departs from the other cultural representations of Peterloo that depict women as victims of the yeomanry, embodiment of the state. The starving mother challenges the teachings of the church that uses religion as a weapon of class warfare:

> Will you say God said this to frighten the rich?
> He will only damn the poor?

That the deadly sins are alone those which
There are many temptations for.[45]

At this point in the poem the persona of the mother shifts from that of a woman begging for food to a mode of articulating Shelley's views on how the church is used in the repression of the people, a familiar argument in his other Peterloo poems. As she shifts from narrating her own sufferings to those of her class, she assumes bardic qualities in becoming the voice of a culture. Through using the language of religious teachings, such as 'sins' and 'temptations', she lucidly accuses the church of criminalizing the activities to which the poor are more prone.

The mother condemns the double standards of church and state:

O God! This poor dear child did I
At thy command bear and cherish –
Thou bad'st us increase and multiply –
And our tyrants bid us perish.[46]

The poem, which begins with a starving mother confronting a cruel and uncaring parson, becomes an attack on the state in its treatment of women before turning its focus on another parson – Thomas Malthus – whose views on the expendability of the poor were abhorrent to Shelley. The shift from first person singular to plural in the stanza above mirrors the broadening scope of Shelley's argument. Even though Shelley is clearly using the character of the mother to articulate his own views on Malthus and the church, the employment of direct address and an intellectually confident argument are heightened through the use of a female voice. Shelley highlights the hypocrisy of a religion, symbolized by the parson, which calls on the people to multiply whilst the state desires a decrease in population growth. Through their shared clerical profession, Shelley implies that Parson Richards is the personification of Malthusian cant. This is not a poem about the plight of one woman or even many women but a savage critique on the methods by which a state subjugates its people.

The exposition at the end of the tale demands that the reader re-evaluate the poem. The parson's cruelty towards the woman is not just that of a clergy indifferent to the sufferings of its parishioners, but of a man who refuses to accept his responsibilities towards his own child. His lack of morality and humanity are total; his supposed Christianity is yet another mask, one which hides a distortion of humanity akin to the grotesque figures in 'The Mask of Anarchy'.

Shelley's choice of mother and child for 'Ballad of the starving mother', his most intimate poem in this genre, was occasioned, according to Richard Holmes, by the death of William Fildes in the arms of his mother at Peterloo.[47] This child's death had even greater resonance with the Shelleys given that they had lost their own son, also named William, only two months prior to Peterloo. The plethora of representations of

Peterloo incorporating the trope of mother and child demonstrates the centrality of this motif to the radical expression of state brutality. As the extent of Shelley's access to the post-Peterloo poems and caricatures is unknown, this shared discourse must be attributed to deeper structures within these genres. The starving mother is simultaneously victim and protester with female agency at the core. Her articulation of suffering and condemnation of hypocrisy, interrupted by her demise, can be read as a challenge to the reader to continue her struggle. Whereas Hope and the other women seen here fight violence with passivity, the starving mother fights indifference with outrage. Perhaps she is 'Despair', the antithesis to Hope, with her solitary battle and death another argument for collective action.[48]

## Conclusion

This brief study of the female victim serves to illustrate the ways in which radical discourse evolved in the weeks and months following 16 August 1819. Galvanized into action on learning of the terrible events in Manchester, radical writers, artists and journalists united in their desire to produce texts and artefacts that would not only honour the dead and injured but also serve as a reminder to a present and future audience of just how far the state was prepared to go to defend its interests. Despite being in Italy, Shelley understood the need for a collective response and, as he had previously shown in his Irish poems a few years previously, appreciated the power of shared motifs in reinforcing cultural opposition to the state.[49] The widespread use of maternal imagery in the cultural responses to Peterloo demonstrates the inter-relatedness of texts across a range of genres and print media, with the commonality of the trope strengthening the radical response to Peterloo. Their longevity is testament to their effectiveness. Together these representations evince a cultural collectivity and an organic evolution of motif into iconography, an evolution to which Shelley's poems contributed.

# William Hone and Peterloo[1]

John
Gardner

William Hone, the London-based reforming pamphleteer, produced four main publications that relate to the government-sanctioned killings at St Peter's Field in Manchester on 16 August 1819. His three best-selling and most influential pamphlets, *The Political House that Jack Built*, *The Man in the Moon*, and *A Slap at Slop*, all address the outrage in Manchester. Produced in collaboration with a young George Cruikshank, later made even more famous through his illustrations for Dickens and latterly the temperance movement, these three pamphlets were so successful that they had combined sales of around 250,000 copies[2] and were read by the full spectrum of society, from cabinet ministers to soldiers.[3] However Hone also produced another less well-known poem on the massacre that purported to be by Lord Byron – *Don Juan Canto the Third*. Hone was a prolific writer and publisher; between 1815 and 1821 he produced around 175 publications, the main focus of which is injustice and hypocrisy.[4] Perceived by the authorities as a seditious radical, in 1817 Hone was tried three times for the same charge: twice for blasphemous and seditious libel, and once for blasphemous libel, for printing *The Late John Wilkes's Catechism*, *The Political Litany* and *The Sinecurist's Creed*. The following parody of the Ten Commandments is from *The Late John Wilkes's Catechism*:

> VI. Thou shalt not call starving to death murder.
> VII. Thou shall not call Royal gallivanting adultery.
> VIII. Thou shalt not say, that to rob the Public is to steal.

In court Hone defended himself by arguing that his parodies attacked the state and not the word of God. His acquittal, after three days of questioning, was a great victory for the radical press. It prompted Leigh Hunt to praise him in the *Examiner* on 21 December 1817, and Keats to write to his brothers: 'Hone the publisher's trial you must find very amusing; and as Englishmen very encouraging – his *Not Guilty* is a thing'.[5] Hone's victory did not please everyone though; Dorothy Wordsworth wrote, 'The acquittal of Hone is enough to make one out of love with English Juries.'[6] By 1819 Hone was viewed as a publisher who was difficult to convict and as such his publications became powerful vehicles to transmit radical and reformist ideas. This article will concentrate on examining Hone's four Peterloo publications in the order that they were released, and in particular how they shaped the representation of Peterloo in the minds of the public.

*Don Juan Canto the Third* was Hone's first post-Peterloo publication. It was written for the kind of educated audience that Lord Byron partly appealed to, and, unlike most of Hone's other pamphlets, was published without any woodcuts to help along the story. Despite his aristocratic background Byron also appealed to the poor and oppressed as he was seen as a champion of their causes. In 1812 Byron spoke in the House of Lords against a new bill, which meant that machine breakers, 'Luddites', would be sentenced to death. His speech had no actual effect on legislation, but it did convince many people that Byron belonged in the radical camp, even though that was not strictly true. *Don Juan Canto the Third* actually predates canto three of Byron's *Don Juan* by several months, and is a full length Byronic counterfeit that runs to 114 stanzas written in eight-line iambic stanzas of ottava rima, making it look, to the casual observer, as if the poem was a genuine continuation by the same author as cantos one and two.[7] To many readers it would have seemed as though Hone's *Don Juan* was more credible than many of the forgeries of Byron's poem, eighteen of which were circulating in London by 1832.[8] It was after all entirely possible that Hone could be the publisher of canto three; he had already published Robert Southey's play *Wat Tyler* (written in 1794 when Southey was a confirmed Jacobin) in 1817, much to the now ultra-Tory poet laureate's annoyance. Hone had been angered by Southey's opposition to reform, recently published in the *Quarterly Review* where he had written: 'If the opinions of profligate and mistaken men may be thought to reflect disgrace upon the nation, of which they constitute a part, it might verily be said, that England was never so much disgraced as at this time.'[9] Sherwood, Neely and Jones had printed the poem (which Southey claimed was stolen) without the author's name in February 1817. Their timing was apt as the publication coincided with the march of the Blanketeers from Manchester that resulted in an attempted rising.[10] However it was Hone that put the name of the poet, who had, in his own words, now 'outgrown' 'democratical opinions',[11] or, in Hazlitt's, become a 'servile court fool',[12] on the title page.

*Don Juan Canto the Third* is a complex piece full of contemporary allusions and various points of attack: the hypocrisy of John Murray; Coleridge's relationship with his reading public; the press; the regent; the issue of reform; Peterloo; radical public meetings, and the spy system. The poem begins with Juan's arrival in London after travelling through France, Italy, Spain, Germany and Holland. Juan is now married to

Haidee, and they have twelve children. Juan then becomes a 'News Retailer', first of all dealing in the established papers:

> XVI
> There lay the Chronicle, and there the Sun,
> The Globe, and once a week th' Examiner;
> The Advertiser, the Republican,
> The Herald and the Statesman and the Star;
> The Courier too, enough to startle one,
> The greatest Liar of the whole by far; [...]
> Tiring of the established papers Juan then sets himself up as a publisher of 'Rubbish on Reform', printing a paper called 'The Devilled Biscuit'

> XXV
> And Juan called it so, because concocted
> Of every hot or savoury Ingredient;
> Upholding principles the same as Locke did,
> Who built a paper limit for the obedient:
> After this Peterloo occurs, and Juan goes to a meeting held at Palace Yard, Westminster, on 2 September to condemn the massacre, addressed by Sir Francis Burdett, John Cam Hobhouse and Major Cartwright – where he is arrested as a traitor.

The poem ends with Juan's imprisonment and the suggestion that there may be a canto four 'if Juan shouldn't die in jail' (CXIII).

Don Juan Canto the Third can be dated before The Political House that Jack Built (also published in 1819) because it does not mention the Six Acts, which were announced at the end of November that year. Undoubtedly Hone was incensed by these measures, as can be seen in The Political House, published in December 1819, and The Man in the Moon, which was released around New Year's day, 1820. Unlike Byron's Don Juan, where in the eleventh canto we find the poet present at St Peter's Field, 'I've seen the people ridden o'er like sand / By slaves on horseback' (XI, 85), in Don Juan Canto the Third the poet is not there but in London, the seat of government.

> XXXIV
> I saw no swords, or Yeoman sworn to draw them,
> But I confess at window frame compact,
> High over-head I saw a noble nob –
> They said the owner's name was Irish Bob.

Rather than exclusively blame the Manchester yeomanry for the violence at St Peter's Field, Hone sees their controllers, from a 'window frame compact', as the true villains. In particular Hone identifies 'Irish Bob', Robert Stewart (Lord Castlereagh), and the government, as those whose ruling ideas have set the yeomanry against the people.

XXXV
I often wish this Bob, like Bobadil,
(who struts our stage the very prince of stormers)
Upon *his* plan would just contrive to kill
Some fifty thousand of these vile Reformers;

When Hone introduces the Peterloo massacre in his poem, he does not utilize the emotive statistics of so many dead, or hundreds wounded. Instead he personalizes the experience of the day by focusing on one person, Elizabeth Gaunt, a pregnant woman arrested along with Samuel Bamford and Henry 'Orator' Hunt.

XLII
I'm but a man, but if I were a woman
I should not be so much afraid of Guards,
But like Eliza Gaunt I dread a Yeoman

The Guards, or the regular soldiers, would not be a threat to a woman as they are professional and have a sense of honour, but the yeomanry have none of these virtues. Hone asks if the yeomanry are aware of whom they were attacking. They may feel it is fine to attack the labouring classes, but some of the crowd may be nobler than them: Elizabeth Gaunt may be descended from the aristocracy.

XLIII
Now, that I'm musing on this Betty Gaunt,
I wonder if she's lineally descended
By Father, Mother, Brother, Uncle, Aunt,
From him who Lusitanian Tower defended.

Gaunt, for Hone, is an early champion of freedom of speech because he had supported the Lollards, who had translated the Bible into English, thereby threatening the authority of the church by giving ordinary people access to the word of God. Also the fact that Gaunt was Duke of Lancaster, and that Elizabeth Gaunt is pregnant, perhaps makes Hone think of Gaunt's speech in act 2, scene 1 of Shakespeare's *Richard II*: 'This blessed plot, this earth, this realm, this England, / This nurse, this teeming womb of royal kings ... is now bound in with shame/With inky blots and rotten parchment bonds.'

At Palace Yard Juan hears Burdett condemn the actions of the Manchester authorities, but here he realizes that to associate with radicals and reformers is to risk being set up by one of Lord Sidmouth's many spies who have infiltrated radical groups and find easy pickings at events such as the Palace Yard meeting.

LVIII
I'm cautious now of what Cockade I wear,
I just observed an Oliver who went hence
To build *Reforming Castles* in the air;

And, tho' for ever in a dungeon pent hence,
He'd swear he saw me in St. James's Square
With jumping McGregor, or Simon Bolivar,
And pike-armed Radicals – Oh Judas Oliver!

Sir Francis Burdett's 'speech' to an estimated crowd of 30,000 people describing what happened at Peterloo – a speech for which he was later convicted of seditious libel and sentenced to three months' imprisonment and a £2,000 fine – is then retold in Spenserian stanzas.

LXVII
Even thus met Englishmen in peaceful guise
Upon the firm earth of that saintly field;
Their council hall o'er-domed by rolling skies,
That spread, they rashly deemed, an ample shield,
For those that in the open day-light wield
Petition's olive branch, – the freeman's tongue, –
But ne'er to *Speech* did the oppressor yield, –
Already to their steeds the Yeomen sprung,
And note of maddening charge their hollow bugle rung.

No Riot Act has been read, 'ne'er to *Speech* did the oppressor yield', before Meagher the trumpeter, decides to sound the charge.

LXIX
Fast fell defenceless manhood in that hour,
And womanhood and childhood lost their charm,
Humanity her sceptre, – thought her power;
And justice was a bruised and broken arm,
Upon the rampant field of that *alarm*.
On every side was heard a fiendish cry,
Where slaughter's sickle reaped her crimson farm,
Wreathing the dead ears round her temples high,
As the REFORMER fell, – and saddening sunk to die.

Peterloo has produced an unwelcome result, 'Sleep on – the stainless banner of Reform / Shall never more to thy applauses wave', implying that there is no longer any scope for peaceful demonstrations; all that is left now is more violence, and probably a revolution.

Hone's next response to the Peterloo massacre was *The Political House that Jack Built*. This pamphlet, designed to be consumed by a broad range of readers, with its witty and biting blend of narrative images and poetry, was first published in December 1819, and went on to sell over 100,000 copies. Unsurprisingly the squib elicited a worried response from loyalists, such as Robert Southey who commented, 'It is exactly one of those things which ought to be brought before a jury'.[13] However it never did go in front of a jury, most likely because those who would prosecute feared another embarrassing acquittal after Hone's three previous successes.

Figure 1: George Cruikshank, 'These are the People all tatter and torn', *The Political House that Jack Built* (1819)

*The Political House that Jack Built* is a pamphlet about the impoverished state of the country, the rulers who have brought it to such a pass, and the unrepresented people who suffer:

> These are THE PEOPLE all tatter'd and torn,
> Who curse the day wherein they were born,
> On Account of Taxation to great to be borne,
> And pray for relief, from night to morn;
> Who, in vain, Petition in every form,
> Who, peaceably Meeting to ask for Reform,
> Were sabred by Yeomanry Cavalry, who,
> Were thanked by THE MAN, all shaven and shorn

Hone's verse is accompanied by a George Cruikshank woodcut, which shows 'the people' not angry and seditious, as the Loyalist Association would portray them, but beaten and tired. The people sit in despair while the Manchester yeomanry hack away in the background as if in a bad dream.

As John Wardroper points out, this cut could have been produced for Shelley's 'England in 1819', with its 'A people starved and stabbed in the untilled field'[14] But, for Hone, there exists a means to end their troubles, the new technology of the Stanhope press. The Stanhope appears consistently throughout Hone's publications and is seen as 'The Thing' that 'will set Britain right again':

In Hone's publications an image of the Stanhope press often appears within an illuminating sun; as a lantern spotlighting corruption; or as an eye containing a press – much the same image is used on the cover of the *Manchester Observer*. The Stanhope press, invented in 1800, was a strong cast-iron machine that used a system of levers, which meant that

**MY EYE**

Figure 2: George Cruikshank, 'My Eye' from *The Political Showman – At Home!* (London, 1821)

Figure 3: The eye featured on the front cover of the *Manchester Observer*, 1 January 1820

it could be operated by one person, thereby lowering production costs. For Hone and other radical pluralist pressmen the 'press' had a reciprocal relationship with 'Liberty'; it needs Liberty to exist, and it protects Liberty. It is also an aggressive machine:

> That in spite of the new Acts,
> And attempts to restrain it,
> By Soldiers or tax,
> Will *poison* the Vermin,
> That plunder the Wealth,
> That lay in the House,
> That Jack Built.[15]

The radical press will defy the new taxes placed on it, regardless of any force that the authorities employ, and in doing so Old Corruption will be defeated through the education of the people.

Usually included with *The Political House* is another shorter poem, *The Clerical Magistrate* (see Fig. 3 in 'The Poetry of Peterloo', p. 180). In this Hone attacks the Revd Charles Ethelston, the churchman and magistrate who was reputed to have read the Riot Act at St Peter's Field. The poem states that Ethelston:

> Commits starving vagrants, and orders Distress
> On the poor, for their Rates, – signs warrants to press,
> And beats up for names to a Loyal Address:
> Would indict, for Rebellion, those who Petition;
> And, all who look peaceable, try for Sedition;
> If the People were legally Meeting, in quiet,
> Would pronounce it, decidedly – *sec. Stat.* – a Riot,
> And order the Soldiers 'to aid and assist',
> That is – kill the helpless, who cannot resist.
> He, through vowing 'from all worldly studies to cease',
> Breaks the Peace of the Church, to be Justice of Peace;

Accompanying this is a cut showing a Janus-faced Ethelston. Facing the left he holds a cross and preaches; facing the right he holds a gibbet in one hand and a flail in the other as he 'Commits starving vagrants'. Hone finds Ethelston a hypocrite because he: 'Breaks the Peace of the Church, to be Justice of Peace'. It may seem strange that Hone, who had been tried three times for his parodies on the Ten Commandments, should be bothered about a churchman who was an agent of the state. But in fact Hone was a religious man, who had uniquely and successfully claimed for his defence that he was attacking the state in his parodies, not the church, and this defence was successful with three juries. In Ethelston he sees a 'Perjurer' who has renounced God in favour of the Regent, who once again is associated with Satan. Hone's pamphlet was so successful that it encouraged his opponents to respond by aping the style of his pamphlets. John Stoddart, nicknamed by Hone 'Dr Slop' after Laurence Sterne's cursing obstetrician in *Tristram Shandy,* was editor of the *New Times*, having been sacked from the 'old' *Times* for the vehemence of his ultra-Tory editorial rants. Head of the Loyal Association, Stoddart was behind many crude loyalist copycat pamphlets.[16] These publications, with names such as *The Real House that Jack Built, The Christian House, The Radical-House which Jack would Build, The Real or Constitutional House that Jack Built* and *The Royal House that Jack Built* attempt to challenge Hone at his own game by producing similar pamphlets that also synthesize woodcuts and doggerel. One such attempt is *The True Political House that Jack Built*:

> These are the People, all tatter'd and torn,
> Because they won't work, for which they were born,
> But would live on plunder, from night to morn,
> Who, in vain, endeavouring, in every form,
> To stir up a riot, and raise a storm ...[17]

Such loyalist efforts were usually crass and humourless, as Marcus Wood observes.

They do not capture the combination of fantasy, frivolity, and rage which underpins the originals. This is hardly surprising given that the didactic impulse behind loyalist propaganda was one of reassurance. It is hard to work up a tone of savage indignation when one's basic message is to tell people that, despite appearances, they are really living in an ideal state.[18]

The power of humour as a 'weapon' is something that the Loyal Association had the arrogance to complain about: 'all must be aware that ridicule and ribaldry, caricature and buffoonery, have been weapons used with too great success among the populace, especially by the doggerel but decorated rhymes of Mr. Hone.'[19] Loyalist copies of Hone's innovative style, even when they use George Cruikshank as the artist, miss Hone's timeless humour, whose currency continued well beyond his times. For example, his and Cruikshank's portrayals of the fat ridiculous Regent became infamous and long-lived – he turns up in Dickens's *Bleak House* as Prince Turveydrop the dancing master, and the novelist William Thackeray perpetuated this uncomplimentary image in several publications including *The Four Georges*, *Roundabout Papers* and *Vanity Fair*.

A pamphlet that Hone published but claimed not to have written was *The Man in the Moon*, from New Year 1820. This anonymous verse squib was written in response to the Regent's speech at the opening of Parliament on 23 November 1819 when he said: 'seditious practices so long prevalent in some of the manufacturing districts of the country have [...] led to proceedings incompatible with the public tranquillity, and with the peaceful habits of the industrious classes of the community'.[20] One week later the Six Acts were announced. These measures were particularly oppressive. Unauthorised military drilling was banned; justices were allowed to search houses without warrants; meetings in excess of fifty people were prohibited; newspapers and periodicals were taxed almost out of existence, causing radical papers like the *Medusa* to fold. The fifth and sixth acts extended the powers of the authorities to the extent that a second conviction for libel might incur banishment from the British Empire.

*The Man in the Moon* is a parody that closely follows the Regent's speech and plays on the similarity between 'Lunashire' and Lancashire, the scene of unrest, which is apt given that Lancaster derives its name from the River Lune. In this squib George, a month away from becoming King, is ruler of Earth's regent, the moon. The pamphlet's frontispiece, by George Cruikshank, shows the regent with his back to the reader, facing the 'Commons' in which the individuals are represented as stars, resembling the order of the knight of the garter, pressing the point that commoners are not present in government. The regent is enclosed in a moon-like spotlight and above him is a quotation from

*Figure 4: William Hone's satire on the Prince Regent, soon to be George IV, as the 'Man in the Moon', addressing parliament on the subject of rebellion in 'Lunashire' [Lancashire]: The Man in the Moon (1820)*

Shakespeare's *Cymbeline*: 'If Caesar can hide the Sun with a blanket, or put the Moon in his pocket, we will pay him tribute for light.' The Regent's buttocks are suitably large and moon-like, reminding us of Shelley's 'The Devil's Walk', written in 1812: 'And pantaloons are like half-moons / Upon each brawny haunch'.[21] In his hand the Regent holds a sword bearing a blanket to 'hide the sun', which has a printing press on it. Inside the pamphlet we learn that in this pose he is delivering 'A Speech from the Throne, to the Senate of Lunataria'.

> My *L_rds and G__tl_n*, I grieve to say,
> That poor old Dad, Is just as – bad,
> As when I met you here the other day. [...]
> But lo!
>
> CONSPIRACY and TREASON are abroad!
> Those imps of darkness, gender'd in the wombs
> Of spinning-jennies, winding-wheels, and looms,
> In Lunashire –
> Oh, Lord!
>
> My L__ds and G__tl_n, we've much to fear!
> Reform, Reform, the swinish rabble cry –
> Meaning of course, rebellion, blood, and riot –
> Audacious rascals! you, my Lords, and I,
> Know 'tis their duty to be starved in quiet.

In his speech to parliament the Regent had begun with the state of his father's health. There is then the assertion that it was the Regent himself who instructed the Manchester magistrates to attack the crowd at St Peter's Field:

> I've given orders for a lot of Letters,
> From these seditious, scribbling, scoundrels' betters,
> N[a]d[i]n and N[o]rr[i]S, F[le]ch[e]r, W[righ]t and H[a]y,
> 'To *lie*, for your instruction,' ...
> That some decisive measures must be taken,
> Without delay,
> To quell the *Radicals,* and save our bacon.

The poem then describes the post-war condition of the people, before moving on to the massacre itself, and one of the most powerful images that Cruikshank produced.

'Steel Lozenges' were actually a popular brand of pill, 'Aromatic Lozenges of Steel'. In a metaphorical reference to the new 'gagging acts', all of the people in the cut are having violent remedies, in the form of swords, thrust down their throats. With the battle won the Regent then dances with the devil at his right, and a clergyman at his left, around a pyre consuming Liberty tied to a pole, topped with the Cap of Liberty, on top of a printing press.

STEEL LOZENGES

will stop their pain,

And set the Constitution

right again.

Figure 5: George
Cruikshank,
'Steel Lozenges',
*The Man in the
Moon* (1820)

Figure 6: George
Cruikshank,
'Peterloo Medal',
*A Slap at Slop*
(1821)

Just as the loyalists copied *The Political House*, the same happened with *The Man in the Moon*. *The Loyal Man in the Moon*, published on behalf of the Loyal Association in February 1820, has a cut on the front by an unidentified artist that closely follows Cruikshank's technically superior piece. It shows a murderous John Bull holding a banner saying 'Death or Liberty', topped by a Cap of liberty with snakes emerging from it. In the other hand he holds a dagger as he addresses death-caps of Liberty with daggers for bodies. Above him is the Stanhope press as a light shining down, but a devil squats on this one. A dove with a dagger in its side and a sprig of bay dropping from its beak falls with 'Peace' in its wake. It is a crude and mirthless cut that falls far short of Cruikshank's original effort. Inside, the pamphlet only follows Hone's superficially in that it reverses the roles taken up in *The Man in the Moon*. There are no attempts to justify Peterloo as the pamphlet's main remit is to work as a piece of anti-radical propaganda attacking the usual figures: Henry Hunt, Burdett, Hobhouse, Place, Wooler, John Gale Jones, Cobbett and John Thelwall.

The final Peterloo-related pamphlet produced by Hone is *A Slap at Slop and the Bridge-Street Gang*, published in 1821. This was first released as a broadsheet, made up to resemble Stoddart's *New Times* in format and style, before being re-issued as a pamphlet. This work, which uses a mixture of prose, verse, songs and fake advertising, is Hone's widest ranging attack on the vices of the government and its defenders. It attacks Stoddart, Southey, the Cabinet, the new king, and addresses the Peterloo massacre along with the emerging Queen Caroline affair, which was filling the newspapers with salacious details relating to the king's attempts to divorce his wife. The pamphlet's innovative use of fake advertisements for subscriptions to commemorate the actions of the Manchester yeomanry serves to undermine the symbols of the state and the rewards offered by it, such as one for a Peterloo medal.[22]

This mock advertisement from the front page of *A Slap at Slop* is a copy of the well-known anti-slavery medallion released by Josiah Wedgwood in 1787 showing a black slave on his knees begging, with an inscription above him reading 'AM I NOT A MAN AND A BROTHER?'[23] Cruikshank's mock advertisement for a medal takes advantage of the Waterloo/Peterloo conflation, and deflates the status of the new Waterloo medal which was then the highest-ranking award to have been minted.[24] Hone extends this conceit by asking if the medals can be minted from brass reclaimed from the melted-down remains of the murderous Edward Meagher's trumpet. Hone, wishing to keep the actions of the yeomanry in the public eye, includes another mock advert in this pamphlet, this time proposing the erection of a Peterloo monument 'in commemoration of the achievements of the MANCHESTER YEOMANRY CAVALRY, on the 16<sup>th</sup> *August* 1819'.

Around the monument will be the names of the soldiers who took part and of the people who died: 'It has been called a *battle*, but erroneously; for, the multitude was unarmed, and made no resistance to the heroes *armed;* there was no contest – it was a *victory* [...] This event, more important in its consequences than the Battle of Waterloo, will be recorded on the monument.'[25]

Hone's pamphlets were fairly expensive at a shilling, when the average wage for a hand-loom weaver was only a few shillings a week. One inquiry offered as a typical example, '4s 3½d. per week from which, when the usual expenses for the loom were deducted, there remained no more than 3s 3d. to support human life (in some cases of five persons) for seven days.'[26] It is impossible to imagine that anyone earning this sort of wage would be in a position to buy one of Hone's pamphlets. Being unemployed and 'on the Parish' (poor relief) provided a barely imaginable 4d. per day to a single man of '20 years of age and upwards'.[27] Nevertheless, Hone's works were available to anyone who could travel to his shop at the home of London booksellers at Ludgate Hill and find a position at the

Figure 7: George Cruikshank, 'The Victory of Peterloo', *A Slap at Slop* (1821)

Advertisements.

MANCHESTER AUGUST 16. 1819.

VICTORY OF PETERLOO.

window where the latest squib would be pasted. Here the illustrations could be viewed closely and their narrative discussed. As Thackeray points out, the verses could be recited to the crowd by the literate, such as the 'grinning, good-natured mechanics, who spelt the songs, and spoke them out for the benefit of the company, and who received the points of humour with a general sympathizing roar.'[28] This London scene was replicated in major cities such as Manchester, where squibs could be pasted in the window of the *Manchester Observer* office or Shudehill booksellers.

A function of Hone's verse squibs and Cruikshank's cuts was to educate the public. Both the verse and the cut could exist independently, but together each enhanced the significance of the other, and helped to educate the 'grinning, good-natured mechanics, who spelt the songs'. For those who could neither afford Hone's squibs, nor travel to London, there were the Hampden clubs and radical societies who would club together to buy radical literature, with members usually contributing 1d. per week.[29] These they would take on the road and use to further their political arguments. Samuel Bamford, in London for a radical meeting in January 1817, relates going to Knightsbridge Barracks with his fellow Lancashire delegate Joseph Mitchell and engaging soldiers in a political discussion:

> We were soon in a free conversation on the subject of parliamentary reform. When objections were stated, they listened candidly to our replies, and a good-humoured discussion, half serious, half joking, was prompted on both sides. I and Mitchell had with us, and it was entirely accidental, a few of Cobbett's Registers, and Hone's Political Pamphlets, to which we sometimes appealed, and read extracts from. The soldiers were delighted; they burst into fits of laughter; and on the copies we had, being given them, one of them read the Political Litany through, to the further great amusement of himself and company. [...] Very soon after this a law was passed, making it death to attempt to seduce a soldier from his duty.[30]

It may seem strange then that Hone's first response to Peterloo, *Don Juan Canto the Third*, was written in a more elevated style than he usually employed, but there is a good reason for this. Hone wished to address an elite who pride themselves on gentlemanly conduct, and rash acts of honour such as duelling. While Byron's publisher John Murray would not even put his name to a poem that was unlikely to be prosecuted, people like Richard Carlile, the Hunt brothers, Hobhouse, and Hone had all risked, and at times given up their liberty, to defend freedom of speech. Just as Cobbett calls the ruling classes 'paupers' due to their poor conscience, Hone adds the title of 'coward'. This cowardice is detectable in every facet of the ruling class: the unarmed are stabbed, pregnant women such as Elizabeth Gaunt are feared enough to be imprisoned, and dissent is not allowed to be published.

In the aftermath of Peterloo both the radical press and the authorities engaged in a print battle to establish who could fix a narrative of the event in the minds of the public. Stories and narratives are of course impossible to own, and after an event there is always a process of mythmaking as people turn the event to suit their own agendas. Most people in Britain had never even been to Manchester, never mind St Peter's Field, and for them the only way that they could understand what happened there on 16 August 1819 was through representations in the press, in poetry, and in graphic art. Pamphleteers like Hone used poetry and the pamphlet as mediums that could travel quickly, efficiently, and cheaply. In fact the importance of poetry in the period can be evidenced from statistics which show that more volumes of verse were published in 1819/20 than at any time between 1814 and 1835,[31] and many of them offer representations, whether direct or indirect, of the great narratives of those years. Following the massacre large public meetings were no longer seen as an effective way to lobby for change, and, as a result, many radical republicans found themselves in the strange position of supporting Queen Caroline's attempt to gain the crown alongside her husband, the new King George IV. However this vehicle to promote radical and reformist agendas ended with the death of Caroline in 1821. Britain then had to wait until the rise in Chartism in the late 1830s before the petitions and ideas that had encouraged up to 80,000 people to gather at St Peter's Field would find another popular rallying point.

# Radical banners from Peterloo to Chartism

Matthew
Roberts

On a crisp winter's evening in November 1838 the Chartists of Hyde, Stalybridge, Dukinfield and Ashton held a great torch-lit demonstration at Hyde. From early evening onwards they marched around Hyde six abreast shouting loudly and discharging firearms as they passed the local cotton mills and the adjacent homes of their owners until shortly before the start of the meeting at 9 o'clock.[1] Across the North West, and indeed beyond, nocturnal Chartist meetings were a common occurrence in the winter of 1838 until, that is, the government issued a proclamation banning them in December of that year. Meetings by torchlight served a number of purposes. Compelled by the need to work in the day time, Chartists met in the evening. Meetings by torchlight were truly sublime, gothic occasions, and were deeply threatening to the mill owners (recalling events such as the Swing and Gordon riots, when flames had last swept across portions of England). The Chartist newspaper the *Northern Star* reported that 'the atmosphere for a considerable distance around Hyde ... was illuminated with the effulgent blaze of the torch of liberty'. The demonstration, it continued in gothic language, 'brought the united people into a solid mass of over 60,000 walking skeletons, to raise their feeble voice as the voice of God, to heaven, to claim protection for themselves and their families, against the devouring spirit of monopoly and oppression'. Meetings by torchlight also served practical purposes. In the dimly lit towns of early Victorian England, without some form of artificial illumination the Chartist rank and file would have been prevented from using one of the few modes of expression open to them. How did the assembled crowd that night communicate their grievances and demands? Here the report in the *Northern Star* was revealing: 'We give the mottos upon their several banners, which are more explanatory of their condition, their feelings, their knowledge of right and detestation of wrong, and their determination, than if we were to write volumes.'[2] Judging by the detail with which the report went on to record the images that accompanied the inscriptions, along with the dimensions, materials, and colours of the banners – a common occurrence in reports of this kind – it is clear that importance was also accorded to image as well as text.

The present article represents 'work in progress' from a more comprehensive study of radical banners.[3] The reports in the radical press have been used to construct two databases, each containing details of banner inscriptions and images displayed by Chartists at mass outdoor meetings. The first database is national in scope and records the details of 482 banners displayed at meetings in England and Scotland between May 1838 and December 1839 (the period of early Chartism). The second database contains details of 261 Chartist banners for the Manchester region (defined here as the borough of Manchester and the neighbouring towns of Ashton-under-Lyne, Hyde, Middleton, and Stockport), a geography dictated largely by the availability of detailed press reports. The chronology of the second database covers the period from 1838 to 1843, after which there are very few reports of banners displayed at Chartist demonstrations for the Manchester region – for reasons which remain unclear.

One of the most intriguing discoveries to emerge from this research is that banners appear to have been used more heavily by Chartists in the North West (defined as the historic counties of Cheshire, Cumbria, and Lancashire) than anywhere else in Britain, with the vast majority coming from the Manchester region. This article suggests that one of the main reasons why banners were more prominent in this region was because of the enduring legacy of the Peterloo massacre, a legacy that shaped both Chartist understandings about the public sphere and the way in which the state responded to Chartism. Yet neither Chartism nor the state's response to it was static. While early Chartism was much more of an outdoors and festive movement, from 1842 Chartism moved indoors and sought to distance itself from the effusive but transient political culture of the mass platform, a move that fuelled and was fuelled by the resurgence of a long-standing iconophobic current within radicalism, a current that was just as much a part of mainstream, dominant culture as it was of radicalism.[4]

| Region | Number of banners (%) |
|---|---|
| North West | 219 (45) |
| Midlands | 79 (16) |
| West Riding | 78 (16) |
| North East | 60 (13) |
| Scotland | 46 (10) |

Figure 1: Geographical distribution of Chartist banners arranged by region, 1838–9

Source: compiled from reports in the *Northern Star* and the *Northern Liberator*

As Fig. 1 suggests, banners were used much more heavily by Chartists in the North West: nearly half of the banners are from this region. Before suggesting some reasons for this geographical distribution, a few brief cautionary remarks are in order. Firstly, this database is derived entirely from press reports in two Chartist newspapers – the *Northern Star* and the *Northern Liberator*, both of which were based in the north, in Leeds and Newcastle respectively. It is likely, therefore, that the geographical coverage of these newspapers was skewed, however slightly, to their respective orbits. On the other hand, if geography was the main factor, then we must ask why there are so few banners recorded for the West Riding and the North East, that is, the areas where one would expect the geographical strength of the two newspapers to be at their strongest. In any case, the *Northern Star* was genuinely a national newspaper.[5] Take Chartism in Scotland as an example. A comparison of the *Northern Star* with the organs of Scottish Chartism, the *Scottish Patriot* and the *True Scotsman*, confirms that it was unusual for the *Northern Star* not to carry exactly the same details of banners displayed at Chartist demonstrations in Scotland as reported in the *Scottish Patriot* and the *True Scotsman*.[6] Secondly, another objection could be that aggregating Chartist demonstrations in Cheshire, Cumbria, and Lancashire into one region – the North West – means that in comparison to, say, the West Riding (itself a sub-region of a county), like-for-like is not being compared. Yet the fact remains that nearly half of the banners in the database come from the North West, and of the 219 banners from that region 114 are from the Manchester region – more than double the number for the whole of Scotland. This suggests that early Chartism in the Manchester region was a much more outdoors, festive and ritualistic affair than was perhaps the case elsewhere. The symbolic stakes were higher in the North West, and to understand why we need to consider the relationship between Chartism and pre-Chartist radicalism. The post-war radical platform (1815–19), particularly the repertoire of symbolic communication that grew up around it, did much to shape Chartist modes of expression, especially in the early phase of Chartism. Nowhere was this more evident than in relation to banners.

Radical use of banners seems to have taken off in the aftermath of the Napoleonic Wars when radicalism first emerged as a mass protest movement. In the 1790s many influential radicals, including those in Manchester, had tried to present themselves as respectable, high-minded and untainted by the excesses of the French Revolution. One of the ways they tried to achieve this was by refusing to develop a visual culture along the lines of the French revolutionaries (who demonstrated their revolutionary ardour through icons and symbols such as cockades, tricolour flags and *bonnets rouges*). As heirs to the enlightenment, British radicals believed that their politics should be conducted through the assumed rationality of the printed and spoken word; appealing to the visual senses was seen as primitive and irrational, associated with Catholicism and with low culture such as street entertainment and the fairground. By shunning this visual culture, British radicals demonstrated their fitness for inclusion in the political nation. However, against the background of a growing willingness of the state and its supporters (the loyalists) to develop a visual culture, coupled with 'the military spectacle of the war, the grand displays of regency ritual' there was a sea-change in attitudes towards vision in the early nineteenth century with the result that radicals after 1815 jettisoned their earlier prejudices and began to develop a fully-fledged visual culture.[7]

Banners were first used by radicals in the Manchester region at the mass meetings for parliamentary reform held in the late autumn and winter of 1816. The Oldham authorities reported to the Home Office in December that banners were being prepared bearing the inscriptions 'No taxation without representation' (watchword of the American revolutionaries) and 'England expects every man to do his duty' (Nelson's patriotic injunction issued at the time of Trafalgar).[8] It was also reported that the following banners were displayed at radical meetings in the Manchester region: 'No taxation without equal representation, annual parliaments, true British liberty, may Britons be firm in the cause of reform'.[9] The same, or similar, inscriptions would reappear on Chartist banners.

Initially, it was not in relation to the industrial north that the government came to regard banners as dangerous but in London where the insurrectionary Spencean radicals began holding mass meetings in 1816 and 1817, complete with banners and the insignia of the French Revolution.[10] On one level, this was nothing new by the 1810s. The state and its propertied supporters had been preoccupied to the point of paranoia since the 1790s with the display of ensigns of insurrection – such as the cap of liberty, the tricolour flag, the skull and cross bone and the phrase 'Death or Victory'[11] which were associated with French warships – when it perceived in British radicalism similar designs as those harboured by the French Jacobins. For all this iconophobia the government did not explicitly outlaw the specific use of banners or even imagery; what had been made illegal in 1794 and 1817 was seditious and treasonable language. Peterloo, however, would change that. The graphic satirist George Cruikshank's print 'Death or Liberty' from December 1819 (Fig. 2) reflects what was, no doubt, the view held by the propertied classes of the radicals' true agenda. Note Cruikshank's deciphering of the meaning of the radical banners that were displayed at Peterloo: the seemingly innocuous cloak of Death, with its call for 'Radical Reform', is translated into the far more threatening inscriptions on the banners below - murder, robbery, slavery, blasphemy, and immorality - none of which actually appeared on the banners at Peterloo.

In the aftermath of Peterloo the Tory government of Lord Liverpool tried to exonerate the Manchester magistrates and the yeomanry by

DEATH or LIBERTY! or Britannia & the Virtues of the Constitution in danger of Violation from the gr.t Poisdent Libertine, Radical Reform!

seizing on the banners in desperation as evidence of the assembled crowd's subversive designs. In charging at the crowd the yeomanry were alleged to have cried 'Have at their flags!'[12] The Middleton weaver Samuel Bamford recalled of Peterloo that 'the preservation of our colours ... was a point of honour, worth any sacrifice'.[13] Embarrassingly for the crown, though, it could not produce any of the banners in the trials as they had been ritually destroyed by the military and local authorities.[14] As far as the radicals were concerned, banners were a legitimate accompaniment to the right to petition parliament.[15] As to the charge that the Peterloo banners made unconstitutional and subversive declarations, the radicals responded, as they always did, that they were asking for nothing new: constitutional ends via constitutional means were being pursued.[16]

The government and its supporters, on the other hand, took the view that the banners were evidence of the illegality of Peterloo. Demands such as annual parliaments and universal suffrage inscribed on the flags were seen as 'utterly unconstitutional' while the phrase 'Liberty or Death' was construed as treasonable. As one MP concluded in one of the many parliamentary debates on Peterloo, banners bearing such inscriptions were 'calculated to convey alarm into the minds of the well affected, and inspire those of different dispositions with confidence in an impending revolution'.[17] Words inscribed on a banner, it was argued, were at least as seditious as those spoken by any radical on the platform. George Canning argued that 'banners, ribbons, and other such devices, might be as clear indications of purpose as words'.[18] Crucially for the government's argument, Home Secretary Lord Sidmouth asked, 'can it make a difference, a substantial difference that the multitude assemble under banners speaking for them all, and uttering for them all sedition and treason? Is not the inscription on each banner to be deemed the language of every individual arrayed under it?'[19]

It was not just the words but also the images on the banners which were regarded as illegal. As Charles Warren, MP for Dorchester, told the House of Commons, one of the banners at Peterloo bore an image of a female figure with a bloody dagger in her hand (a false claim, as it happens: the figure was, in fact, justice with sword and scales). This, Warren, concluded, 'was necessarily connected with an alteration of the law'.[20] At the trial of Henry Hunt, the hugely popular radical who chaired and briefly spoke at Peterloo, the crown similarly took the view that this was a declaration by the crowd that 'the dagger was the instrument by which lost rights were to be recovered'.[21] Operating in the context of post-war social unrest it was hardly surprising that the government viewed the display of bloody flags, black flags and inscriptions such as 'Vengeance' and 'Let him who has not a sword sell his garment and buy one'[22] as bold declarations of physical force. The other advantage to the government of using the evidence of banners to vindicate the actions of the magistrates was that they could be used to explain the timing of their actions as well. One of the other controversies surrounding Peterloo was why the local authorities had not acted sooner to prevent the meeting from taking place. The convenient answer, as another MP told the Commons, 'was because those banners and circumstances of terror were not till then displayed, which could justify their interference'.[23]

One of the problems for the government was the ambiguity surrounding the legality of public meetings. The Whig grandee the Marquis of Lansdowne hit on this when addressing the House of Lords on the state of the country in the aftermath of Peterloo. In what must have been a particularly uncomfortable question for the Tory ministers, Lansdowne wanted to know why the conduct of magistrates from different parts of the country appeared to be so different: why were radicals allowed to march in martial array, display banners and listen to speeches of a seditious kind in some parts of the country but not others? Even more uncomfortable was his follow-up question: 'What instructions had the noble secretary of state for the home department given to the magistrates to guide them in the execution of their duty regarding these meetings?'[24] These questions underlined the need for a clear, uniform and all-encompassing repressive policy, one that facilitated a clampdown not just on seditious libel but also on unlawful assembly.[25] This came in the form of the Six Acts which, *inter alia*, prohibited attendance at meetings 'with any flag, banner, or ensign, or displaying or exhibiting any device, badge, or emblem, or with any drum or military or other music'.[26]

AFREE BORN ENGLISHMAN!
THE ADMIRATION of the WORLD!!!
AND THE ENVY OF SURROUNDING NATIONS!!!!!

Figure 3: 'A free born Englishman!', by George Cruikshank, 1819. © Trustees of the British Museum

The Six Acts represented an all-encompassing assault on radicalism and popular politics. Popular assembly and symbolic display were outlawed. The whole period from the 1790s through to the 1810s had witnessed the raising of visual stakes: first the iconic threat posed by the French revolutionaries and their British allies; then the re-emergence of radicalism and its new visual culture after 1815, announced by the re-hoisting of the cap of liberty; and finally the banners at Peterloo. From the state's point of view, message, medium, and context needed to be circumscribed. The Six Acts represented the state's acknowledgement that radicals and their working-class audiences could see and hear as well as speak and read. Cruikshank appreciated, even if historians have not, what the Six Acts truly represented (see Fig. 3 – note the discarded cap of liberty and the broken sword reminiscent of a torn banner).

One of the legacies of Peterloo concerned the right to free public assembly and political expression. The displaying of banners was a crucial component in that struggle after 1819. By focusing on banners in the aftermath of Peterloo, the authorities had unwittingly transformed them into objects of highly charged symbolic significance. Not just at the annual commemoration of Peterloo, but each and every time that a public meeting outdoors took place the radicals reasserted the popular right to petition parliament and hold meetings as a means to express grievances and rights whether through the spoken word on the platform or through the written word on the banners. Ultimately, it was the state rather than the radicals which had done most to widen the discursive field by underlining the symbolic value of visual communication.

In his study of radical displays of the cap of liberty Epstein has argued that 'forms of symbolic resistance continued most strongly in the manufacturing districts of Lancashire and Cheshire'.[27] This much was evident at the time of the Reform Bill demonstrations in the early 1830s when popular radicals (notably the members of the Manchester Political Union of the Working Classes) used banners to voice their demands for genuinely democratic reform. When the moderate reformer Benjamin Heywood came to Manchester in May 1831 as part of his election campaign for the county of Lancashire the radical crowd made clear their far-reaching demands via their banners: 'Annual Parliaments and Universal Suffrage' – a reminder that not all popular radicals in 1830–1 were swept along with the rising tide of middle-class support for a moderate Reform Bill.[28] A month earlier when Hunt had visited Manchester, the radicals exhibited a banner which depicted the yeomanry cutting down a female – a banner that would reappear in Chartist demonstrations a few years later.[29] So worried had the Manchester authorities been when Hunt visited the town the year before, which coincided with the anniversary of Peterloo, that they had 'put the military and police in readiness at an early hour of the morning'.[30] At the great reform meeting held on St Peter's Field in May 1832 the radicals were bold enough to hoist once again a tricoloured flag accompanied by the motto 'The Rights of Man', while another read 'Those who will not work, shall not eat' – again, inscriptions that would reappear on Chartist banners.[31]

We begin to see, then, the legacy of the post-war mass platform and the Reform Bill demonstrations for Chartism. Not just the content of the radical banners, but the forms in which the banners were displayed were also inherited from this period, the torch-lit meeting being one notable example, a practice that appears to date from the time of the Reform Bill demonstrations. In 1832 the radicals of Manchester decided to make the anniversary of Peterloo more spectacular than was usually the case, perhaps to assuage their feelings of frustration at the Reform Act, the limited nature of which had left most of the working class without the vote. As the report in the *Manchester Times* observed, Hunt's arrival in Manchester took place 'under somewhat novel circumstances'. While previous commemorations had taken place during the day, this one commenced at 8 o'clock in the evening. Hunt was met at Pendlebury by hundreds of workers, a band and 'a few flags and banners'. Hunt was then escorted in procession to St Peter's Field 'amid the blaze of torches and the din of drums, fifes, and other instruments of music'. On reaching the Field, the hackney coach in which he was seated was wheeled to the centre of the ground and a square was formed by flags and torch-bearers. Even though it was raining that evening, the reporter in the *Manchester Times* observed that the multitude was nonetheless 'very considerable in number ... as many people were attracted to the spot by curiosity, a meeting by torch-light being a novelty'. The novelty of the spectacle was not yet exhausted. At regular intervals during Hunt's speech, fire-arms were discharged and at the conclusion of his speech gunshot salutes were sounded 'and to the noise of the shouts were added the rolling of the drums' – all rituals that had come to be associated with state pageantry. The report noted that weapons had never been displayed, much less discharged, at Hunt's daytime processions, the practice being all the more nefarious at 'night time, when concealment is easy'.[32]

Epstein claims that by the time of Chartism 'there was no longer the same intensity surrounding acts of symbolic display'.[33] He provides little evidence to support this assertion. The fact that banners were much more in evidence at Chartist meetings in the Manchester region suggests that the symbolic stakes were higher there than was perhaps the case elsewhere. As Chartism's first historian Robert Gammage observed, 'Nothing ever excites a Lancashire audience like the name of Peterloo'.[34] At the great meeting on Kersal Moor in 1838 the Rochdale Chartists brought with them a 'blood stained flag of Peterloo'. Another (the Middleton banner, which still survives) bore the inscription 'Liberty and Fraternity, Unity and Strength – a flag that was at Peterloo'. The Manchester Chartists displayed at least one flag commemorating Peterloo at almost every demonstration held between 1838 and 1843.

The local authorities in their many anxious letters to the Home Office made frequent reference to the presence of banners at Chartist demonstrations just as they, or their forebears, had done between 1816 and 1819. As keepers of the public peace, it was the duty of magistrates to provide the Home Office with evidence of suspect individuals and groups, and so it was only to be expected that inscriptions and insignia continued to form part of this evidence gathering operation. When Lord John Russell was Home Secretary (1835–9) he instructed magistrates to record how many people were present at Chartist meetings, the character of the language used by speakers, whether firearms were discharged and the nature of the emblems on any banners.[35]

The alleged ensigns of revolution – the cap of liberty and the tricolour flag – continued to be hoisted at Chartist demonstrations in the Manchester region in 1838 and 1839, as did banners bearing inscriptions such as 'Liberty or Death', 'Universal suffrage or death'.[36] Indeed, the basic content of early Chartist banners was little different from that of the post-war mass platform. Radicalism was still conceived as a critique of political corruption and elitism even though events such as the 1832 Reform Act (which deliberately excluded the working class) were conspiring to make radicalism more of a working-class movement. While there is little overt evidence of hostility towards the middle class on Chartist banners (the only banner to mention them explicitly read 'Middle classes! make common cause with the industrious millions, and give freedom to your country') many of the banners do, nevertheless, assert the distinctive rights of labour. Thanks largely to the presence of trades societies in Chartist processions, a number of banners celebrated 'labour, the source of all wealth' and demanded protection for it, but there is no sense of class exclusivity: 'Equal rights and equal laws for all classes'. The unity of the productive classes is called for, as is an end to class legislation. It was the idle and tyrannical who attracted most hostility (usually attacked abstractly, though there were occasional references to pensioned clergy and 'tyrant landlords'). It would, of course, be facile to imply that the absence of overt class warfare on Chartist banners is evidence of the movement's non-class character. Context was all important. As Epstein has perceptively asked of the torch light demonstrations, 'What does it mean when 20,000 factory workers ... lay siege to their factory town by night?' 'Such actions', Epstein rightly concludes, 'dramatically underscored the isolation of the mill owner'.[37]

A crude index of the novelty of Chartist banners is the number of banners that make explicit reference to 'The People's Charter': only fourteen out of the 261 banners from the Manchester region, and only a further three banners listed all six points of the Charter. By contrast twenty-six banners listed five or fewer individual points (with equal electoral districts featuring the least often), the most frequent being 'universal suffrage' and 'annual parliaments', both of which had predominated between 1815 and 1819. This suggests that Chartists were re-using banners. Another clue that Chartists re-used radical banners from earlier campaigns is the reference to 'equitable adjustment' on a number of banners, the policy advocated by Cobbett in the aftermath of the French wars of scaling down debts and contracts to prevent inflation. When Feargus O'Connor visited Manchester after his release from prison in the autumn of 1841 one of the banners read 'Universal suffrage, Annual Parliaments, and Equitable adjustment' and on the reverse 'Repeal of the New Poor Law'. This suggests that old banners were amended, and in this case it is quite possible that the same banner had been used during the period of the post-war mass platform, the anti-Poor Law demonstrations in the mid-1830s and finally in the Chartist demonstrations in the 1840s.

Whatever the content of Chartist banners, the fact that local magistrates and other members of the propertied classes in the Manchester region still went to the trouble of detailing the inscriptions and images on the banners in 1838 and 1839 suggests that they continued to regard banners as declarations of subversive intent. Similarly, the depositions of eye witnesses taken by magistrates, such as those at Hyde after the great torch-lit demonstration in November 1838, also make detailed reference to the flags and banners displayed at the meeting.[38] In cases brought against Chartists by the crown, these depositions formed part of the prosecution brief. In the trial of the radical leader Joseph Rayner Stephens at Liverpool in the summer of 1839, the Attorney General told the court how, on 14 November last, the Chartists of Hyde and region had marched, discharged fire-arms and displayed 'banners of a most inflammatory and culpable nature'.[39] As late as 1848 magistrates were reminded that banner inscriptions could be used as evidence against rioters.[40] It is hardly surprising, therefore, that no Chartist banners have survived.[41]

What *had* changed by the time of Chartism was not so much the state's attitude towards radical banners, which it still regarded as evidence of subversive intent, but its nerve. The state, at least on a national level, had come to realize the danger of needlessly provoking crowds, however threatening they appeared to anxious local magistrates. As far as central government was concerned, in matters relating to public order, what Peterloo had made all too clear was the need to restrain local magistrates (who were too easily unnerved and too ready to apply to the Home Office for military aid).[42] It had also highlighted the unsuitability, except as an absolute last resort, of using the military for civilian crowd control. This was one of the reasons why arguments for a professional police force gained ground in the 1820s and 1830s.[43]

This view was expressed by General Napier who was appointed commander of the Northern District in April 1839. Though based in Nottingham, Napier spent a good deal of his time dealing with Chartism in the Manchester region. On assuming the command Napier confided that in dealing with any civil violence the 'great point is to defeat without killing'. When it came to crowd control Napier was adamant that a police force was much more suitable, though one that was centrally controlled like the Metropolitan Police on the grounds that if 'turned over to the town...it will become a means for oppression in the hands of faction'.[44] Most tellingly of all, on the eve of the second great Chartist meeting on Kersal Moor (held on 25 May 1839), Napier told the Home Office that he had 'entreated the boroughreeve [of Manchester] not to interfere with flags'. Though Napier made it well understood that any civil violence which escalated would be put down by force, he added that 'when men assemble to express their political opinions it is unjust as well as foolish to disperse them'.[45] Where Napier was perhaps less astute was in his failure to understand the reluctance of magistrates in the Manchester region to use the yeomanry whom, even leaving aside the legacy of Peterloo, they deemed unreliable and expensive.[46]

Occasionally when dispersing Chartist meetings the police attempted to confiscate banners belonging to the crowd and this led to scuffles, as at Macclesfield in 1839 when the police tried to commandeer a banner belonging to the female Chartists of the area. As the *Northern Star* gleefully reported, the banner – inscribed 'The Patriotic Females of Macclesfield' on one side with an image of a woman wearing the cap of liberty on the reverse – was carried by a 'valiant female Chartist' who 'refused to give it up, accompanying the refusal with much impudent language'. When the police tried to 'take it from her she held fast with one hand and fought desperately with the other; and the policemen were ultimately compelled to take her to the lock-ups, with the banner in her hand'.[47] This is not to suggest that the authorities or the military always exercised restraint when dealing with Chartists, but it is telling that there was no repeat of Peterloo in the Manchester region. The state may well have honed its repressive apparatus in response to Chartism and it may also have won the propaganda battle in uniting the propertied classes against the Chartists,[48] but as Napier and the saner heads in government knew only too well, Chartism would not be defeated by repression alone. Learning how to effectively manage popular protest also involved knowing when to leave well alone (not interfering with banners), of selecting the most appropriate type of force and using just the right amount, in short of walking the tightrope between containing and inflaming.

Changes to the ways in which Chartists used banners may also have been a factor in the state's growing tolerance. Where Epstein is perhaps correct is in his assertion that *after* 1839 there was no longer the same intensity surrounding banners and symbols. Writing against the background of Chartism, Samuel Bamford hit on this theme when describing the constructions that the prosecution had attached to the Peterloo banners, 'constructions which if followed in these days, would place some of the Chartist exhibitors in a rather perilous position'.[49] Why had this change come about? It is surely no coincidence that from 1839, when local magistrates from the Manchester region wrote to the Home Office complaining of the Chartists, there was a marked tendency towards summary statements, typically describing banners displayed 'with the usual inflammatory inscriptions and devices' rather than detailing individual inscriptions.[50] This suggests that banners were becoming less controversial or at the very least less original, which is understandable: as we have already seen, the basic content of Chartist banners was little different from that displayed at Peterloo.

Neither, perhaps, is it a coincidence that banners and mass outdoor demonstrations were much more prevalent in the early phase of Chartism in 1838 and 1839. When Chartism first emerged, the form and content of the movement was little different from that of the post-war mass platform. It was only to be expected that before the new movement took its distinctive shape local radicals would cling to what they knew, and that they literally dug out their old banners: we know that radicals from Skelmanthorpe (in the West Riding) buried their banner to keep it from falling into the hands of the authorities, and that it was used at various radical demonstrations from 1819 through to the 1880s.[51]

Just as Chartist poetry helped to generate emotional bonds and common feelings and was particularly important in the early days of the movement when the infrastructure was at its weakest,[52] commemorative banners performed a similar integrative function. As a means of legitimizing themselves the Chartists clothed themselves in the language and symbols of their forebears. But from 1839, once it became clear that the Chartists were not going to realize their goals overnight, the movement evolved into something different. In the first instance frustration with the failure of the General Convention and the rejection of the first Chartist petition in July 1839 pushed many further along the

Figure 4:
Skelmanthorpe
Banner,
commemorating
'The Manchester
sufferers'.
Kirklees
Museums and
Galleries

physical force trajectory, with many Chartists in the Manchester region supporting the idea of a general strike and some even willing to drill and take up arms. Not surprisingly, the local authorities then became much more preoccupied with preventing arming and foiling any plots, and so banners began to recede into the background, though occasionally Chartists clutched for them as evidence of their peaceable intent. When confronted with the charge that pikes had been present at one of the meetings at which he had spoken, Rayner Stephens retorted that the pikes served merely functional purposes: as banner poles and for affixing aloft a loaf of bread and a red herring.[53]

After the heady days of winter 1839–40 had forced the Chartists to reassess once again their strategy and tactics, and the movement began to realize the need to put down firm foundations in preparation for 'embarking on an indefinite agitation',[54] there was a marked tendency from the early 1840s to hold more meetings indoors.[55] The only notable and sustained exception was the period of the 'plug plots' in 1842, though banners do not appear to have been carried by the Chartists on this occasion. Neither, it seems, were banners much on display when Chartism revived in 1847 and 1848. When the Chartists of Lancashire and Cheshire held a great camp meeting on Oldham Edge in March 1848 all they carried with them was their lunches and umbrellas.[56] Banners were conspicuously absent at other outdoor Chartist meetings in 1848.[57] The minority of Chartists in the Manchester region who did issue challenges to the authorities in 1848 reached not for banners but guns, pistols, pikes, brickbats and other weapons.[58] Reports of meetings at which banners were displayed are very few, notable exceptions being at a meeting of Chartists and unemployed workmen in early April when a tricolour flag was hoisted;[59] a meeting of Chartists at Oldham when two flags belonging to the Royton Political Union were displayed,[60] and at the demonstrations and riots protesting against the conviction of John Mitchel, the Irish revolutionary, when the Chartists and Repealers of Oldham displayed 'several printed banners, with mottoes, such as "Mitchel, liberty or death"'.[61] But in each of these instances, only a very small number of banners were reported. On the whole, banners were either absent or else had ceased to be newsworthy (even in the *Northern Star*), or perhaps both. We might also note that the new cross-class reforming initiatives, such as the People's League, which were designed to bring Chartists and middle-class reformers together in support of parliamentary reform met indoors.[62]

The move indoors from the early 1840s coincided with a turn away from the mass platform. Martin Hewitt has detected a questioning by Manchester Chartists of what he terms the 'threat/overthrow' strategy associated with the mass platform as early as the disappointments of 1839, a questioning that the revival of 1848 did little, ultimately, to stem.[63] From 1840 there was a greater stress by Manchester Chartists on education, and so the accent shifted back to privileging the printed and spoken word (as it had in the 1820s) – a commitment to what might be termed 'deep Chartism' as opposed to the assumed transitory and fleeting Chartism associated with mass demonstrations and banner waving. This cerebral Chartism was personified at a national level by Bronterre O'Brien who bemoaned the 'thousands of pounds of hard earned money squandered upon flags and banners and coaches and triumphal cars – and such like trumpery'.[64] The London Chartist leader William Lovett similarly lamented the 'wasted glorious means of usefulness in foolish displays and gaudy trappings, seeking to captivate the sense rather than inform the mind'. In such trappings Lovett detected an 'aping...of a tinselled and corrupt aristocracy, rather than aspiring to the mental and moral dignity of a pure democracy'.[65] Indoor lectures, tea parties, dinners and classes were the staple fare of Manchester Chartism from 1842. It could be argued, therefore, that the 1840s saw a resurgence of radical iconophobia and an enlightened condescension towards visual culture, a culture in which early Chartism had revelled.

As Chartism moved indoors it began to use banners in much more controlled ways, more in line with middle-class movements like the Anti-Corn Law League which used banners as decorative backdrops to stages or suspended them from the ceilings (Fig. 5).[66]

Used in this manner, the organizers of events exerted far more control over the form and content of banners than they did during the earlier

Figure 5: 'Great National Anti-Corn Law Bazaar at Theatre Royal', 1842. Photo ref. M09367. Courtesy of Manchester Libraries, Information and Archives, Manchester City Council

outdoors phase of Chartism where anyone was free to bring along a banner. Small wonder that the organizing committee of the 1838 Kersal Moor demonstration had been 'anxious to learn from the Organized Trades and other bodies in Manchester and the neighbouring Towns and Villages ... the number of their principal Flags and Banners – their inscriptions and devices ... to be used on the occasion'.[67]

With the move indoors the emphasis shifted even further towards the local Chartist leadership with the result that some of the spontaneous festivity associated with the mass platform was lost – symbolized by the homemade banner – and thus became part of the process by which the Chartist crowd was mobilized, yet disciplined, at the same time.[68] It may be a chance coincidence but all references to 'death' on Chartist banners in the Manchester region database disappear after 1839 (save for the single instance of the Mitchel riots), though the cap of liberty was still being hoisted in 1842. This is not to suggest that the rank and file had no input into the decision-making process about the use of banners, not least because it seems that official banners were often paid for by soliciting subscriptions from the wider membership, but the fact remains that banners became fewer and their content was formally decided upon by a committee that met beforehand. Whereas the banners belonging to the rank and file had tended to be homemade those belonging to associations were more likely to be professionally produced by manufacturers like George Tutill and the Manchester based J.W. Whaite, and were much more expensive.[69] This shift towards the more controlled and circumscribed use of banners, therefore, may have contributed towards the process by which banners became less controversial (not that there seems to have been any changes to the inscriptions and imagery on the banners; just that the same inscriptions and images were no longer as controversial). Occasionally, Chartist banners continued to excite controversy after 1840, such as at general election campaigns or at meetings held by the Anti-Corn Law League when Chartists announced their presence and objectives through their banners,[70] but the context had changed: no longer were banners being used to threaten the propertied classes, as had been the case at the torch-lit meetings; now they were being used as part of a much more focused strategy of what Hewitt describes as 'paralyzing the effectiveness of traditional middle-class pressure groups ... by seizing control of the local platform'.[71]

As the relationship between text, image and context changed in the first half of the nineteenth century the symbolic power of radical banners rose and fell with the mass platform. This suggests that it is perhaps more helpful to think in terms of cycles rather than watersheds when it comes to radical attitudes towards visual culture, though further work exploring the relationship between radicalism and the politics of sight, which takes in the whole period from the 1760s through to the 1840s (and beyond) is needed. We know that before the French Revolution, the radical supporters of the mercurial John Wilkes had been quick to exploit the commercial potential of visual and material culture in the 1760s and 1770s,[72] but the French Revolution seems to have forced many British radicals to distance themselves from a politics that was too closely associated with the excesses of the revolutionaries. To a new generation of self-improving radicals, who came to believe in the totalizing and rational power of the word,[73] appealing to the visual sense was, in any case, deeply suspect. Nonetheless, as the state came to realize the patriotic 'pay-off' of developing a rich feast of visual culture, so the post-war radicals of the mass platform came to appreciate the importance of developing their own spectacles to rival that of the state's.

As Robert Poole has shown in his study 'The March to Peterloo', in developing this culture radicals delved deep into the 'flourishing popular culture of the weaving communities' of the North West where banner waving had long formed part of the religious and associated calendric culture. Poole argues that radicalism and community were virtually co-extensive: the rich repertoire of rituals, symbols and iconography associated with wakes, rushbearing, which 'embodied the pride, cohesion, prosperity and skill of the whole community' were pressed into service for the radical cause. Banners were just as much a part of this popular culture as they were of radicalism. Under the combined impact of state repression, a rejection of the mass platform and the rise of a more ascetic radical politics, Poole argues that radicalism began to shed its association with the popular culture of the weaving communities, a culture that was, in any case, in decline. By the time of Chartism, the context had changed: Chartist rituals of fellowship were 'increasingly those of a sub-culture rather than of a community'. Radicalism, Poole concludes, had become 'more of a class movement' and 'accepted the reduced status of a counter-culture'. Yet as this article has suggested, it is important to distinguish between early and late Chartism. There is a case for seeing in early Chartism (festive, communal, open), not the post-war years, 'a late flowering of an older style of popular politics, marked by an unstable mixture of legitimism and insurrection'.[74] Before Peterloo, radicals had only just begun to develop a visual culture. The repressive response by the state to Peterloo transformed banners into objects of charged symbolic value: no longer were they merely message boards, they were now part of the armoury through which radicals asserted the popular right to free assembly and to petition parliament. But in the face of repression, radicalism fragmented and the visual culture of the 1815–19 period was driven underground. As we have seen, this visual culture experienced a partial revival in the Reform Bill agitations of 1830–2, but under the restrained tutelage of the middle class there was little space for this demotic radical politics, though this did not stop it from bursting forth on occasions.

When Chartism first emerged there was a revival of the mass platform and old banners were dug out and in some cases amended. But if the initial strategies and tactics of Chartism had not significantly evolved from those practiced by the radicals of the post-war mass platform, the attitude of the state had – at least at a national level. The never-to-be-forgotten 16 August 1819 was lodged just as firmly in the official mind as it was in the radical mind. Once it became clear to the Chartists in 1839 that they were not going to achieve their objectives overnight the efficacy of the mass platform was called into question, even though it would take the defeat of 1848 to underline its utter bankruptcy as radical strategy. It was at this point that many Chartists seemed to turn their backs on the festive and communal politics of the mass platform. In the mid-1840s, Chartism moved indoors as it tried to put down firmer roots, and banners began to be used in different ways. When Chartism revived in 1847 and 1848 there was a conspicuous absence of banners in the Manchester region. We will probably never really know why no Chartist banners have survived, but if the evidence – or to be more accurate the absence of evidence – from the Manchester region is anything to go by, Chartist banners seem to have disappeared even before the movement went into terminal decline.

# Remembering
# the Manchester Massacre

Terry
Wyke

Berthold Brecht memorably wrote in 'A Worker Reads History' of the biases and silences that characterize historians' constructions of the past. 'So many particulars' are ignored, 'So many questions' are overlooked, unintentionally or otherwise. This essay about the memory and commemoration of Peterloo in Manchester is prompted by one of those questions: Where are those who were killed at Peterloo buried? What is now widely referred to as the Peterloo Massacre – some writers continue to enclose the word massacre in quotation marks to indicate its contentious usage and to distance themselves from it – has been studied extensively,[1] and although few would seriously dispute that it is those who were killed at or around St Peter's Field in Manchester that endows it with its irrefutable power, its special place is in the long struggle for democratic rights in Britain. But whilst we are now able to name with greater certainty those who died,[2] exactly when, where and with what ceremony they were buried remains unclear. As the bi-centenary of Peterloo comes ever closer, there are no individual memorials to those who were killed, nor, and even more surprisingly in the light of the impressive memorials at Amritsar (1919) and Sharpeville (1960), is there a public memorial in Manchester. The principal purpose of this essay is to trace the efforts to memorialize Peterloo in Manchester from 1819 to the present day.

The memories of Peterloo began to be forged on the afternoon of Monday, 16 August 1819. Politically-charged polarized versions of the day were soon being widely circulated in the stamped and unstamped press, in prints, in verses and songs, and by word of mouth. At the heart of the event was blood – the dead and wounded cut by the sabres and trampled by the horses of the yeomanry and cavalry. This memory remained needle sharp for many years as the Peterloo trials took place. Peterloo artefacts helped to bolster narratives of the massacre.

Both sides kept artefacts directly connected to the day as well as other memorabilia.[3] Peterloo artefacts were added by John Crossley to his personal collection of historical objects and documents.[4] Objects in his 'Armoury and Trophies of Antiquity' included 'Part of one of the

Figure 1:
Broadside verse
supportive
of Hunt and
remembering
the dead of
Peterloo, printed
by George Innes,
a Manchester
jobbing
printer. Photo:
Manchester
Archives and
Local Studies

## A Tribute to the Immortal

## Memory of the Reformers,
### Who fell on the 16th of August, 1819.

HAIL Sons of Freedom who in Britain's cause
Fell victims to the Usurpers of her Laws;
The muse shall pay her tribute to your worth,
And in your cause the nations of the earth,
E're long shall join ; and Liberty's blest sound,
Shall thro' each Tyrants land with joy resound,
What tho' in proverty's rude grasp ye lay,
Unmark'd with vain distinctions of the day,
No titles, honours, pomp, proclaim'd you brave,
Yet your memorials shall survive the grave,
Tho' not in conflicts with a foreign foe,
Ye felt contending death's resistless blow,
At home ye fell, at home your blood was shed,
Thrice honour'd few who for your country bled,
No more cou'd you have done, no more have
   lost,
If you in foreign fleids had join'd the host
Of warlike heroes in their country's cause,
And crown'd with laurels gain'd, deserv'd ap-
   plause,
Lamented Friends, your suffering country
   mourns,
That her brave sons shou'd meet such base
   returns,
But shall Barbarians with a savage hand,
Destroy the bud of freedom in our land,
Shall kindred hands be wanton in the blood
Of her brave Sons, who for their country's good,
Have advocated Liberty's blest cause,
Her glorious Rights, her Charter, and her Laws,
Rest you in Peace, ye much lamented Dead,

And may your name throughout the land be
   spread,
May your example fire the noblest breast,
Until with Liberty, this Nation's blest,
Your names shall live whilst truths resistless
   light,
Refulgent shall be shed, on freedom's night,
Thus when the Sun of Liberty bursts forth,
With beaming radiance o'er this joyous earth,
Then shall Oppression end, then each be free,
And in the bonds of love united be,
Weep not ye lonely widows of the Dead,
Whose brave remains have claim'd their dusty
   bed,
Ye yet shall smile in freedom and in peace,
When proud Oppressors and your wrongs shall
   cease,
And Tyrant's hurl'd from rule by Heaven's
   command,
And freedom's Banner's wave throughout our
   land,
Your smiling babes shall hail the auspicious
   reign,
Of Liberty, and ENGLAND'S RIGHTS
   MAINTAIN.

### AN ACROSTIC.

H ail noble Champion of thy Country's cause,
U nlike the base corrupters of her Laws,
N onedare like thee their sinking country save,
T hou Son of Liberty bothrenowned and brave.

*Innes, Printer, 3, Back Turner-street, Manchester.*

Flags taken on the 16th August', a 'Bugle supposed to have belonged
to the Radical Reformers 1819' and a 'Truncheon used by Mr John
Pilling, as one of the Special Constables, on the memorable 16th August
1819'.[5] Appointed a magistrate in 1819 Crossley had been at Peterloo –
and later swore a statement of having seen men near the Manchester

Infirmary wearing military uniform – 'the cloth being of a French gray colour' – two of whom were carrying what he referred to as 'the great drum'.[6] Crossley's antiquarianism and collecting passion must have been widely known for he also acquired a 'Stone (or Missile) thrown by one of the Radical Reformers on the 16th August 1819'. Horsfield, one of the special constables, authenticated the object, explaining that it was a broken paving stone thrown at Major Trafford of the Cheshire yeomanry at New Cross, but which, missing its target, struck Horsfield. A pike made by and carried by the radical Amos Ogden when drilling men at Royton must have been another incongruous object among the more ornate weapons in Crossley's collection.[7] The radicals also preserved mementoes of the day, though of the 'strewed caps, bonnets, hats, shawls, and shoes, and other parts of male and female dress, lying where they had fallen trampled, torn and bloody', little was to survive. Articles such as the black petticoat worn by Nancy Clayton, which was later made into a radical flag and subsequently seized by the authorities, have not come down to the present day.[8] They have disappeared, along with the bloodstains on the floor of the Friends' Meeting House where the injured sought safety.[9]

Peterloo sharpened the contempt that the Tories and their supporters had for the new working class – 'the sons of bitches' who 'had eaten up all the nettles for ten miles round Manchester, and now they had no greens to their broth'[10] – whose politics threatened revolution. Loyalists took every opportunity in public and in private to support the action of the magistrates and military.[11] Meetings of the Pitt Clubs in and around Manchester saw Peterloo toasts added to the long list of those drunk on the anniversary of their hero's birth.[12] Further toasts were included as the authorities continued their attacks – in 1823 glasses were raised to the jury that found Hunt guilty at York. The Manchester yeomanry met and toasted their actions as did their brothers in other towns.[13] Hugh Hornby Birley was fêted and presented with an engraved sword by those under his command, whilst the Cheshire yeomanry looked to appoint William Hulton as their colonel.[14] Anniversaries such as the king's birthday and occasions such as the coronation allowed the yeomanry to show themselves in public, drawing their sabres and waving them 'a la mode de Peterloo'.[15]

For Manchester's radicals the process of commemorating the 'Manchester Massacre' saw the anniversary become part of their calendar, the day on which they gathered to remember the event and the dead. Dinners were organized at which Peterloo was re-lived in speeches, songs and toasts. Guests might bring news of the condition of Hunt and other prisoners. There were presentations – a white counterpane with embroidered verses referring to Peterloo was sent to Hunt in prison by the Bolton's radicals.[16] The centrepiece of the commemoration in Manchester was the gathering at St Peter's Field which for that day became a sacred space. There was a public procession to St Peter's Field, the crowd falling silent at the exact time of the attack. Banners were carried and hymns sung. In 1821 the procession marched from St Peter's Field to Scholefield's radical church in Hulme where parents had their infants christened Henry Hunt.[17]

Meetings on St Peter's Field continued but there was always the possibility of a disturbance. In 1826 the anniversary meeting was abandoned when it was discovered that stones had been deliberately spread on the field.[18] St Peter's Field was also used for the holding of other political meetings. In the very heart of the reform crisis – May 1832 – a large public meeting took place on what the *Poor Man's Guardian* dubbed the 'Plains of Peterloo'.[19] Radicals and reformers gathered, parading banners rich in symbolism and declarations. Mary Fildes was reported carrying a flag with a representation of the massacre. Later in the same year, Henry Hunt spoke on what he referred to as 'the field of blood'.[20] However by the mid 1830s such meetings were moving to St George's Field, Camp Field, Stevenson Square and other open spaces in Manchester as buildings began to be erected on St Peter's Field. One of the last Peterloo anniversary meetings to be held there was in 1836 when Feargus O'Connor described it as 'having been the great scene of the century in which they lived'.[21] Yet, important as it had become as a radical site, the idea of placing a memorial on or near it does not appear to have been seriously considered.

Building on and around St Peter's Field quickened in the following years, most notably with the erection of some of the city's most impressive public buildings: the Gentlemen's Concert Hall, Natural History Museum, Theatre Royal and Free Trade Hall.[22] The first Free Trade Hall was opened in 1840. The League's largely middle-class supporters took pride in being on the very site of Peterloo, an event that had become part of their own narrative of Manchester radicalism. At the same time this huge meeting hall was contributing to the removal of the most politically charged outdoor meeting place in the city centre, encouraging the public platform to move indoors. In short, the 'Plains of Peterloo' were being appropriated. Peter Street was rapidly becoming one of Manchester's principal bourgeois streets, a street sufficiently impressive for Queen Victoria to be driven along it when visiting the city in 1851.

Peterloo remained embedded in the popular memory.[23] What Carlyle identified as 'the treasury of rage, burning hidden or visible in all hearts ever since' marked out Peterloo as the single most important event in the making of radical consciousness.[24] But whilst Peterloo was not forgotten by pugnacious Tories supping at John Shaw's, as Pickering and others have argued, Peterloo and Henry Hunt became a cardinal point of reference in the Chartist movement. Manchester Chartists, some of whom had been at Peterloo, continued to remember the 16th of August as well as the anniversary of the birthday of Hunt.[25]

Figure 2:
Monument to
the memory of
Henry Hunt
at Every Street
Chapel, Ancoats,
as portrayed
in a special
number of the
Leeds-based
Chartist paper
*Northern Star*,
20 August 1842,
to mark the
unveiling of
the monument.
Arriving too late
from London, the
engraving was
only included
in the second
edition of the
paper. The statue
of Hunt on top of
the obelisk was
never realized.
Courtesy of the
late Victor Innes
Tomlinson

ERECTED IN THE CHAPEL YARD, EVERY ST' MANCHESTER, BY THE WORKING PEOPLE.

Hunt's death in 1835 became the catalyst in Manchester for the raising of a memorial to him, but in the city where his name was inseparable from Peterloo, the project also became one of remembering 'the never to be forgotten 16th August'. The memorial took the form of a stone obelisk surmounted by a statue of Hunt. One of Manchester's foremost radicals, Revd James Scholefield, who had been at Peterloo and given evidence at Hunt's trial, was a leading figure in the project and, presumably, in the absence of a more public location on or near to the fast disappearing St Peter's Field, it was decided to site the monument in the burial ground of Scholefield's chapel in Every Street, Ancoats. Thousands of people attended the ceremony for the laying of the foundation stone on Good Friday 1842, many of whom having walked to Manchester carrying flags and banners, along the same roads used in 1819. Before reaching Ancoats the main procession stopped respectfully by what remained of the open space of St Peter's Field, and the 'Dead March' was played.

Feargus O'Connor, who had taken on the mantle of Hunt,[26] presided at the laying of the foundation stone in a ceremony that was attended by many of the leading Chartists.[27] Among the commemorative items buried was a copy of 'An Account of the Massacre at Peterloo' and 'other tokens of that bloody day'. A vault was prepared beneath the monument to receive those who had fought for the people's rights.[28] That the monument was commemorating the massacre as much as Hunt was made doubly clear in the formal address, a copy of which was also placed inside the monument. It began:

> A few friends of liberty, animated by the love of justice, and having witnessed the dreadful massacre of their fellow-men on the field of St Peter's, when they were assembled for a perfectly legal purpose, namely to petition the British Parliament for Universal Suffrage and a repeal of the Corn Laws, Vote by Ballot and a reform of the people's House of Commons, they were assailed by a drunken and infuriated Yeomanry Cavalry, and slaughtered without mercy ...[29]

Speakers referred back to 1819 and in what was one of the most emotive moments on one of the most important days in the Christian church, Scholefield linked the blood of Christ to that spilt at Peterloo.

The plan to unveil the monument on the forthcoming anniversary of Peterloo, however, was overtaken by the industrial unrest of August 1842, an episode that again revealed the potency of the memory of Peterloo, most notably in the attention paid by the 'lawless mob' to Hugh Hornby Birley's mills on Oxford Road.[30] Memories of Peterloo also helped to raise the anxieties and determine the actions of the authorities during the crisis and the subsequent trials.[31] As a consequence the monument erected to perpetuate the memory of Hunt and the victims of Peterloo was never inaugurated, nor fully realized, a shortage of funds preventing the commissioning of the statue of Hunt.[32]

In the following decades Peterloo became an event that was more readily remembered in Manchester and the North West than in other parts of the country. At political meetings in the Free Trade Hall, Liberal and radical speakers in particular continued to acknowledge the significance of the site on which a now far grander building had replaced the earlier halls. At the famous meeting in 1862 to send support to Abraham Lincoln, the tone was set by the reminder that they were meeting on the very spot 'consecrated to liberty by the blood of their forefathers'.[33] At election time, Liberal speakers understood that audiences could still be roused by referring to the Tories as the 'Butchers of Peterloo'.[34] John Bright was ever ready to quote Shelley's 'Masque of Anarchy' as befitted the Rochdale nonconformist who as a young man had clashed with Parson Hay. Bright's personal possessions included a Peterloo jug.[35] Sometimes the reference to Peterloo was little more than a local courtesy, but on other occasions, as in 1889 when Gladstone spoke about the shooting of civilians at Mitchelstown, it had an additional resonance.[36]

For Manchester's radical Liberals Peterloo was an event to be revered, as were those who had been there. At the funeral of Ernest Jones, one of the most important radical occasions in Manchester in the 1860s, the cortege was led by four Peterloo veterans.[37] There was pride in being able to claim family associations with Peterloo. There was political capital in arranging reunions of those who had been at the massacre.[38] Thirty Peterloo veterans were prominent in a reform demonstration in Manchester in 1867, parading behind a banner that read 'The Fathers of Reform. The Heroes of Peterloo'.[39] And it was not just men: four women were among the Peterloo survivors photographed at a political demonstration in 1884.[40]

By the 1860s of the thousands who had marched to St Peter's Field in 1819 no one was better known than Samuel Bamford. His first-person narrative of the massacre in his *Passages in the Life of a Radical* (1844) was the most widely referred to account of Peterloo, painting in its cool prose, as effectively as Cruickshank had done in his 'Manchester Heroes', the sudden and shocking brutality of the day. Bamford died in 1872 when his description of Peterloo was quoted in a number of newspapers.[41] Most obituarists however took their lead from James Fraser, Bishop of Manchester, who found in the *Passages* the reassuring trope of a radical who came to moderate his views and reject direct action. Such was the swell of feeling following Bamford's death that it was decided to raise a memorial. Significantly, the proposal that it be put on the site of Peterloo rather than in Middleton was dismissed, in part because it would be 'keeping an old sore green'.[42] However Peterloo was not to be forgotten and the inscription on the memorial obelisk in Middleton churchyard began: 'Bamford was a Reformer when to be so was unsafe, and he suffered for his faith', a clear reference to 1819 and his subsequent imprisonment.[43] Two monuments to individuals deeply associated with the Manchester Massacre had now been raised, both in somewhat remote locations, away from St Peter's Field.

That Peterloo was widely regarded as a 'sore' seems to be borne out by the decision not to include it as one of the murals depicting the history of the city in Manchester's new town hall.[44] Although Peterloo was on the original lengthy list of possible subjects, its omission can be largely explained by the general policy of not including recent incidents in Manchester's history – the only nineteenth-century subject being a singularly bucolic scene featuring the scientist John Dalton. To what extent Peterloo contributed to this avoidance of modern subjects is less clear. The presence of older liberal radicals, notably John Thompson and Abel Heywood, at the centre of the commissioning scheme might have been expected to have made Peterloo a probable rather than a possible subject. The minutes of the New Town Hall Committee are silent on the matter but the decision not to feature modern subjects may be read as a recognition that they were more likely be contentious. The political squabbling over the statue of Cromwell in the city was also still fresh in the minds of Heywood and other older liberals.[45] Had the choice of subject been left to Ford Madox Brown then he would have preferred to have worked on a composition of Peterloo rather than on Dalton discovering marsh gas.

By the closing decades of the century, the memory of Peterloo burned brightest in Manchester and textile Lancashire. The last of the Peterloo veterans had died and with them the opportunity of learning directly about the massacre. The Lancashire labour journalist, James Haslam, recalled of how he had heard of Peterloo from an old weaver who had been there:

> Peterloo, lad! I know. I were theer as a young mon. We were howdin' a meetin' i' Manchester – on Peter's Field – a meetin' for eawr reets – for reets o' mon, for liberty to vote, an' speak, an' write, an' be eawrsels – honest, hard-workin' folk ... Bournes [Burns] says as 'Liberty's a glorious feast.' But th' upper classes wouldn't let us poor folk get a taste on it. When we cried for freedom o' action they gav' us t' point of a sword. Never forget, lad! Let it sink i' thi blood. Ston up an' feight for t'reets o' mon – t' reets o' poor folk![46]

For others, Peterloo was learned of in those history books that were now ordering the recent events of the past. The space given to the event revealed their author's political sympathies, many histories making slight or no reference at all.[47] Among Manchester writers W.E.A. Axon's description of the yeomanry as 'hot-headed young men who were more or less intoxicated' in his much consulted account of Peterloo did not go unchallenged in Manchester's Conservative press.[48] John Ashton in his *Social England under the Regency* (1890) prefaced his unvarnished account of the meeting with the observation that 'There are some people who still regard "Peterloo" as a massacre of the innocents: they must be either very wrong-headed, or very badly informed', whilst for Henry de Beltgens Gibbins, one of the most widely read of economic and social historians, the term massacre was 'grossly misapplied'.[49] The labour movement saw Peterloo differently, regarding it, increasingly alongside other events – Tolpuddle in 1834 – as one of the key moments in the ongoing struggle for political and economic rights. Others learned of Peterloo through historical fiction. The Manchester massacre was a central episode in Mrs Linnaeus Banks's novel *The Manchester Man* (1876). Isabella Varley (as she was born) had family members at the meeting and had witnessed the anniversary demonstrations as a child, connexions which help explain her sympathetic interest and original researches into Peterloo.[50]

In these years the Hunt monument in Ancoats, long one of Manchester's poorest districts, became neglected. Both the graveyard and the church were closed, and in 1888 following the sale of the chapel the monument was demolished and the churchyard cleared. The act did not go entirely unnoticed but an appeal to erect a new monument faltered.[51] One idea had been to place a tablet on the land between the Central Station and the rear of the Free Trade Hall. Some twenty years later the idea of a memorial to Hunt in Manchester was revived by Manchester Liberals. It took the form of a bronze medallion portrait, commissioned from the local sculptor, John Cassidy. The idea of fixing it on the site of

St Peter's Field was again mooted but the entrance hall of the Manchester Reform Club was the location eventually agreed upon. C.P. Scott, editor of the *Manchester Guardian*, unveiled the bronze tablet in June 1908. The inscription read: 'Henry Hunt who for his part in the Great Reform Meeting in St Peter's Fields Manchester (Peterloo) Aug. 16 1819 suffered two years' imprisonment.' Scott pointed to the now established Liberal historical timeline from 1819 to 1832 before commenting, rather surprisingly given the occasion, that although Hunt deserved a memorial, he did not consider him to be a great man – 'He certainly was not a man of as fine character as Samuel Bamford'.[52] Manchester now had its second quasi-Peterloo memorial via Hunt, but, as in 1842, while the Reform Club in King Street was only a few hundred yards from St Peter's Field, for the majority of the city's population it was even more inaccessible than the Chartists' monument in Ancoats.[53]

Figure 3: The bronze memorial to Henry Hunt by the Manchester sculptor John Cassidy, placed in the entrance hall of Manchester Reform Club in 1908. Courtesy of Stephen Yates, Manchester Metropolitan University

But by the early twentieth century it was not only the Liberals and the recently established Labour party that were shaping the social memory of Peterloo. The suffragettes also came to regard it as part of their history, recognizing that women had been prominent at Peterloo and that by 1819 they were already establishing their own political organisations. Peterloo had an additional relevance to the movement in that the Free Trade Hall had seen the decisive protest by Christabel Pankhurst and Annie Kenney. For the Pankhursts there was also a family memory – Emmeline's paternal grandfather having been at Peterloo.[54]

The centenary of Peterloo was commemorated in Manchester where the economic landscape – post-war shortages and unemployment – was reminiscent of the years after Waterloo. The political landscape, of course, had changed dramatically, the general election having seen the return of sixty-three Labour MPs, who were now the main opposition to the coalition government. It was to be in these years that the Left became the undisputed keepers of the memory of Peterloo, a process that was to see attention shifting away from the heroic Hunt to the crowd. In Manchester an alliance of left-wing groups – Manchester and Salford Trades Council, Manchester and Salford Labour Party, the Independent Labour Party, the British Socialist Party and the Women's International Socialist Council – established a Peterloo Centenary Committee to make arrangements to mark the anniversary over the weekend of August 16/17th. Platt Fields, a park south of the city centre, hosted a large outdoor public meeting on the Saturday with Tom Mann, Ben Turner and W.H. Hutchinson, chairman of the Labour Party, among the speakers. The celebrations began with a march of trade unionists, socialists, co-operators and other supporters from the city centre to Platt Fields. A red cap of liberty carried on a pole at the front of the procession and banners with inscriptions reading 'Labour is the Scourge of All Wealth', 'Peterloo 1819. Labourloo 1919' and quotations from Shelley's 'Masque of Anarchy' set the tone. A band played tunes from the time of Peterloo.[55] In Peter Street the marchers stopped, removed their hats, and sang 'The Red Flag'.[56] Speakers at Platt Fields paid appropriate tribute to Peterloo as a key event in the history of the working class, but it was the unfinished reform agenda of Peterloo and the current problems facing ordinary people that preoccupied speakers. The tenor of the Sunday meeting at the Free Trade Hall was similar, with Philip Snowden, chairman of the ILP, calling on the working classes to use their political and industrial power to return a Labour government. Other speakers included Katherine Bruce Glasier, Annot Robinson and Councillor Rhys Davies.[57] A pamphlet about Peterloo written by the Swinton socialist, J.H. Hudson was published by the Centenary Committee.[58] Its sub-title 'A story for working people to teach their children' was suggestive. Outside the Labour press,[59] there was little to suggest that Peterloo was regarded as an important anniversary.[60] Coverage of the anniversary in Manchester's Conservative newspapers was slight, seemingly determined not to perpetuate its afterlife.[61] But from within the Left the centenary did not prompt a call for a Peterloo monument in the city, a surprising omission, especially given the discussions surrounding the statue of Abraham Lincoln which was about to be unveiled in Platt Fields. It was reported that a 'well-known firm, whose offices stand on the site of Peterloo' had decided to install a plaque on its building, but there is no record of this being done.[62] The Peterloo centenary came and went but, unlike in the later centenary commemoration of the Tolpuddle martyrs, there was not even to be the legacy of an anniversary rally.[63]

The centenary was noteworthy in seeing the publication of new accounts of Peterloo. Frederick Bruton, a schoolmaster at Manchester Grammar School with a long interest in the history of the city, wrote a short account of the massacre, *The Story of Peterloo*.[64] Uncontentious and uncomplicated as far as any narrative of Peterloo could be, Bruton had the good sense to include for his readers a map of the long built over St Peter's Field, helping to clarify the spatial memory of Peterloo. The account prompted the liberal Lord Sheffield of Alderley to provide the John Rylands Library with funds to publish a contemporary account of Peterloo written by a family member (Bishop Stanley). This was done by Bruton in his second and more original publication, *Three Accounts of Peterloo by eye-witnesses* (Manchester, 1921), a review of which was to prompt the eminent historian G.M. Trevelyan to write a short article about the casualties of Peterloo.[65] Trevelyan had a personal as well as professional interest in the event, his mother being a member of the

Philips family who had been prominent in the reform movement in Manchester.[66]

But in the interwar years, although the importance of Peterloo was recognized by the radical Liberal historians such as the Hammonds,[67] it was the Left that continued to claim Peterloo as part of their history, and it became, along with Tolpuddle and Tonypandy, one of the stations of the cross on the forward march of Labour. More particularly, Peterloo became part of the history of the radical Left of the Plebs League and the Communist Party.[68] Their attitude towards conventional accounts of British history was neatly reflected in a poem copied out on the inside cover of a copy of Mark Starr's *A Worker Looks at History*.[69]

**On Historians**
They tell us tales of England's glory
Of battle knights of yore;
But not the shameful sordid story
Of Britain's social sore

Of how the wretched slums and cities
Arose on the fruitful fields;
A lot of wanton wartime ditties
But not the harvest's yield.

But if they must talk of fights in history,
Then forget Waterloo;
A little less of sophistry
And more of Peterloo!

Whilst the Left in Manchester were confident about the importance of Peterloo, Manchester Conservatives seemed generally content to ignore it, unless it was directly raised. Forgetting, as historians of cultural memory have argued, can be as significant as that of remembering. That Peterloo was still a part of the city's history that was alive and important enough to be fought over became evident in the historical pageants which were a feature of interwar Manchester, a means of expressing local pride as well as boosting flagging economies.

Peterloo did not feature in the historical pageant organised by the council as part of its Civic Week in 1926 when the narrative of the city's history was largely determined by Ford Madox Brown's murals, a now widely accepted public history, even though a number of its picturesque episodes were tangential to the city's history.[70] Peterloo however did feature in the Lancashire Cotton Pageant held at Belle Vue in 1932. Supported by the main cotton associations, its purpose was to boost what was still the region's largest but now chronically depressed industry.

The recreation of Peterloo was one of the most spectacular of the pageant's twelve episodes. It featured 5,000 mainly voluntary performers, some recruited from the satellite towns that had been prominent in the original demonstration. The re-enactment began with processions singing and dancing, making their way to St Peter's Field. There the crowd welcomed and listened to Hunt before the cry of 'The Soldiers! The Soldiers!' heralded the arrival of mounted troops and the mayhem of the massacre. Matthew Anderson's script drew on contemporary accounts, ending with verses from the 'Masque of Anarchy'. He possibly drew on the knowledge of the *Manchester Guardian* industrial journalist and historian, A.P. Wadsworth, whom Anderson knew through the centenary pageant for the Liverpool and Manchester Railway. Peterloo was one of Wadsworth's particular interests, especially in his native Rochdale.[71] The Peterloo set was carefully researched, the props including sixteen banners, based on reported designs, and five caps of liberty. Brass band music and excerpts from Sibelius's great symphonic protest 'Finlandia' provided the soundtrack of the spectacle.[72] The Peterloo episode was not as directly related to the story of the cotton industry as many of the others in the pageant, and it could be argued that it was included more for the spectacle that audiences had come to expect on such occasions than for its historical relevance. Even so, whatever impressions the audience and participants took away with them about the history of Lancashire's cotton industry, only one interpretation of the moral topography of Peterloo could be drawn from this presentation.[73] Yet, unambiguous as this depiction of Peterloo was, there was little discussion or criticism in the press, possibly a reflection of the seriousness of the ongoing crisis in the cotton industry.

That political sensitivities surrounded Peterloo in Manchester was evident once more in 1938, when it was announced that it was not to be one of the historical events represented in the official pageant which was to be the centrepiece of the celebrations to mark the centenary of the municipal charter. For some Conservative Mancunians Peterloo clearly continued to be regarded as a contentious and best-forgotten episode in the city's history, in opposition to those who believed that 'the blood of the martyrs of Peterloo is in our quick independence and our insistence on democratic freedom and fairness'.[74] The pageant committee's initial refusal to include the 'dark event of Peterloo' prompted protests.[75] The Manchester and Salford Trades Council pressured the council to reinstate the event which they regarded 'perhaps the most important in the last hundred years of Manchester history'.[76] The *Manchester Evening News* editorialized on the significance of Peterloo in establishing the 'free and independent city we know today'.[77] The outcome was that the 'sad events of "Peterloo"' were re-instated, though it was placed towards the end of 'A Cavalcade of Progress', a crammed scene covering Manchester's history from the 1750s to 1830s.[78] In contrast to 1932, Peterloo, represented by Hunt in his carriage followed by a small number of workers flanked by yeomanry, was treated as almost inconsequential in what was one of the most perplexing scenes in a pageant that one reviewer generously described as 'a bit bewildering'.[79] Less controversial was the Repertory

Theatre's production, 'They Build A City', written by George Mould and Armitage Owen. This developed from an earlier project in which Mould worked with the documentary film maker John Grierson on a script for a film to mark Manchester's centenary. The film was never made but like the play it took the aftermath of Peterloo to be the starting point of the city's modern history.[80] Among left-wing groups such interpretations were seen as degenerate, and when Manchester Communists staged an alternative historical pageant, their Peterloo banner was prominent.[81] Similarly, when Manchester women, led by communists but including women from other political associations, celebrated International Women's Day in 1939, they did so with a pageant which acknowledged women's role at Peterloo.[82]

But for large numbers of people in the 1930s Peterloo, if remembered at all, was merely one of the many disconnected events that had occurred in the past. The further away from Manchester the fainter was the memory of Peterloo though by now even the Manchester press could let the anniversary pass without an article. Peterloo was rarely referred to in the London press.[83]

Again, for some people it was through fiction that they learned of Peterloo. Howard Spring's *Fame is the Spur* was published in 1940, a sweeping account of the rise of Labour from the 1870s to the 1930s. A Peterloo sabre flashes through its pages, a powerful symbol in Hamer Shawcross's political journey which see his socialist ideals compromised. Given the centrality of the telling of the massacre by Shawcross's 'grandfather' in the novel, an alternative title might have been 'Peterloo is the Spur'. As in other of his novels, Spring drew on his considerable knowledge of Manchester acquired during his years working for the *Manchester Guardian*.[84] The novel sold well and after the war the story reached a wider audience as a film.[85]

The priority given to the rebuilding of the Free Trade Hall after its almost complete destruction in the December blitz of 1940 confirmed the centrality and symbolically charged nature of the building to Mancunians. Leonard Howitt, appointed City Architect in 1946, was the architect of the new building. Art commissions were at best a secondary consideration in a project where budgets were tight and central government approval was needed to release basic building materials, but once construction eventually started it was decided to include a number of art works, reflecting the building's special place in the city's history. Two works were installed: first, stone figurative statues representing activities associated with the hall were placed on the rear wall in Windmill Street; second, a painting depicting the Peterloo massacre was placed inside the hall. The idea of commemorating Peterloo in the new building had been raised by local trade unionists but details of the commissioning process are opaque except that Howitt played a leading part. Financial considerations ruled out organizing a competition and both commissions were given to Arthur Sherwood Edwards, an artist employed in the City Architect's department. Howitt's close interest in the project was evident in requesting information about the uniforms worn by the 15th Hussars at Peterloo from the commanding officer of the regiment.[86] An illustration of the completed Peterloo 'mural' (in fact an oil on canvas, measuring 16 feet by 5 feet) published in the press[87] resulted in a volley of criticisms. Artistic rather than political considerations predominated. Margaret Pilkington, Director of the Whitworth Art Gallery, led the critics, arguing that the painting was a failure, not worthy of either the building or the city. Howitt defended Edwards and the painting was installed in the rear foyer. The official commemorative booklet to mark the opening of the new hall made only passing mention of Peterloo. The Left in Manchester was less reticent, and a pamphlet remembering 'the British martyrs for liberty and justice' at Peterloo was published by the Lancashire and Cheshire Federation of Trades Councils. Its author was its president and Labour MP Ellis Smith who had been born in Eccles and whose socialist politics had been shaped as a shop steward at Metropolitan Vickers in Trafford Park in the 1920s.[88] Amidst the criticisms directed at the painting, it was easy to overlook the main significance of Edwards's work: after 132 years, Peterloo had been finally officially recognized on the site of the massacre.

In the 1960s a re-invigorated Left in Manchester continued its custodianship of the Peterloo flame but that the massacre remained a divisive event was confirmed in the public arguments surrounding the sesquicentenary in 1969. It was marked by the publication of two new books about Peterloo, which, once more, revealed the ideological fault lines beneath Peterloo.[89] Both books were by competent amateur historians with strong connections to Manchester. Robert Walmsley's *Peterloo: the case reopened* attacked the received radical version of Peterloo, arguing that generations of commentators and historians had misunderstood, deliberately or otherwise, the actions of the magistrates, in particular William Hulton. Westhoughton-born Walmsley was an antiquarian bookseller with a shop in Manchester city centre, a reminder that Manchester booksellers had long taken an interest in Peterloo items. Ira Hewkin, a well-known Manchester bookseller, left his collection of Saddleworth material, including Peterloo items, to the people of his native Saddleworth.[90] Walmsley was encouraged in his researches by W.H. Chaloner, economic history lecturer at the University of Manchester. Chaloner's right-wing views were well known, having been highlighted by the publication (with W.O. Henderson) of a new translation of Friedrich Engels's *The condition of the working classes in England*, in which Engels's reliability as a witness and analyst of the new industrial society were questioned. Marxist historians rushed to defend this attack on a revered text.[91] Both Chaloner and Walmsley regarded the new book as a long overdue correction to an incident that had been too long in the hands of left-wing historians. They speculated on reviewers in the leading papers.[92] Some reviewers were generous in recognizing Walmsley's labours and new findings, though for many it proved impossible to excuse the spilling of innocent blood.[93] An unusually long review of Walmsley's lengthy study by the Marxist historian Edward Thompson in the *Times Literary Supplement* was especially devastating, showing no sympathy for Walmsley's attempt to rescue Hulton from the enormous contempt of posterity.[94] Yet, discussed as Walmsley's book was in the press and by academics, it did not find a wide readership. In part this was because of the publication of *The Peterloo massacre*, the first book-length account of Peterloo aimed at the general reader. The author was the Manchester-born actress, novelist and committed Labour supporter, Joyce Marlow. Her account followed the radical version of Peterloo, making adroit use of contemporary sources as well as incorporating some original research. Its success led to a book-club edition. It was not reviewed in the *TLS* but was summed up by Michael Foot as 'a good popular statement of the popular cause'.[95] A Granada TV documentary on Peterloo narrated by Marlow was also commissioned but its broadcast was delayed because of an ongoing dispute with the television trade unions.[96]

That Peterloo was still capable of stirring up controversy was also evident in the Manchester council chamber. As in 1919 it was the local labour movement which made sure that the anniversary did not pass unnoticed. The principal event was an entertainment of contemporary songs and commentary performed on the day of the anniversary in the Free Trade Hall. One highlight of the evening was the displaying of Middleton's Peterloo banner.[97] But as in 1919 there was to be no official municipal celebration, although Labour had pushed for this. The idea of an official celebration had been discussed by the Manchester Labour Party in 1968 and early in 1969 Labour councillors pressed the now Conservative-controlled council about organizing a civic celebration of the anniversary.[98] The Conservatives refused, Alderman Nellie Beer suggesting that any civic celebration in 1969 was more likely to recognize the fiftieth anniversary of Alcock and Brown's first transatlantic flight – 'the fine achievement of two very young people'. Labour pressed on, reviving the idea that both Peter Street and St Peter's Square be renamed after Peterloo.[99] Manchester Conservatives were determined not to allow Labour a civic platform to propagate their own version of the city's history. Labour's proposal was easily defeated in the council chamber.[100] But there was a limit to the council's power in the city and the anniversary was marked by lectures and exhibitions. Manchester Communists remembered the anniversary by organizing a Peterloo exhibition at Belle Vue, as well as publishing a pamphlet and articles in their press, while a folk concert was organized at the Free Trade Hall on the anniversary itself, with a speech from Michael Foot.[101] Somewhat more unusual was the stamping of local mail with a 'Peterloo

Remembered' slogan at the city's main post office. The year ended with the Manchester premiere of Malcolm Arnold's 'Peterloo Overture' at the Free Trade Hall, a work commissioned by the Trades Union Congress to commemorate its foundation in Manchester in 1868.[102]

When Labour took back control of the council the idea of renaming Peter Street was revived. Once again, it was met with strong and organized opposition, led by the businesses in the street. This opposition went far beyond concerns over the inconvenience of altering letterheads. A petition challenging the proposed name change presented by the main Peter Street businesses (these included the Midland Hotel, YMCA, Theatre Royal and legal firms) was followed by a legal challenge, using the Public Health Act of 1925 to oppose the alteration in the name of the street. Labour was not going to be allowed to appropriate the city's history unopposed. 'Will Deansgate become Tolpuddle Martyrs Way? Will Piccadilly become Engels Square, and what about Marx Street for Market Street?' asked one local historian.[103] What the press headlined as the 'Battle of Peterloo Street' reached court where the stipendiary magistrate, John Bamber, was persuaded by the opposition arguments, concluding that Peterloo was a significant but shameful incident, 'one of which the city has little reason to be proud'.[104] Having unexpectedly lost, the council decided not to continue the fight, taking some satisfaction in fixing a plaque about Peterloo on the exterior of the council-owned Free Trade Hall. 153 years after Peterloo, people passing along Peter Street had some indication of the momentous event that had taken place there. The cautious wording of the inscription on the plaque reflected the sensitivities surrounding the more recent struggle over the site as much as the actual massacre of 1819.[105]

Figure 4: Free Trade Hall commemoration poster, 1969. Courtesy Geoff Bridson

In the following years, difficult as it is to gauge the extent to which Peterloo was rooted in Manchester's sense of its own history, it appears that the social memory was fading. Peterloo had certainly become a less important part of the national political memory, its echoes fainter, for example, in parliamentary debates on subjects such as the use of the military by the state in industrial disputes. Indeed, reference to Peterloo in the Westminster parliament was now confined mainly to the maiden speeches of MPs whose constituencies had a Peterloo association.[106] This was in contrast to Scotland where a resurgence of nationalism saw the 1820 Society (established in 1989) elevate the 1820 insurrection into one of the key events in modern Scottish history. SNP politicians joined the 1820 Society, and its annual commemorations in Edinburgh became gatherings of leading Scottish nationalists. The insurrection

Figure 5:
The cautiously worded blue Peterloo plaque, installed on the Free Trade Hall by the Labour-controlled council in 1972, itself became the subject of protest and was replaced in 2007

became a part of the nationalist debate over the teaching of Scottish history in Scottish schools, the general view being that whilst schoolchildren were taught about Peterloo in 1819, they were told nothing of its aftermath in Scotland in 1820.[107]

In Manchester the 'never to be forgotten 16th August' passed each year with little public notice, unlike the annual procession organized by the Irish community to remember the Manchester Martyrs which culminated at the memorial in Moston cemetery. Peterloo had no equivalent to the Manchester Martyrs Memorial Committee.[108] There was certainly no plan to organize an anniversary meeting or raise a memorial. This was in spite of the fact that prominent Manchester Labour politicians were aware that the labour history of the city was not publicly acknowledged. Graham Stringer, who became council leader in 1984, was conscious of the importance of such symbolic capital.[109] But initiatives involving Peterloo were few and minor, as when the idea of renaming the Free Trade Hall after Peterloo was mooted, criticized in the press, and quickly dropped. The declaration of Manchester as the world's first nuclear-free city was followed by a set of commissions for politically-charged public art. Among these was Philip Jackson's 'Struggle for Peace and Freedom', which could be read as a statement in bronze of the city's radical traditions. It was not explicitly linked to Peterloo, even when its eventual location in St Peter's Square encouraged such an interpretation.[110]

That the key moment in the city's radical past might be finally recognized seemed more likely when the council agreed to support the move of the National Museum of Labour History from London to Manchester in 1987. Peterloo was the subject of the museum's first major exhibition in Manchester, Michael Foot opening it on the day that the international news was dominated by the killings in Tiananmen Square.[111] Public understanding of Peterloo in Manchester, however, remained patchy. Gerald Kaufman, one of Manchester's longest-serving MPs, lamented the neglect of this part of Manchester's history in his evidence to the National Heritage Select Committee, of which he was chairman:

> You go to the United States and every little bit of history is exploited even if it has not happened. You go to Kansas and find Dorothy's cottage out of the Wizard of Oz, whereas if you go shopping in Manchester which is ruled by a Socialist council, there is nothing to tell you that you are shopping on the site of St Peter's Field where the Peterloo massacre, one of the cardinal events in British social history, took place.[112]

Although the absence of any shops on the site suggested an uncertainty about its actual location, the idea that Peterloo had been neglected was beginning to be officially recognized.

By the 1990s Peterloo had become part of the programme of official guided walks, a tour that could be traced back to those led by the communist historians Eddie and Ruth Frow, if not earlier.[113] Heritage tourism, however, was peripheral to the urban regeneration strategies being developed by the council. Neither in the council nor among local trade unions was there any strong feeling to recognize Peterloo, let alone raise a prominent memorial. This was especially evident in the debates and subsequent public inquiry surrounding the plan to demolish the bulk of the Free Trade Hall to build a luxury hotel behind the retained facade. Peterloo was barely mentioned in the arguments over the building's future, the debate focusing more on its role as a famous concert venue in the nineteenth and twentieth centuries. The opportunity to provide a memorial was allowed to pass – Manchester City Council had never pursued a per cent for art policy – and the developer only had to display a number of saved artefacts from the old hall in the new building. Among these was Sherwood Edwards' painting of the massacre.

Academic interest in Peterloo continued, not least among Manchester-based historians. E.P. Thompson's interpretation of the massacre continued to be influential, making it a pivotal episode in popular accounts of modern radicalism.[114] Conservative historians were generally content to relegate it to the margins of their national political narratives.[115] Social

Figure 6: Terry Wyke leading a Peterloo walk outside Manchester Central at the Manchester Histories Festival, March 2009, veteran Peterloo historian Donald Read (left) looking on. Photo: Robert Poole

historians brought new perspectives to what many mistakenly assumed was already an exhaustively researched subject. The endlessly reproduced contemporary prints of Peterloo were finally contextualized and analyzed by Diana Donald, an art historian at Manchester Metropolitan University.[116] The role of women at Peterloo was given more prominence by feminist historians who looked more closely at those on the platform and in the crowd, some whose aprons were 'weighted with stones'.[117] The eminent public historian G.M. Trevelyan, whose last words were said to have been 'Peterloo 1819',[118] would have found pleasure in reading Michael Bush's painstaking post-mortem of Peterloo casualties.[119] Works on Peterloo written by those with a family interest in the massacre, as well as by local socialists, were also

Figure 7: Handbill advertising Mike Harris's 1994 community play that set the massacre of 1819 firmly in the politics and policing of the Thatcher years. The play was performed in the Upper Campfield Market, a hall built by the local state in the 1870s in its efforts to control the saturnalia of the Knott Mill fair. Photo: Chetham's Library

published.[120] Peterloo as a symbol of the struggle between the powerful and powerless also attracted, as it had done in the 1930s, other media. 'The Peterloo Massacre' directed by Justin Hardy (Channel 4, 2003) made telling use of the compelling evidence of the witnesses at the inquest of John Lees, leaving the viewer to reach a single conclusion.[121] Radical theatre groups also found in Peterloo an event with strong modern resonances.[122]

A Peterloo Memorial Campaign was finally established in 2007 and enjoyed early success in persuading the council to replace the blue Peterloo plaque on the front of what was now the Manchester Radisson Edwardian hotel with one whose inscription referred directly to the massacre and the blood spilt.[123] This was part of the group's wider campaign for a 'prominent explanatory and respectful' memorial in the city centre.[124] Each year the group organized an anniversary meeting on the open space close to St Peter's Field. Supporters came from the surrounding towns, and local councillors and MPs also attended. Other groups supported the campaign. One public meeting, held in the city council chamber, to discuss the proposed memorial, was organized by the Manchester branch of the Historical Association.[125] A Peterloo memorial finally seemed to be within reach when the council announced plans to commission three public artworks to mark the city's radical past: the Abolition of the Slave Trade, the Suffragettes and Peterloo.[126] Details about the commissioning process, location and budget were not specified. Subsequently, in 2010, the 'Manchester Manifest' identified three of the six 'key narratives' of Manchester's identity as 'Manchester Merchant and Maker', 'Manchester Radical and Revolutionary' and 'Manchester Democrat and Activist', all with obvious relevance to Peterloo.[127]

It seemed unlikely that any memorial would be sited on St Peter's Field itself, in spite of the re-naming of the area as Petersfield as part of a continued reorganisation of the city centre into distinctive districts – what the council's consultants described as a 'brand identity'.[128] But having revived and then compressed the place name, they remained curiously silent about the event which had made the area famous. Neither was any reference made to a Peterloo memorial. The likely location of a memorial became clearer when the city council announced plans to transform St Peter's Square into a 'high quality public space destination' in 2012. The intended memorial would be in the new world-class square, although arguably the square's only direct connection to the massacre was that it was the burial place of Hugh Hornby Birley.[129] Its commissioning was to be closely overseen by the city council. In 2013, in spite of pressure from the Peterloo Memorial Campaign to open up the commissioning process – a further chapter in the struggle over the memory of Peterloo – the exact form and precise location of the memorial remains uncertain and the process opaque.[130]

Figure 8: Jeremy Deller's 'Procession' at the 2009 Manchester Histories Festival involved an attempt to bring together people whose ancestors had been at Peterloo (promotional leaflet)

The remembrance and commemoration of historical events and individuals has been the subject of much historical writing in recent years. Social scientists and historians have adopted different theoretical approaches to clarify the complexities of the relationship between history and memory, and the cultural politics of commemoration.[131] Historians have been important figures in determining the Peterloo narrative, often providing strong oppositional narratives, that has left little middle ground between the 'victims' and the 'villains'. The legacy of Peterloo continues to be fought over. But in this contestation of the making and defence of the popular memory of Peterloo, it is also important to recognize the part played by others, not least in the form of novels, film, poetry and song. Institutions have also contributed to that memory, most recently seen when the John Rylands Library submitted the Peterloo Relief Fund Account Book (which it had acquired in 1919) to be one of the first items to be entered in the United Kingdom section of UNESCO's Memory of the World Register, the documentary archive equivalent of its programme of world heritage sites.[132]

Just how deep rooted the popular memory of Peterloo is remains problematic. It is noteworthy that Peterloo has never had an automatic place in those changing history syllabuses that since late Victorian times have set out to teach schoolchildren the story of British history, even though most agree that parliamentary democracy is an essential part of the story.[133] This essay has argued that the memory of Peterloo waxed and waned. Communal acts of remembrance in the decades after Peterloo did not continue, and except for significant anniversaries, Peterloo has been marked by minimal public remembrance in the twentieth century. Although Peterloo was to be remembered by the Left, it has not been memorialized as other significant events in working-class and labour history, notably Tolpuddle and the Newport rising – a reminder, should it be needed, of the limitations of studying the memory of Peterloo from a Manchester-centric perspective. There has been nothing comparable with recent events in Scotland where the three martyrs of the 1820 insurrection – John Baird, Andrew Hardie and James Wilson – were honoured by a debate in the Scottish parliament.[134] Important as Peterloo has been to the Left, especially the radical Left, attempts to fix its place more firmly in the social memory of Manchester have been episodic and weak. Until the present century there had never been an organized campaign to raise funds, either locally or nationally, to provide a specific Peterloo memorial in the city centre. This absence cannot be explained entirely in terms of the opposition, though, as we have seen, Conservatives have been resolute and effective in denying the simplest forms of public memorialization. Neither is the absence of a memory due to the loss of St Peter's Field, which became contested space and was quickly built over, dominated by public buildings that themselves became politically and culturally significant in the city, adding new interest groups to any memorialization project. Manchester's indifference to provide an appropriate memorial was rooted in its ambiguous attitude towards its own past, which is evident to outsiders in its modest collection of public monuments relating directly to its own history, and, even more obviously, in the absence of a museum devoted to the history of a city that claims to be the world's first modern city, a radical city prominent in the fight for human rights and justice.

*My thanks to Tilman Frasch, Alan Kidd, Robert Poole and Michael Powell for helpful suggestions on an earlier draft of this essay.*

# Three new accounts of Peterloo

When the Manchester Grammar School teacher Francis Bruton gave a Peterloo centenary lecture at the John Rylands Library in 1919, he launched himself on researches which led to the publication two years later of his *Three Accounts of Peterloo* (Manchester, 1921). His chosen witnesses were respectable and credible figures: the Revd Edward Stanley, Rector of Alderley (later a bishop); Lieutenant William Joliffe, a young hussar (later a lord); and John Benjamin Smith, a Manchester merchant (later a leading anti-corn law campaigner, and MP for Stockport). None supported the magistrates' view of events, and Bruton saw all three as reliable, independent accounts which established the facts about a disputed episode.

Nearly a century later many more accounts have come to light. This second set of three are from the reformer and Peterloo defendant George Swift; the magistrates themselves, compiled by their senior colleague William Hay; and the Manchester cotton merchant Joseph Barrett. Swift and Hay are strongly partisan, while Barrett, although independent, is if anything the angriest. Historians no longer expect to find wholly independent and reliable information with which to arbitrate on historical disputes. These three new accounts all consciously present a point of view, and it is this that makes them valuable. It is in the attitudes of those involved, more than in the traditional quibbles over issues such as who cast the first stone, that an understanding of the extreme events of 16 August 1819 can be found.

There are over three hundred surviving eye-witness accounts. Nearly all of these have now been captured in the Peterloo Witness Project, which aims to recover and make available every eye-witness account of the Peterloo massacre. Thanks are due to all participants in the project, particularly those who joined the programme at the 2012 Manchester Histories Festival, whether or not their particular transcripts appear here.

*Robert Poole*

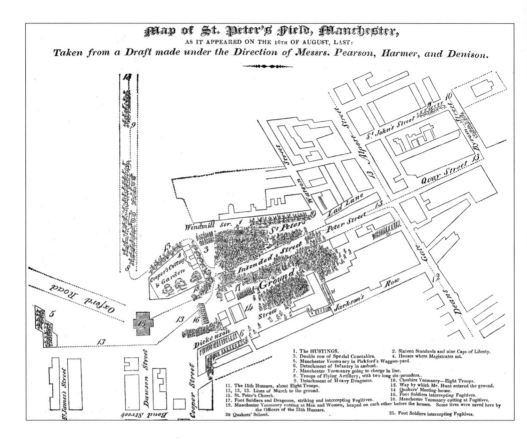

Figure 1:
A plan of
Peterloo
published in
the *Manchester
Observer*,
23 October 1819

## Joseph Barrett

*Joseph Barrett was a Newton Heath manufacturer who kept a warehouse in Market Street, Manchester, and he saw Peterloo from a vantage point close to that of the magistrates. Born around 1788, he was about thirty at the time. His account of Peterloo is part of a memoir of his life, written apparently in the mid-1830s. The early part deals mainly with the Luddism of 1812 and the activities of spies and radicals in Failsworth and Newton Heath; the spies tried to entrap people, including himself. He was related to the pioneer cotton spinner Samuel Crompton and married into the family of his colleague Jonathan Hobson.*

 *Barrett has been identified as the author of the memoir by Chris Westhead of the Peterloo Witness Project. The memoir reveals that Barrett gave evidence at both the trial of Henry Hunt and others in York in 1820 and the* Redford vs Birley *action in 1822, which narrows the field down to six people. His position in the upper room of a house close behind the hustings with his brother and a Mr Hobson identifies him as Joseph Barrett. With his brother Thomas and his friend Jonathan Hobson he watched from the second floor of the house next to the Windmill public house, near Buxton's house where the magistrates sat, some thirty yards*

*behind the speakers' platform. Both Barrett and Hobson gave evidence*
*that the demonstrators had been entirely peaceful and orderly until after*
*they were attacked.*

*Barrett's memoir is written in an exercise book, with additions here*
*and there which have been placed in the order he seems to have intended.*
*His spelling is imperfect and occasionally phonetic and he has a habit of*
*missing out words; corrections and omissions have been supplied in square*
*brackets. It seems to have been an effort to recall and write. Some fifteen*
*years after Peterloo, Barrett's memory is hazy on the exact order of events;*
*his recollection that the speakers had been peacefully arrested before*
*the attack by the yeomanry does not match any of the other eye-witness*
*accounts. But his recall of individual incidents and conversations seems*
*clear and vivid, and there is no reason to doubt his account of the episodes*
*which left such a powerful impression on his mind.*

I am now come to give an account of the Manchester Massacre, or Peter
Loo affair, as it was often called because it took place in St Peters Square.

It was on the 16 August 1819 that a meeting was announced to take
place of Reformers at that place.

A few days before Mr Jonathan Hobson, a merchant in that place, & he
came to my brothers house, and asked if my eldest brother would obtain
a room where it could be seen. My brother said he would try to do so,
& fortunately he met with a gentleman that had an untenanted house
nearly opposite to where the platform for the speakers was to be placed,
& he gave my brother the key of it, & my brother brought it home, and
gave it to Mr Hobson. Mr Hobson got some refreshments taken to an
upper room in the house, & on the morning of the meeting Mr Hobson,
myself & eldest brother were together. We saw the people arrive, among
whom were many young women, dressed in white. There were persons
from all the neighbouring towns and villages, with flags and bands of
music, & persons with long white rods, who seemed to be the directors of
each separate procession, but no weapons of any [kind] not even walking
sticks, for they had been left in some house before the men entered
Manchester lest it might be thought they were weapons.

The people continued to arrive until the square was filled, & there were
calculated to be 80,000 & they [were] all quite peacable and orderly. We
were in one of the best positions to see the whole of the meeting, & all
the proceedings.

The speakers came about one o'clock on to the Platform & were about
to address the meeting, when the Manchester Yeomanry began to come
towards the Platform, headed by Meager a drill sergeant to Captain
Withington, whom we knew, as he had often sold us yarn.

The Yeomanry looked very pale & frightened, except Captain
Withington, who was – . The speakers were taken off the platform, &
the people remained quiet. It was said that the riot act was read, but

if so, no one seemed to know. It was said afterwards it had been read from a chamber window at some distance. After the speakers had been removed, the people began to go away, and then the Yeomanry got courage, and began to strike the people, but no [Resistance?] was mad[e]. The confusion, and panic became general, & we continued at the window to watch the proceedings of the Yeomanry, but soon a soldier or two pointed a musket, & said that they would shoot us, unless we shut the window & went from it.

After some time we return[ed] when the Yeomanry were not to be seen, but the appearance of the square was such as it is impossible to give an adequate idea; there were heaps of people lying, who seemed dead, but had got into this state, by being stuck & frightened, though a many of them were wounded. All over the place there were Flags & several instruments lying. There were only two persons killed on the field, one was John Lees, whose father we knew, as he had supplied us with cotton weft, & he lived at Oldham. The other was a special constable from the Bull's Head in Manchester. There were about three hundred stationed under the house where we were, & the Manchester & Cheshire Yeomanry were so drunk & excited that they did not know what they were doing. One thing I must mention that while the people were lying as I have stated, one of the Cathedral Ministers high in office, kept walking about in the field, & seemed highly pleased with the seen [sic], for he strutted about like a cock that had beaten his opponent.

The Yeomanry after this brilient victory went completely mad; the[y] made about the streets of Manchester striking at every person, that was in their way, and even went to one Cotton Mill, & wished to strike the people that were coming out, & hacked at the doors to make them come out. Myself and brother returned home very much astonished, & [amazed?] at the proceedings. After we got home persons who had been to the meeting began to pass our house, & to them that were wounded my brother Thomas gave money.

The Yeomanry went about the streets of Manchester in the mad[d]ist manner.

The morning after an ultra Tory came into our Warehouse, & my brother said to him: 'You made sad work with the people yesterday.' He replied, 'We could do it better, if [we] had to do it again.' My brother said, 'How would you do it better?' He answered, 'by stopping up the end of the streets leading from the meeting, & planting cannon, & killing ever[y] devil of them.' My brother then said: What would you do for workmen, after that?' He made no reply. There were about 80,000 persons assembled at the meeting.

We had supplied the Colledge, & the Infirmary with Bed Ticking for some time, & the buyer for the Infirmary came in one day about a week before the Meeting & said, You have a large pile of Gray Ticks there, send them to the Infirmary. We did so, but my brother was surprised at this offhand order. We learned after that the Ticking were made up into beds in readiness for the wounded at Peterloo.

This circumstance has not been related often before & I do it now to shew the extreme madness & [illeg.] of the Tories at this time.

## An Account of the Oldham inquest

After the Peterloo affair, I will relate a little of the Oldham inquest on the body of John Lees killed there, which took place soon after, and continued until the Government stopped it, a most illegal proceeding, and one which made Reformers more than ever opposed to the Government. Then came the trial of Henry Hunt & his associates at York. I, Jon^n Hobson & his nephew were supenoed to be witnesses for the defence. My eldest brother would have gone instead of me but he was unwell. When we came into the court, & saw the jury that had been selected, we all of us were certain that H. Hunt & his associates would be found guilty, for they all seemed of the Tory stamp.

The prosecution affirmed that the prisoners had instigated the people to excesses before the meeting, which was not true, for it was the spies that had done this.

The defence was that the meeting was perfectly peacable, and the defence was corroborated [by] the testimony of the witnesses, and the rest. Serjeant Scarlet was the leading councill for the prosecution, & it seemed by the passionate [violence?] as if he might have a personal spite against Hunt. Hunt, who defended himself, and his defence was mild & argumen[t]ative, the reverse of Scarlet's. The prisoners were, of course, all found guilty, and were imprisoned a year.

1822. The next year I was supeonied to Lancaster assize to give evidence in the case of an old man out at Droylsden, near Manchester, who was hurt at Peterloo. The man had no recompence. Thus ends the account of the Manchester Massacre.

# The Magistrates

*This account was drawn up on behalf of the joint committee of magistrates by the Revd William Robert Hay, its most experienced member. Hay lived mainly at his parish of Ackworth in Yorkshire and left most day-to-day business to his Manchester-based colleagues, leaving him with the time to oversee action on political unrest and to correspond with the Home Office. The chairman of the joint committee, and the man who gave instructions to the troops, was the much younger William Hulton, but Hay remained the master strategist. He was also the archivist, his extensive collection of correspondence, cuttings and ephemera now distributed between Chetham's Library and the John Ryland's Library.*

*Hay had written the first account of Peterloo in a hurried letter to the Home Office on the evening of 16 August (HO 42/192, folios 174, 348–50, reprinted in the* Manchester Observer's *'Peterloo Massacre', pp. 55–61). 'The Riot Act was read, and the mob was completely dispersed, but not without very serious and lamentable effects' he wrote then. His estimate was that five people had died (one special constable 'cause unknown' and four women crushed in the crowd), although he had heard that there might have been one or two more. He claimed that pistols had been fired at the troops, and conceded that 'a variety of instances of sabre wounds occurred but I hope none mortal.' 'We cannot but deeply regret all this serious attendant on this transaction', he concluded, 'but we have the satisfaction of witnessing the very grateful and cheering countenances of the whole town; in fact, they consider themselves as saved by our exertions.'*

*A much fuller and more carefully-rehearsed account appears in a letter to in the Home Offices disturbances papers in The National Archives (HO42/196, folios 19–22 and 44–9). It was prepared in response to a request from the Home Secretary for the authorities' side of the story, and compiled by Hay from written notes made at the time in consultation with his magistrate colleagues – particularly James Norris, who*

Figure 2: William Robert Hay. Courtesty Chetham's Library

*wrote out one of the versions and presumably therefore endorsed it all. It is very much a document for the record, intended to address legal points identified by the Home Office advance of the York trial and to vindicate the magistrates' treatment of the St Peter's Field rally as if it were a riot. The details of the military action do not concern Hay: 'the meeting was quickly dispersed' he writes. William Hulton, the chairman of the magistrates on the day, sent a note of clarification to the Home Secretary claiming that he delayed longer before sending the regular troops in; significantly, his comment is added as a rider but not actually incorporated, suggesting dissent between the magistrates.*

*Here, Hay explains that the magistrates had always*

*regarded the meeting as illegal and dispersed it at the earliest credible opportunity. The magistrates' account is of most value in showing how the authorities viewed the mass meeting, what they thought was an adequate justification for the use of military force, and how they polished their story. A similar set of justifications can be found in the Manchester yeomanry's account of Peterloo in the Wadsworth papers in the John Ryland's Library (Eng. Mss 1197), which may also have been ghosted by Hay.*

*This account was transcribed by Yvonne Jez, Mike Jenkinson and Ryan Jones in the Peterloo Witness Project workshops at the Manchester Histories Festival in February 2012. In the version used then the names were left blank, but they have been filled in from an almost identical later draft, dated 9 October, in the same bundle of correspondence. For minor details of punctuation and spelling the most logical choice has been made between the two. This is therefore a composite version.*

<u>Private</u>

Manchester 7 Oct 1819

My Lord,

I have the honour to state to your Lordship that your letter of the 4th inst. to Mr Norris has this morning been laid before the committee of Magistrates at the New Bailey. There were present Mr Hulton, Mr Tatton, Colonel Fletcher, Mr Norris and myself. Considering that your Lordship's wish applied itself to a summary narrative of such occurrences as took place on the morning of the 16th, with certain preliminary circumstances necessary to the explanation of them, we have shaped our notes with reference to such wish. The time would not admit of our adopting any other method than that which we have followed. The Gentlemen living in the Country being gone out of town, assisted by Mr Norris I have drawn out the following narrative from the joint notes of the Committee.

Your Lordship will have received from Mr Norris from time to time, previously to the 11th July, various statements respecting the private movements of the disaffected. On that day he came over to me and communicated several particulars to me, and on the next day we went over to Sir John Byng. It was clear from Mr Norris's account that some support would be necessary for the magistrates here, and that it would be proper that the districts should be put on their guard. Our Sessions commenced here on the 19th July and one of the first measures adopted by the Bench was to issue directions to the magistrates of neighbouring parts of Cheshire and the more distant districts of Lancashire to attend on the following Friday. A very numerous attendance was then given. I hope to be able to furnish your Lordship with the names. Mr Egerton was in the Chair, & amongst other proceedings a Select Committee of magistrates from both counties was appointed, the names of which were privately communicated to Your Lordship. At our Sessions it appeared that some spirited resolutions had been passed at the lately held Knutsford sessions, at which Lord Stamford attended; that these had been communicated to Lord Derby who in strong terms expressed his approbation of them. From the information received the Sessions signified to the Grand Jury the necessity they felt for an armed Association, and such proposition was also forwarded to Your Lordship and to Lord Derby.

The Select Committee of Magistrates met from time to time. After the first two meetings three of the committee were unable to attend and the remainder continued to act regularly, the name of Mr Wright being added to the Committee. These Magistrates of course amongst other matters received information in respect of different particulars connected with the views of the disaffected. It was soon made known that a meeting on which great stress was laid by the disaffected was fixed for the 9th August, but when the purposes of the meeting were published, the Magistrates issued a notification of their sense that it would be an unlawful meeting and of their intention to stop it. After consulting Counsel, one Sax[t]on, assistant to the Editor of the Observer, gave notice that the meeting was abandoned, but in that notice there was a peculiar expression, which caused the Committee and others whether or no the abandonment was real. The unexpected arrival of Hunt with Sir C. Wolseley at Stockport on the evening of the 8th and their proceeding to Manchester on the forenoon of the 9th, and going through the streets with an evident wish to court popularity strengthened our suspicion. In truth information was brought to us that emissaries had been dispatched to their friends to order their attendance at St. Peter's that afternoon at 4 o'clock; this however proved unfounded. The parties proceeded to Johnson's at Smedley, with a seeming intention to stay there; and as meetings were to be held at Leigh and at other places, the Magistrates thought that they meant to travel about to those places for the whole week, and to harrass the military by attendance previous to the 16th on which day the meeting was proposed to be held. These circumstances were communicated to General Byng. However the apprehension was false. Sir Chas. Wolseley left Smedley and Hunt was principally engaged in writing and other Business.

On Saturday the 14th Hunt came with Johnson to the New Bailey and enquired for Mr Norris or me, we were not there; Mr Tatton and Mr Trafford were. Applying himself to Mr Tatton Hunt said, 'I understand there is a warrant against me.' Mr Tatton replied 'I am not aware that there is one.' Hunt said, 'I merely have to say that that if there is a Warrant out against me I am ready to deliver myself up.' Before Dinner Mr Norris returned home and found Johnson writing a note to him. On Mr Norris's appearing, Johnson stated the purpose of his enquiry was to know whether any warrant was out against Hunt. Mr Norris answered, 'I have issued none nor do I know of any.'

The Committee continued to meet and did so on Saturday the 14th, Sunday & Monday. Prior to Saturday different points had been discussed, as to the propensity or expediency of stopping the meeting, and the manner of doing so. They were of opinion that multitudes coming in columns, with flags, and marching in military array, were even in the approach to the meeting, a tumultuous assembly, and it was for a little time under consideration, whether each column should not be stopped at their respective entrances into the Town; but this was given up; it was considered that the military might thus be distracted, & it was wished that the Town should see what the meeting was when assembled, and also that those who came, should be satisfied that they were assembled in an unlawful manner. In truth our information was such, that we could have little doubt but that the parties would assemble in an illegal manner. In addition to the general information of training from time to time there was specific information of the training to be at White Moss on the 15th early in the morning: we had also information that the parties were there told that it would be the last training that would be necessary before the meeting. Your Lordship will be aware that it was at this meeting on the 15th that Murray and Shawcross met with the treatment which was at the time detailed to you.

Under this information and being satisfied that in point of Law, that meeting if assembled, as it was expected, would be an illegal meeting we gave notice to Lieut. Col L'Estrange the commanding Officer here of our wish to have the assistance of the Military on the 16th and in the evening of the 15th the arrangements in respect of the military were made. What the arrangements were, was unknown to the Magistrates: our advice and assistance as friends had been wished for in this respect but we declined giving them. They were made between him & other Officers and Gentlemen in another room, so that we were total strangers to what was settled. In the morning of the 16th, we requested that the Town Constables & special Constables should be in attendance, but none of them knew in what particular instance, or for what particular purpose that might be employed: they attended in consequence. The Magistrates got to the ground, and were in a house fronting the area of St Peters, whence we could have a full view of what passed at the Hustings, though we could not hear. The Area is computed to be about 14,000 Square Yards – this space was occupied very closely near the Hustings and in other parts more or less so. We compute the numbers of those collected who took part in the meeting to be about 30,000. Of these at least 20,000 were strangers to Manchester: we saw 5 or 6 columns march in these were from 2000 to 5000 each if not more: they marched in to quick time, with martial music, banners, and Ensigns. The representation on several of the Banners have been communicated to Your Lordship: each column as it came in view marched directly up to the Hustings, as they came they were received with three cheers: their Banners were then arranged in front & they were cheered again. This took place in every instance – after all the columns had arrived. Hunt came with his party, and the same reception took place. Prior to Hunt's appearance on the Ground one Owen came to us and gave information as to the parties in Hunts company. His information was taken in form, and a warrant filled up in consequence, and signed by ten Magistrates.

Before this the Magistrates had been not only on their own view convinced that the meeting was in terror of his Majesty's subjects, but they had also taken the information of about 50 inhabitants who were to the same effect. In addition to this the Shops at the lower part of the Town at a quarter of a mile from St Peters, had been shut all the morning and but a very few could be prevailed on in the afternoon to take down their shutters.

The warrant was filled up about the time of Hunts arrival: Mr Andrew one of the town constables, came in the Magistrates room and told Mr Hulton that it could not be served without military aid. Nadin was in the room. Mr Hulton laid hold of Nadin by the arm and asked him whether it was possible for the Police aided by the special Constables to execute the warrant. Nadin replied neither with those special constables, nor with 10 times the number, nor with all the special constables in England. Mr Hulton asked him 'cannot it be executed without military force?' Nadin answered it cannot. Mr Hulton said 'then you shall have military Power, for God's sake don't sacrifice the lives of the special constables.'

The special Constables in the first instance were formed on one side of the Hustings; and an alley of them was formed up to the House where the Magistrates were agreeably to a Plan, which will hereinafter be forwarded to Your Lordship. As soon as the reformers came and saw the situation of the special constables they moved the Hustings twice: the first movement was about 8 yards distance: by this means they got between the special constables & the Hustings, and pushed them back: the second movement was merely to arrange the fronting of the Hustings. These men were 10 or 12 deep, linked together, their hats off & evidently placed to prevent the special constables from having access to the Hustings. The warrant was delivered into the hands of Mr Moore the towns constable, he delivered it over to Nadin the Deputy Constable.

Mr Hulton on learning that the civil power was inadequate to execute the warrant, sent notices by two gentlemen to the military in different situations, informing them of such inadequacy, and requesting their presence, in front of the Magistrates house. Mr Andrew & Nadin & were now together; Mr Andrew headed the Yeomanry on foot towards the Hustings; but as the Yeomanry advanced on a trot, they got first to the Hustings, surrounded them, and Mr Andrew found himself mixed with them directly. He brought Johnson off – Nadin seized Hunt.

The cavalry on coming up to the House had to form – prior to their forming, we observed the mob to wave their hats, and sticks and to defy them – they formed. Whilst they were forming and before they went up, Mr Ethelstone read the riot Act, out of the window. Mr Silvester went down stairs, proceeded as far as he could into the Crowd and read the Riot

*Vide Trial Redford, v. Birley and Others.*
Printed and Published by J. T. Saxton, Nightingale-street, Port-street, Manchester

Figure 3: Revds Hay and Ethelston, caricatured reading the Riot Act, with Ethelston leaning as far as he dared out of an upstairs window as they claimed. If the act was indeed read, very few heard it. Courtesy of Manchester Libraries, Information and Archives, Manchester City Council

Act, but before he had quite finished, he was pressed down by the Mob. As the Cavalry were advancing, Mr Hulton saw the Cavalry were assailed by Brick-bats &c. &c. several pistols were fired. Colonel L'Estrange and Colonel Dalrymple at this instant rode up with Mr Trafford (a Magistrate who attended the commanding Officer) and asked what they were about. Mr Hulton said, 'don't you see they are attacking the Cavalry – Disperse the Mob.' They were instantly dispersed. The Cavalry had been attacked about ¼ minute* before Col L'Estrange came up. From the time of forming the Cavalry to the dispersion of the Body of the Mob above ¼ of an hour did not elapse. The Magistrates in general, afterwards went about the town with different bodies of Troops. I went to the infirmary with Mr Silvester to learn the state of the patients who had been brought in. Mr Ransome the Surgeon, a very eminent one, a Quaker, observed to me that the Cavalry must have studied to do as little mischief as they could for the wounds were so slight.

I am to apologise for the haste in which this is written, but we can Barely save the Post, and we are most anxious that Your Lordship should not be disappointed. Mr Norris is so good as to write the letter from my copy and I trust Your Lordship will excuse my only signing it. Should any further information be required, it will be readily afforded. As I return home on Saturday should any communication become necessary may I request that it should be made to Mr Norris.

I have the Honor to be
with Sincere respect
My Lord
Your Lordships faithful
Humble Servant
W. R. Hay.

* Memorandum. Mr Hulton in a letter addressed to Lord Sidmouth on the 17th October 1819, states that instead of having witnessed the attack of the mob on the Yeomanry Cavalry for ¼ minute only when Col. L'Estrange, Col. Dalrymple and Mr Trafford the Magistrate arrived, the Manchester Yeomanry, had then been assailed four or five minutes and were (as he firmly believes) exposed to the most imminent danger of being sacrifised, and he remained in conversation with Col L'Estrange &c. for a quarter of a minute: that is had only time to point out the point, in which he conceived the Yeomanry were exposed.

# George Swift

*George Swift was one of the least-known of the ten Peterloo defendants tried at York. He was described then as a Manchester shoemaker, yet he talks here of having journeyed into his native county for the meeting. Swift was on the hustings for Hunt's speech and was probably arrested for his actions before the start of the meeting, when he was seen to address part of the crowd from the platform and to get those around it to link arms – an action which Hulton and the other magistrates took to be a sign of aggressive intent. Swift was observed by others, and was the 'unknown man' whose impromptu speech was later rewritten by Charles Dickens (see 'Dickens on Peterloo' in this volume). Cowdroy's Manchester Gazette (28 August 1819) noted that about twelve o'clock, as a column marched in with a band of music and flags flying, 'George Swift, a Reform orator, now addressed the meeting, and on ending his speech four or five huzzas were given by order.' John Tyas of The Times observed that 'A young lad, not more than seventeen or eighteen, was addressing the meeting with great vehemence of action and gesture, and with great effect, if we may judge from the cheers which he every now and then extracted from his audience.'*

*Swift defended himself at York and was acquitted. On the fourth day of the trial he told the court:*

> My situation in life has given me little opportunity of becoming acquainted with the rules of a Court of Justice ... I positively affirm, I had no concern in erecting the hustings whatever; neither should I have been upon the hustings at all, had it not been from what observed in the conduct of the constables, I was very apprehensive they might excite some to acts of violence – therefore, I determined to do my utmost to induct the people to give them no pretext. I have been but a short time in Manchester, but long enough to learn the general character of the Police Officers. When I was but a child, I volunteered my service in my country's defence ... and I consider I am no longer worthy to live, than whilst I retain the character of a worthy Briton ... I defy any one to prove that I had any connection with any of the Defendants. I never saw any of them, with the exception of Mr. Hunt until we were confined together, and he never saw me in his life before to his knowledge.

*Although dated 16 August the letter seems to have been written up over several days while Swift was in the New Bailey prison awaiting examination. The first hearing took place on 20 August and the charge of High Treason mentioned by Swift had been dropped by the final hearing on 27th. His account is cast in the form of a letter intended for publication, and was probably modelled on Henry Hunt's open letters to the Lancashire reformers. Swift's manuscript is in Manchester Central Library, MSC 920, with a copy at BR 942 730731 P92. His handwriting is strong and clear and his English good. It was transcribed as part of the Peterloo Witness Project by Chris Westhead.*

Dear Brothers,

You will in the course of a few hours hear of the abominable proceedings and the unexpected result of this day. A more shameful attempt to support an aristocracy never was heard of – nor could anything more cruel have been contemplated to support the most absolute tyrant or to crush at one blow a faithful and loyal people. To stop the mouths and deafen the cries of an oppressed nation. To add new burdens on the already overloaded shoulders of the middle and working classes. To sacrifice the interest the liberty and life of nine tenths of [the] community to support in the vilest profligacy of the other one tenth. Oh how shocked will be the inhabitants of every town in the empire when they hear this is done with the edge of the sabre and the point of the bayonet with the loss of scores of our fellow creatures lives and the blood and limbs of hundreds more. As the painful news will reach you long before anything I can send you, I will commence making memorandums and will transmit them to you as brief and early as I possibly can. My last letter informed you of my journey into my native county and this will inform you of my living in a Dungeon six feet by seven, under no less a charge than that of High Treason awaiting the opinion of the Crown Officers on the probability of a conviction on the adduced evidence. On my arrival at Manchester I was informed the public meeting had been postponed to 16 of August from reasons assigned by a Mr Raincock of Liverpool. The circumstance is mentioned by that base hireling the Editor of the Manchester Chronicle in the following words,

> Our readers are well aware that a meeting of the Radical Reformers was appointed to take place near St Peter's Church in the town on Monday next. The probable occurrence of such a meeting had engaged the serious attention of the Right Hon the Earl of Derby, the active and vigilant Lord Lieutenant of the County of the Magistrates, the Boroughreeve, the Constables and the whole of the civil authorities.

Government had also not been inactive in its contemplation but had directed to the Town and neighbourhood of Manchester and Salford a formidable force of Artillery, Cavalry and Infantry under the superintendence of General Sir John Byng, military commander of the District, and Sir John had regulated in person a proper distribution of this extensive armament. A very great addition to the civil power had also been provided by swearing in extra constables and on Saturday last nine Magistrates acting for the counties palatine of Lancaster and Chester issued a public notice dated from the New Bailey Courthouse, cautioning all persons to abstain at their peril attending the illegal meeting convened for Monday the 9<sup>th</sup> of August. So this succeeded the admirable proclamation of his Royal Highness the Prince Regent declaring the various objects of mischief which the country had to apprehend and His Royal determination to repress the practices once merated [merited]. The Reformers now thought it high time to betake themselves to consideration and one of their notorious chiefs whose name is Saxton was commissioned to apply to that eminent Counsel Mr Raincock for an opinion on the legality of their notice for their intended meeting and his answer was that the intention of choosing Representatives contrary to the existing law tends greatly to render the proposed meeting seditious under those circumstances it would be deemed justifiable in the Magistrates to prevent such meeting. Saxton announced this in a very inflammatory [sic] printed bill in which he throws doubt upon the legal conclusion of Mr Raincock but says, he (Saxton) is induced to recommend the Requisitionists to pause merely in consideration of the cruel threats of violence issued in a paper from the Bench of Magistrates and because in a question of Right they, the Requisitionists are not prepared to defend themselves, but recomend [sic] St Peters area as the place and Monday the 16th of August as the day for a meeting to consider the propriety of adopting the most legal means of obtaining a Reform in the commons house of Parliament. So far so good Mr Wheeler of the Chronicle. Mr Hunt having been invited to take the Chair, he arrived at the Bullock Smithy near Stockport on the 8th and came to Manchester on the 9th of August attended by thousands of people. They made a stand at the end of Blakeley Street where Mr Hunt animadverted very strongly on those who caused the postponement of the meeting, describing Mr Raincock as a pettifogger and nine Magistrates as nine Tailors. He then proceeded in company of Sir Chas Wollesley [sic], Mr Moorhouse of Stockport and Mr Johnson to Smedley Cottage, the country seat of the latter Gentleman where he remained the following week, having promised to preside on the 16th. The authorities was so much agitated as to induce a observer to think the most serious revolt might be expected from a meeting to petition the legislature to remove certain grievances, the existence of which all agree but vary in the mode of removing them. The Magistrates describing the meeting for the 16th seditious if not treasonable and assured the public that every person composing the meeting would be provided with firearms. This proclamation was contradicted by Mr Hunt in a most Gentleman like manner he assured no-one would come there with any other weapon than a self-approving conscience. This had a powerful effect in more ways than one. He invited the Magistrates and minor authorities, and if not inclined to take an active part in the business of the day use their influence and keep the peace. 'I need not say what will men do for money.' So those men has done all they ought not to have done and left undone all they ought to have done. That talent they are endowed with has been most grossly misapplied. Mischief has been their object all through and to carry their point the press forever in some part has not rendered them a trifling assistance. I have now before me a paragraph of Wheeler of the Chronicle in alluding to Mr Hunt, he says,

> To say the best we can of this popular Democrat is, that he is a profane irreligious libertine, a penurious, proud, revengeful Coward, capable and accustomed to insult his inferiors to defraud his servants and tenants defraud his Creditors and prostitute his public faith for protection. Now only observe if a man should be capable of all this where shall we find a human being that may be said to be his inferior

but I must proceed with facts and not surmises.

I was walking up Market Street with Saxton on Sunday morning. Let us said he go to the Union School and prevent the women going tomorrow for it will be a bloody day, every yeoman's sword is ground on purpose. I would not go and I mention this here as an introduction to other matters for I do apprehend that Mr Saxton knew more than he dare tell me of at that time. However the Monday morning arrived and I went to the different Barracks (for there were several places fitted up as temporary barracks) to ascertain the orders of the Military, but nothing could I illicit that appeared of importance. I went to the meeting about quarter to twelve o'clock and found they had not finished the hustings. I found fault with a joiner who had undertook the work, for the numbers increased so fast that I apprehended they would not get their work done, the pressure became so great. At this time I got upon the wood already erected and caused to be formed a ring of about thirty yards diameter and to maintain their position in spite of the pressure. I requested they would link Arms six or eight deep all around and place a flag at the only place where an opening was to be made. Some people came to me and advised I would strive to allay the fears of some that was exited [sic] by the arrival of the posse of special Constables, who have but just then formed a line extending from the hustings. I stop'd on the top of the now finished temporary Rostrom [sic] with feelings bordering on contempt for the busy fools and on pity for those who feared them, and dispensed with the subject in as few words as I possibly could, but short as they are, they, and the instructions given in forming the before mentioned circle, are the paltry grounds of the evidence that detained me on a charge of so high a nature, that Death is the inevitable consequence of conviction. Mr Hunt arrived about ten minutes after One o'clock in a coach accompanied by Mr Johnson, Mr Knight and others. Mr Johnson proposed Mr Hunt do take the Chair. This was carried unanimously. The Hustings was formed of deal planks with vacancies so that all but the speaker might be seated. I sat betwixt Saxton and Edward Baines Junior of Leeds. At this moment the sight was beautiful. Mr Hunt now rose to address this immense mass of human beings who after the accustomed salute stood motionless and in breathless silence. Here then commenced the oration that is to end – where? – with its consequences I know not. Speaking of the postponement being generally known he had only to say that it had caused double the number to attend. Alluding to the resolutions formed for the consideration of the meeting and now in the act of pulling a paper out of his pocket the Yeomen cavalry made their appearance at the top of the ground. At this moment a very apparent sensation pervaded the whole assembly so sudden an appearance of Military without the least warning in word or deed induced me to think they was come to intimidate all they could and not to act from authority, for not a word had been spoken on that field to the public by anyone in authority - civil or military. Mr Hunt now set himself off to advantage, he had 130 thousand people under command, he gave signal for a general cheer and ordered the people to stand fast. If they want me said Mr Hunt let me go - don't resist, stand fast; don't resist, pointing to a near him if them fellows won't be quiet put them down and keep them down and again exerted himself as a Masterpiece [sic] in managing a public assembly. The Cavalry formed in front of a range of buildings at the top of the area. After a pause of about two minutes they dashed forward towards us as well as they could, closing in as they got faster into the crowd. Their swords was lifted up and struck down all the way but I could not at that instance see whether they cut anyone or not. They was a considerable time getting through the dense crowd considering the distance so short. They came to the cordon or well of men round the Hustings but no resistance was made to their progress there more than at any other place. The inside of this circle we had filled with Woemen [sic] from the Union Schools, music and flags. The Cavalry surrounded the Hustings and made a full stand for the space of one minute and then turned round to the unoffending multitude most of which near them was women and [illegible] and in the most confused brutal undicipled [sic] manner rode circuitously about the Hustings chopping down all before them. The confusion and bloodshed now became so general that I cannot describe anywhere but just around the place I stood. The Hustings was about eight feet high. I stood up when the Cavalry surrounded us and during the moment they stood still I anxiously looked for some of the Magistrates in execution of some legal document but guess my surprise when the Cavalry turned round and no-one appeared with a specific charge. They cut at our legs and but for dextrously leaping backwards I must have lost a foot that fellows sword entered the plank on which I stood two inches in a sloping direction. There was scores of those special constables amongst the Horse Soldiers who appeared to share of the fury of the Soldiers same as those who were not of their party, those fellows had staves or Bludgeons with which they struck everyone they come near who had not one of the same sort but when the horses came round they paid no respect to a truncheon but down they went amonst [sic] others and the Cavalry cut at them indiscriminately. I saw several of those fellows showing their staves and beging [sic] them to observe they were constables. Not so they slashed amongst them and they squealed out like young brisk Pigs, there was no way for those to get away from the ground as every street end was blocked by Infantry with the power of the Bayonet. I called to those constables to take me in custody and was getting off the Hustings to them but the cavalry come on so rapidly that I got up again. I took the immediate advantage and got hold of two of those constables but before I had time to say 'Jack Robinson' I had lost the fellows and was under the Horses amongst thousands. I took hold of a young woman at this time that was bleeding very much and nearly senseless. I dragged her somewhere and a woman in the place washed her. She told us where she came from and I took her home. I said to her Mother, here is your Daughter, I will call presently. I had left the door perhaps one hundred yards when a Mr Edge took my Arm and as we was going towards St Peters area we met Mr Hunt Mr Johnson and others under an escort of light Dragoons and Constables going to the New Bailey. The Constables surrounded me and amongst them to Prison I went. On our arrival we were called our names which were Henry Hunt, Jos[ep]h Johnson, John Thacker Saxton, George Swift, Robert Wilde, J^no Jones, W^m [sic] Tyas and a young woman. We were all put in one yard at ten minutes past two o'clock. On examining Saxton [sic] clothes we found one of the Yeoman had cut his coat laps off, through the wilt that covers the Pocket, through the pocket into his trowsers and entered his thigh an inch and a half. The sword that cut it must have been as sharp as a Rasor [sic] or it could not have cut it so clean. Mr Saxton here had good proof of the truth of his assertion made to me in Market Street last Sunday morning. Mr Hunt could not lift his left arm to his head he was so abused with the Constables Staves. Mr W^m Tyas who is a reporter for the London Times wrote to the Magistrates for his liberation that he might haste to town with his notes but he was detained untill his report was too late for insertion. This man has given such a strict and true account of this day's proceedings as I am afraid the Editor will not allow to appear in its original form; this man has since admited his report was materially softened down respecting the Yeomanry.

During this afternoon they brought in Mr James Moorhouse who had been taken into custody at the Flying Horse, the office where his Stage Coaches stops at, a lolly [sic] old man he is, there is something in this person which I am told commands the respect of all good men. I will obtain further knowledge of him and them. Mr Hunt and Mr Saxton who is the manager of the Manchester Observer was busy examining Mr Tyas reports and preparing them for the compositor expecting his liberation, but not so all. At 10 Minutes to 6 to o'clock we called and put [end of account missing].

# The objects of Peterloo

Chris
Burgess

'Popular prints for a dozen years to come made all men familiar with the symbolic figure of a mounted yeoman in his shako, prancing over a heap of shrieking women and sabring them on the ground.'[1] So wrote G.M. Trevelyan on how the vast quantity of visual material produced following the massacre helped cement it as the key event in early-nineteenth-century radical history. Writing in this very journal twenty-three years ago Diana Donald echoed Trevelyan's view, arguing that 'engravings have ultimately had the greatest influence in creating a mental picture of the 'Peterloo massacre.'[2]

So strong is the visual legacy of the prints of Peterloo, that it has become almost impossible to consider the massacre outside of their frame. While Robert Poole has done much to redress the balance, visually reconstructing the day beyond the massacre and reconstituting 'Peterloo' within the broader context of Georgian popular political culture, the event remains wedded to the image of slaughter.[3] And yet the cultural – and that is to say artefactual – legacy of 16 August 1819 is more than the prints produced after the event. Surviving objects from the day and the family history that accompanies them potentially offer the historian new insights into events of the day, notably the actions or intentions of the crowd. Moreover the objects produced after Peterloo demonstrate the nature of commemoration by both working-class and middle-class reformers.

The article in the 1989 *Manchester Region History Review* highlighted the quantity of surviving Peterloo artefacts, which the anonymous author described as 'less appreciated and less well known' than manuscript sources.[4] Since that article's publication extra objects have come to light and, more is known about the original ones mentioned. Moreover, it is no longer fair to say that the objects are less well known. As a result of major refurbishment at Touchstones in Rochdale and the People's History Museum in Manchester, there are now two significant displays of Peterloo material – both containing original artefacts – seen by tens of thousands of members of the general public every year. This is aside from the material held in other collections around the north-west of England. Geographic spread does mean that more people can see Peterloo collections and learn about the day, but it also makes it impossible to consider the artefacts as a whole. This article attempts to do this. Surviving material is broken down into two groups, objects that were (or supposedly were) at Peterloo, and objects produced in the aftermath. Through such a structure we can get some grasp on the surviving object legacy of the event.

Given the bloody violence of Peterloo, many of the objects that survive from the day are weapons of one form or another. The problem with much of this material is that any knowledge of its actual presence on the day relies on oral testimony, and often this information has passed through the tangled branches of family trees. For instance Salford Museum and Art Gallery has Captain Robert Hindley's sword. Whether Hindley used that particular sword at Peterloo remains unclear but we know he was in the field, and commanded a group of yeomanry.[5] In more recent years two more sabres that could potentially have been at Peterloo have come to light. These came down through the family of a yeoman from Droylsden. Again as with Hindley's sword locating them at the event is problematic, though it is a weapon contemporaneous with the period and the family history of the lender does prove the yeomanry link. Whatever the truth, the swords remain tantalizing objects.

Swords aren't the only weapons surviving from Peterloo. Several of the truncheons carried by special constables also survive. The example at Rochdale Touchstones was carried by an unknown special constable, but more is known about the example at the Greater Manchester Police Museum. Richard Jones, pawn broker and special constable, carried this long baton at Peterloo. In his 1909 *Manchester Streets and Manchester Men* T. Swindells mentions another of these long coshes. Swindells states that the club was given to him by a descendent of James Fildes, a grocer from Shudehill. On the staff was an inscription 'A relic of Peterloo. Special constable's staff which belonged to the late James and Thomas Fildes, grocers Shudehill, Manchester.'[6] Alas the whereabouts

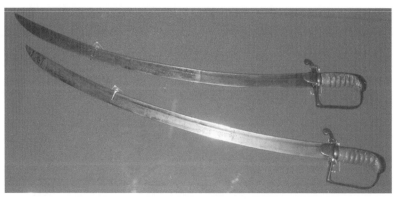

Figure 1: Sabres owned by a yeoman from Droylsden. Picture courtesy of the People's History Museum Manchester

of this item is unknown, although Swindells's interest in the 'relic' demonstrates just how long such items have held attraction for those interested in understanding the event. Another example can be found at the People's History Museum, although this is shorter and more club like than the longer ones at Touchstones and at the Police Museum. A detailed examination of the John Slack design that appears on the numerous surviving calico handkerchiefs, shows both the long and short truncheons – see below.

These museum artefacts provide the public with an insight into the horrors of Peterloo, an extension of the visible manifestations of the massacre so familiar from the prints to the actual objects that were wielded during the day. The ability of such objects to create resonance between visitors and a past they did not experience remains an intrinsic and powerful factor of any museum display.[7] As the world become increasingly more digital the weapons of the Peterloo massacre render the physicality of violence concrete. As objects in themselves, whether the surviving weapons from Peterloo open new lines of enquiry for the historian is questionable. New evidence is, however, available if the pre-history of these objects can be established – not just who owned them but how they were used. Although there is no verifiable documentation to connect the pike head displayed in the People's History Museum with Peterloo, there are objects which suggest that sections of the crowd were not entirely passive. For instance the truncheon in the People's History Museum collection came from the descendants of a former lord mayor of Manchester, Thomas Stone Williams. Family testimony asserts that Stone's great-great-grandfather stole the truncheon from a special constable on the day of Peterloo in order to fight back. He then, supposedly, hid the truncheon in a pub on the corner of Factory Lane and Rochdale Road in the Moston area, and after three days he went to collect the offending article.

Ceremonial objects from Peterloo also survive. In Rochdale there is a finial which would have a stood atop a banner poll. It takes the form of a Phrygian cap and bears the words Hunt and Liberty.

Samuel Bamford described two banners leaving from Middleton to attend the demonstration at Peterloo. One blue, with the words 'Liberty and Fraternity' and 'Unity and Strength', the other green with the slogan 'Parliaments Annual' and 'Suffrage Universal'. The 'Unity and Strength' banner survives and is now in the care of Touchstones Rochdale (as discussed in Robert Poole's article on the banner in this volume). Intriguingly, in his 1921 *Three Accounts of Peterloo* Bruton wrote that there was another surviving banner, the one from Chadderton, but its owner had moved to Blackpool and its whereabouts were unknown. Nor were there just ceremonial objects belonging to protestors that survive. Touchstones also contains a horse hair plume supposedly from the helmet of a 15th Hussar. Like the finial this was collected from the field

Figure 2: Banner finial in the form of a Phrygian cap, or cap of liberty. Image courtesy of Rochdale Arts and Heritage Service – Museum Collection

by a Mr Mansfield, who on the day had seen the people streaming from the field and with his son picked up the items (and a truncheon, the whereabouts of which are now unknown).[8] Manchester City Galleries hold another interesting survivor from Peterloo. Included in the collection of costume at Platt Hall is a dress worn on the day by Mrs Mabbott, a confectioner with premises in Shudehill. Rather than being an active participant in the protest it seems Mrs Mabbott was swept up in the violence. The dress, a type worn by a lower-middle-class shop keeper of the period, shows just how much the violence of the day swept through the centre of city and affecting all.[9]

As the previous section shows, objects that were actually at Peterloo are something of a rarity. Much more common are items produced afterwards to commemorate the day in some way. Material sympathetic to the carnage inflicted at Peterloo survives in significant quantity, but commemorative objects related to the yeomen's actions on the day also exist.

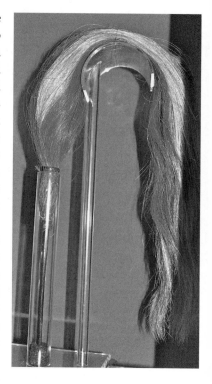

Figure 3: Plume from the helmet of a 15th Hussar. Image courtesy of Rochdale Arts and Heritage Service – Museum Collection

The most notable of this latter group is a sword held at the Museum of Lancashire and from the collection of the Duke of Lancaster's own yeomanry. The blade was a presentation from the men who served at Peterloo under Hugh Hornby Birley in the Manchester and Salford yeomanry. The present marked Birley's acquittal at the Lancaster Assizes, following charges brought by Redford for the Captain's actions at Peterloo. It remains unclear whether a mug held by the National Army Museum and stating the words 'Success to the Manchester Cavalry' was produced just before or just after the Peterloo massacre. The cup's other slogans – 'In defence of our king and country' and 'To protect our families and prosper' – show that, whether produced just before or just after the 'massacre', it was an object produced in resolute support of the government forces.

The majority of objects produced in commemoration of Peterloo were, however, resolutely in support of the martyrs. Of all objects the most numerous are commemorative jugs, and are held in several collections across the region. Given the mass production of pottery, it is perhaps unsurprising that the same example is seen in the collection of several institutions. Manchester Art Gallery holds two jugs with the transfer 'Murdered on the plains of Peterloo' above an image of a yeoman slashing at a woman on the floor. She in turn is holding a banner entitled 'Liberty or Death'. (See Fig. 4 in Alison Morgan's article, p. 72). Below this image are the words 'Manchester 16th August'. There is a similar example at Saddleworth Museum.[10] An examination of the surviving ceramics shows just how erratic their production was. Many of the jugs came from the Herculaneum Pottery in Toxteth, Liverpool, and it was clear that the factory had several shapes and several transfers and they were applying them randomly to meet demand.

Evidence of the haste with which many of the ceramics commemorating Peterloo were produced can be seen in a series of jugs bearing the supposed image of the 'Orator' Hunt. Two examples at the People's History Museum, one at Manchester's Museum of Science and Industry and one in Rochdale picture 'Hunt' with a variety of different slogans including 'Hunt and Liberty' and 'Bad Luck to the Manchester Butchers'. The figure shown on the jugs, however, is not Hunt but Commodore William Bainbridge, a United States naval hero. Why Bainbridge rather than Hunt appears on the jug is not entirely clear. Possibly the factory had an over-run of the Bainbridge image, or in response to the massacre they needed to produce an object quickly and in the absence of an image of Hunt, applied Bainbridge instead. Quite what those purchasers thought, or if they even understood, that the man on their jug was not who it purported to be is again unclear. But surely there would have been some questioning of the appearance of ships of war in an image about an event which occurred in a landlocked city, and of a man who was better known for his white hat than for his seafaring qualities.

Figure 4: Bainbridge-as-Hunt. There is a similar jug in Touchstones, Rochdale. Image courtesy of the People's History Museum, Manchester

There do exist some ceramics which feature accurate depictions of Hunt. The People's History Museum has on display a jug on loan from Manchester Museum and Art Gallery featuring Hunt and the Phrygian cap, or 'cap of liberty'. The same institution holds two lustre wear jugs that feature a small depiction of Hunt. The legend 'To the memory of the unfortunate Suffers at Manchester' appears below Hunt, while an image of the editor of *Black Dwarf*, T.J. Wooler, and a weeping Britannia also appear, all of which sit on a monumental pediment; the jug, itself a commemoration, depicts one also. One jug at Rochdale rather than being a memorial to those at Peterloo promises revenge. Under an image of the yeomanry charging the people – an image labelled simply 'murder'– a statement reads 'The scripture crys out life for life and God ordain'd it so. We'll not forget to repay the debt incurred at PETERLOO'.

Aside from ceramics, two other items appear to have been mass produced in the aftermath of Peterloo. There are a number of commemorative medals, produced following the massacre. The People's History Museum and Manchester Art Gallery museum all contain examples. The front of the medal depicts a scene of the yeomanry riding into the crowd, one of whom holds up a cap of liberty on a pole. On the reverse of the medal is the 37th Psalm 'The wicked have drawn out the sword. They have cut down the poor and needy and such as be of upright conversation'. Another version of the medal has recently been turned up by a dealer, Tim Millett, with a different slogan on the reverse: 'The magistrates and Yeomanry of Manchester God confound them', and round the edge: 'These things will not endure nor be endured.' [11] As this is the only such copy to survive a reasonable guess would be that this is an early version, and that the more aggressive slogan was replaced by the quotation from the psalms. Such medals, or coins at least, were an integral part of the radical tradition. And tokens referencing the London Corresponding Society and the Spencean Philanthropists may well have been familiar to those purchasing the Peterloo medal. Whether the sale of this item was produced to raise money for the victims is unknown.

Figure 5: An alternative, and probably earlier, version of the Peterloo medal. Photo courtesy of Tim Millett, www. historicmedals. com

By far the most numerous of surviving Peterloo artefacts is the calico handkerchief printed with John Slack's image of the massacre (see Fig. 1, p. 69). Examples of this can be found at the Working Class Movement Library, People's History Museum, Manchester Art Gallery and Saddleworth Museum, as well as numerous private collections. Ruth and Edmund Frow always said that the object was produced to raise money for the victims of Peterloo. Certainly the production of serviettes and ceramics to commemorate, but also raise money for, victims of pit disasters was occurring in the 1870s, and the technique of raising money must have begun somewhere.

As well as the multitude of mass-produced ceramics and handker-chiefs, those seeking to commemorate Peterloo also commissioned unique objects. In the case of the Skelmanthorpe flag, produced three months after the massacre, these objects could themselves participate in the radical cause; the site of commemoration itself becoming part of the movement for reform. The banner, held at the Tolson Museum, includes the supplicating figure of the slave movement and the message 'Truth and justice pouring balm into the wounds of the Manchester sufferers'. The banner was carried at reform and Chartist meetings throughout the nineteenth century, and buried in between in order to avoid confiscation.[12]

Other unique sites of commemoration exist. The Museum of Science of

Industry hold a long case clock by the maker W. Stancliffe of Barkisland, Calderdale. Above the clock face is a painting of the massacre, and surrounding it are portraits of Henry Hunt, T.J. Wooler, William Cobbett and Major John Cartwright. The commissioning of such a clock demonstrates that the commemoration of Peterloo extended beyond the material culture of working-class reformers, to the middle-class drawing rooms of those well off enough to commission such pieces.

Nor is the clock the only object representing high-end and expensive commemoration. The Museum of Science and Industry also contains a bronze plaque of Henry Hunt executed by the Manchester sculptor John Cassidy for the Manchester Reform Club and unveiled on 29 June 1908. In the People's History Museum there is a snuff mull previously belonging to the St Peter's Field Society, an object which would have been passed around the table by members of the society during the annual Peterloo dinner.

There is one surviving object which does not fit into the binary separation of objects present and those produced after. In the collection of the Working Class Movement Library is a map once owned by William Hulton, the magistrate who ordered the yeomanry to arrest Hunt. The map, produced in 1819, possibly for one of the inquests, shows the positions of the various yeomanry, infantry, and cavalry in the streets surrounding St Peter's Fields. It is a remarkable survival, and makes an interesting comparison with the *Manchester Observer* map (Fig. 1, p. 134).

What then do the Peterloo objects tell us about the massacre? Certainly there is some paradox about the nature of the evidence. While documentary research is increasingly revealing more about the nature of the violence at Peterloo, the actual objects of that violence, the

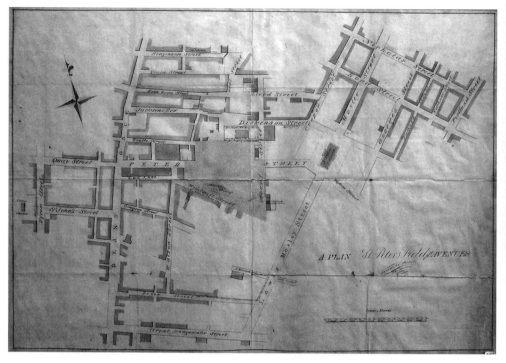

swords and truncheons, in themselves offer little new evidence for the
historian. However, when contextualized, the People's History Museum's
truncheon could potentially open new avenues of enquiry into the nature
of the crowd's self-defence, or indeed attack. Such considerations rely
on the oral traditions of family history. Admittedly this is a severely
problematic type of evidence, the actualities of fact and fiction are too
easily blurred, but this does not mean we should reject them out of hand.
While the prints of the day have become the recognizable image of the
massacre, surviving objects show if nothing else, that if we want to better
understand the historic context we might do well to move beyond the
two-dimensional.

Figure 8: Map
of the streets
surrounding
St Peter's Field
once owned by
William Hulton.
Photo courtesy
of the Working
Class Movement
Library, Salford

# The Middleton
# Peterloo banner

Robert
Poole

The Middleton Peterloo banner is England's oldest political protest banner. It fortunes have varied with those of the wider labour movement: paraded on the great reformers' march to Manchester in 1819, rescued from yeomanry sabres, brought out on occasion to mark advances in democracy, painstakingly conserved during the 'winter of discontent' in 1978–9, and now sheltering in a corrugated iron storage shed in a Rochdale trading estate as the public sector itself lies under siege. Like democracy itself, the Middleton Peterloo banner has been through a lot.

The nineteenth century's best-documented political banner is described by its best-documented working man: the Middleton radical Samuel Bamford. It was in Middleton, at Barrowfields below the churchyard, next to the cottages of the handloom weavers who formed the backbone of the movement, that the reformers rallied on the morning of Monday 16 August 1819. As the contingents from Rochdale and Heywood poured in, the Middleton crowds awaited them, all dressed in their Sunday best clothes. The procession then drew itself into order.

> First were selected twelve of the most comely and decent-looking youths, who were placed in two rows of six each, with each a branch of laurel held presented in his hand, as a token or amity and peace, – then followed the men of several districts in fives, – then the band of music, an excellent one, – then the colours; a blue one of silk, with inscriptions in golden letters, "UNITY AND STRENGTH." "LIBERTY AND FRATERNITY." A green one of silk, with inscriptions in golden letters, "PARLIAMENTS ANNUAL." "SUFFRAGE UNIVERSAL;" and betwixt them on a staff, a handsome cap of crimson velvet, with a tuft of laurel, and the cap tastefully braided with the word, LIBERTAS, in front. Next were placed the remainder of the men of the districts in fives ... Our whole column, with the Rochdale people, would probably consist of six thousand men. [1]

As they set off, recalled Bamford, 'the banners flashed in the sunlight.' With a hundred or so women at the front, and thousands of stragglers walking or dancing alongside, and under orders to maintain peace and order at all costs, the column marched towards Manchester.

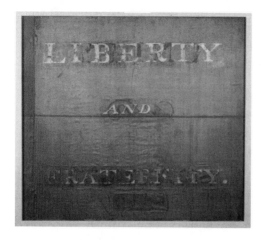

Several miles of country lanes then lay between Middleton and Manchester, and the procession grew in numbers as it proceeded. They passed the tollbar to Manchester unmolested, and after an unplanned diversion to rendezvous with orator Hunt, the principal speaker, they entered Manchester through Newton, the Irish quarter. The green banner had an electric effect on the poor Irish weavers who had also turned out in their best dress. 'Some of them danced, and others stood with clasped hands and tearful eyes, adoring almost, that banner whose colour was their national one, and the emblem of their green island home', recalled Bamford. The march then proceeded through Oldham Street, Piccadilly and Mosley Street, but became detached from Hunt's party (which went via Shudehill and Deansgate) and so arrived at St Peter's Field as it had left Middleton: as a local contingent from what were then called 'the country areas'. *The Times* described the procession as it arrived:

> The Reformers from Rochdale and Middleton marched to the sound of the bugle, and in very regular time, closing and expanding their ranks, with two green banners, between which they hoisted, on a red pole, the cap of liberty, crowned with wreaths of laurel, and bearing the inscription 'Hunt and Liberty'.[2]

The John Slack commemorative print of the St Peter's Fields meeting (Fig. 1, p. 2) shows the local banners clustered near the platform. The Middleton banner, withdrawn to the edge of the field by Bamford, is not included.

As well as proclaiming reform principles the coloured banners had a practical purpose, as Bamford had instructed the marchers:

> When at the meeting, they were to keep themselves as select as possible, with their banners in the centre, so that if individuals straggled, or got away from the main body, they would know where to find them again by seeing their banners; and when the meeting was dissolved, they were to get close

Figure 1:
The banner photographed during conservation in the late 1970s. Photo: North West Area Museum Servic With thanks to Vivian Lochhea Textile Conservation Studio, People's History Museu Manchester

around their banners and leave the town as soon as possible, lest should they stay drinking, or loitering about the streets, their enemies should take advantage, and send some of them to the New Bailey.

The colours were first taken to the hustings, to join the band and all the other colours in the centre of the field. Bamford however did not like the look of the unknown group of men who occupied the speakers' platform and ordered both band and banners to be reunited with the Middleton contingent on the other side of Peter Street. James Dyson of Middleton confirmed this: 'On arriving at St. Peter's-field, I saw many flags and banners on the hustings; ours were taken to the hustings, but Mr Bamford ordered them back again.'[3] They stood 'forming an almost unbroken line, with our colours in the centre'. The banners, bearing a mixture of slogans and the names of disenfranchized localities such as Saddleworth and Stockport, symbolized the readiness for citizenship of the communities that bore them.[4] The disposition of the banners around the hustings can be seen in the *Manchester Observer* print, which corresponds with written descriptions. The absence of the Middleton banners, which had been withdrawn from the centre, increases our confidence in this visual source.

What the reformers did not appreciate at the time was that their impressive display of orderliness and common purpose was exactly what spooked the authorities. 'The flags, 18 in number, were ranged in a line, across the ground, and made a most formidable appearance' wrote James Garnett to the Home Office. 'The party with the blue and green banners came onto the field in beautiful order', testified a magistrate, adding: 'not until then did he become alarmed.'[5] It was the good organisation of the reformers, symbolized by the banners, that the authorities found most threatening.

As Hunt began speaking, the troops were sent in. Witnesses reported that the yeomanry were particularly concerned to seize and destroy the banners. The reformers were equally anxious to preserve them, and Bamford was in the thick of it:

> On the first rush of the crowd, I called to our men to break their flag-staves, and secure their banners, but probably I was not heard, or understood, all being then, inextricable confusion. He with the blue banner, saved it, – the cap of liberty was dropped and left behind – indeed woe to him who stooped, he would never have risen again – and, Thomas Redford, who carried the green banner, held it aloft until the staff was cut in his hand, and his shoulder was divided by the sabre of one of the Manchester yeomanry.[6]

Redford's mother 'saw the severed bone gaping in the wound'. Others of the yeomanry were observed 'cutting down the flag-staves, and demolishing the flags at the hustings'. As Bamford made his way home through Collyhurst he saw a party of yeomanry hunting for stragglers, one of them sporting a broad green sash made from one of the two Middleton banners. The blue banner somehow survived: according to a family story passed down four generations to the present day it was hidden under her clothes by a young Middleton woman, later known as Mrs Mather.[7] Many of the Middleton and Rochdale contingent gathered at the Red Lion at Harpurhey and regrouped about a thousand-strong around the surviving banner. 'We set off to the sound of fife and drum', recalled Bamford, 'with our only banner waving, and in that form we re-entered the town of Middleton'. A blacksmith, Joseph Fletcher of Blackley, saw the march pass by in both directions. On the way back the man carrying the flag called out 'here's another borough-monger lives here!' Fletcher duly reported the incident to the magistrates, claiming that the flag had carried the threatening slogan 'liberty or death'.[8] The real banner, bearing the slogan 'Liberty and Fraternity', was displayed in the window of the radicals' meeting-place, the Suffield Arms in Middleton. A young man from Chadderton returned the cap of liberty, which he had picked up on the outskirts of the field.[9]

Bamford was to spend a year in Lincoln gaol in 1820–1 for his part in organizing the Peterloo rally. An incident that occurred while he was imprisoned demonstrated the importance attached to the banner.

> One hoary-headed slanderer, who hated me because I had prevented him from imposing on the relief fund, and obtaining money to which he had no right, circulated a report that I was actually a government spy; that I had sold the Middleton blue banner to the authorities at Manchester for twelve pounds, and that if the banner were sought for, it would be traced to the police office at the said town. The fellow actually went about the town swearing most confidently that such was the case. A committee was appointed to investigate the charge, and a deputation waited upon my wife, who opened a chest, and pulling out the banner, displayed it; and yet the scoundrel afterwards went up and down persisting in what he had said.[10]

After this period the banner disappears from history for a time. As Terry Wyke and Matthew Roberts show in this volume, the memory of Peterloo remained strong through the Chartist period and beyond, and a later Chartist banner survives from Galston in Scotland bearing the date 1819. But if the Middleton Peterloo banner was displayed either at Chartist rallies or during the first or second reform act campaigns of 1831–2 and 1866–7, no record of it has so far turned up. In 1884, however, at the time of the third reform act, the banner was photographed alongside a group of Peterloo veterans at a spectacular reform rally in Failsworth, between Oldham and Manchester. Earlier in the century Failsworth had been sharply divided between loyalists and radicals, but on 27 September 1884, reported the *Oldham Chronicle*, 'Almost every inhabitant turned out either to participate in or follow with sympathy the demonstration in favour of the extension of the franchise.' The grand procession featured a waggon carrying aged reformers from earlier years, including a group of about ten veterans of Peterloo. The reporter was moved:

Figure 2: Peterloo
veterans at a
reform rally in
Failsworth, 1884.
The Middleton
banner can
be seen in the
background.
Oldham Local
Studies

Who did not, when he rapidly glanced back at the history of the last fifty or sixty years, feel an uncontrollable sensation in the throat as he heard the strains of 'Auld Lang Syne,' and gazed upon those aged, worn, and furrowed faces which saw the making of history at Peterloo? Nine or ten of those veterans – amongst them a lady – formed an honoured and venerated part of the procession. What a contrast between then and now – between the time when the Yeomanry rushed sword in hand upon a peaceable crowd, and now, when the officers of the law are calmly looking on or assisting the marshals to keep order? … Conspicuous amongst the flags was an old and tattered one borne by Sam Bamford's contingent on their march to Peterloo.[11]

The Peterloo veterans, including one woman, had begun their day by posing for a photograph behind an old loom house, bearing portraits of Gladstone in their hats. According to an account by two local reporters, 'In the background of the picture the outlines of Bamford's banner and the old handlooms can be seen, the whole surroundings being in harmony with the courage and rugged determination of these early pioneers.' The dialect writer Ben Brierley was there, and he later used the photograph as the frontispiece to his memoir of the township. The banner has been remounted, suspended from a pole running along the top, but the outline of the word 'Liberty' can be discerned.[12] There is no evidence of who owned the banner at that time.

After this outing the Middleton banner again disappears from view. It at first eluded a brief centenary survey of the surviving Peterloo artefacts in 1919 by the Manchester schoolmaster F.A. Bruton in connection with his Peterloo centenary lecture at the John Rylands Library. The lecture however elicited further information, and in the appendix to his subsequent *Three Accounts of Peterloo* Bruton printed a photograph of the 'Unity and Strength' side of the Middleton banner, now 'carefully preserved between sheets of glass', 'taken under considerable difficulties as regards light by Mr. R.H. Fletcher, of Eccles'.[13] He also noted another survivor: 'The Chadderton banner is still in existence. It was made of white and green silk, measured about 12 feet by 9 feet, and bore the usual mottoes of the Reformers.' Attempting to track it down in Chadderton, Bruton learned that the banner's owner had moved to Blackpool, address unknown; at this point, the Chadderton banner disappears from the historical record.[14]

The Middleton banner finally became public property in 1937, when it was donated by Middleton Liberal Club to the local library. It was put on public display, only one side showing, in the children's section of the lending library, a few hundred yards from where the march had set off in 1819. (An 1856 photographic portrait of Bamford, hand coloured and framed in copper, hung nearby.)[15] But how did the banner end up in the hands of the Liberal Club? The story emerged in the mid-1970s when it was removed from Middleton Library to Rochdale for conservation. One Christmas, around 1975, Harry Johnson of Middleton and his father were at Harry's uncle Tom's house in Church Street, along with three of his aunts. Harry Johnson recalled the conversation:

Figure 3:
The banner,
photographed
soon after
1919, probably
in Middleton
Liberal Club.
Rochdale Local
Studies, Arts &
Heritage Service,
Link4Life

> I was dozing in a chair whilst they were discussing the rumours that the restored Peterloo banner would be moved to Rochdale rather than remain in Middleton library. I heard my father, now in his indignant and argumentative mood, exclaim that 'they can't do that, it's ours!' Now very interested I asked for an explanation. All the brothers and sisters were aware of the story which was related to me by my uncle Thomas who was best on fact.
>
> Their great Uncle Harry Johnson had lent the banner to the Liberal Club for some kind of exhibition. It had never been returned to him despite requests. The banner had subsequently made its way to the Middleton library. Great Uncle Harry had married a Mary Ann Mather who had received the banner from her mother Mrs Mather.

Mary Ann Mather had lived in Edward Street. Her mother had when young been at the St Peter's Field rally and had the banner, smuggling it away from the field wrapped around her waist under her corset. Great Uncle Harry, who lived in Samuel Street, had lent the banner in 1937 to a Mr Thorpe, owner of a silk factory in Cheapside, for the Liberal Club exhibition, but despite several requests it had never been returned. Harry's uncle Tom was subsequently interviewed by Mr G. Thornber of Rochdale Libraries and his story published in the *Middleton Guardian*.[16] There seems no reason to doubt the basic story, which was generally known in the 1970s by family members only three generations down from a Peterloo survivor.

By 1975 the banner was in urgent need of conservation. The North Western Museum and Art Gallery service estimated that the work could be done for £60: fifty hours' work at £1 an hour, plus £10 for materials. This seems to have been optimistic, for it was another three years before the work was actually begun. During the 'winter of discontent' of 1978–9, conservator Vivian Lochhead spent 184¼ hours painstakingly conserving the Middleton Peterloo banner. This was how it was described on receipt.

> Fine, hand-woven silk banner ... Originally dark blue, the silk has faded to a greenish blue.
>
> The banner is made from two widths of silk, with a central french seam running horizontally. The stitching is done by hand, with fine matching silk thread. The words 'UNITY AND STRENGTH', with the date 1819, on the face side, and 'LIBERTY AND FRATERNITY' on the reverse side, are painted in gold. All the lettering except the date is shadowed with darker paint. The banner is clamped between two sheets of ½" thick plate glass and mounted in an extremely heavy, painted wood frame.

The banner was quite small, 48" by 43". It was made from two strips of silk, running horizontally, of standard two foot width, with finished edges. It was almost certainly locally woven, for Middleton was a centre of fine and silk weaving. When removed from the frame it could be seen that there had originally been two vertical sleeves, one at each side to hold the banner poles, but that one sleeve had been crushed inside the frame. The original blue colour, which had since faded to green, could be seen in places. Light damage and atmospheric spoiling had caused the silk to fade and split. The painted part of the silk was brittle and cracking, and the gold lettering was mainly held together by strips of gold coloured adhesive paper. The banner had been crushed inside the glass sheets and one edge had been glued to the glass during framing, causing it to disintegrate. There were various darns and patches.

The conservation work took weeks, and was a minor saga in its own right. After checking that the dye was colourfast (which it was), the banner was gently sponge-washed, rinsed, rolled, smoothed and dried, five times over. The painted areas were treated to stabilize them, and most of the old repairs removed. Conservation of the gold lettering was an extremely slow procedure: identifiable fragments were put back in place, and the other tiny loose fragments used to build up other letters which had fallen away. The whole banner was sandwiched between two layers of transparent, plain-woven silk crepeline material, taking care to align the warp and weft threads of banner and conservation support fabrics exactly. The conservation support was then stitched with the finest dyed Chinese silk. Finally the banner was mounted in a wooden subframe, and then in a larger wooden frame, and glazed with Perspex manufactured to resist ultra-violet light. The work was completed in late April 1979, just after the fall of the last old-style Labour government. The whole operation had taken 184¼ hours, but this most fragile of Peterloo relics had been rescued.[17]

For the next twenty-two years the Middleton Peterloo banner was displayed high among the roofbeams of Middleton Local Studies Library, confounding earlier fears that it might be lost to the town. In 1996 a full-size replica was made, thanks to the efforts of Bill Johnson of Mottram (no relation to the Peterloo descendant). An active conservationist and local historian, Mr Johnson came across the banner in Middleton library and became

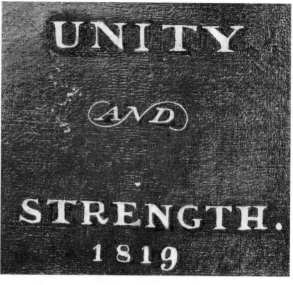

concerned about its state. A chance meeting with Councillor Henry West, chairman of Middletown town council, led to a £250 grant from the Middleton Community Chest, and work began. Bill Johnson spent some time up a ladder in Middleton Local Studies Library, taking measurements and making drawings of the original banner, from which he produced an accurate coloured picture.

Figure 4: The measured drawing of the Middleton banner made by Bill Johnson as a pattern for the 1996 replica. Courtesy of Bill Johnson

He made contact with the National Museum of Labour History (now the People's History Museum), where the original conservator Vivian Lochhead now worked, and borrowed a small folded piece of the banner fabric which had been retained, preserving its original blue colour. This he gave to banner maker Renata Hargreaves of Glossop, who took it on a visit to a Manchester warehouse and used it to select some silk of the same type and colour. The lettering this time was made of gold material, rather than painted on. There being virtually no visible trace of the original second sleeve a single sleeve was included (technically making it a flag rather than a banner). The finished reproduction was proudly displayed at a civic ceremony at Middleton Library on 16 August 1996, and has remained at Middleton Library ever since, its brilliant colours a reminder of the spectacle of the march from St Peter's Field.[18]

The making of the replica prompted Rochdale Museum Service to inspect the original once again. Suggestions were made about labelling and displaying it better, perhaps one side at a time to limit light damage, but nothing seems to have happened. By late 2001 however concerns about the condition of the banner led to another visit from the conservator Vivian Lochhead. She found that while the 1979 conservation work was still in good order, the UV-absorbing property of the glazing had probably lost its effectiveness. Up in the roof beams, near a window, the banner had been well-protected from knocks and shocks but subjected

Figure 5: The replica banner displayed outside Middleton library on 16 Aug. 1996, held by Middleton Township chairman Henry West and Bill Johnson, accompanied by Rochdale Council Leader Jim Dobbin and colleagues, MEP Glyn Ford, and MP James Callaghan. Photograph: *Middleton Guardian*; Local Studies, Arts & Heritage Service, Link4Life

Figure 6: The banner was taken on the 190th anniversary march from Middleton to Manchester. Martin Gittins, family and friends gathered at the Middleton Peterloo plaque, 16 Aug. 2009. Photo: Robert Poole

for over twenty years to sharply varying levels of heat and cold, light, dryness and humidity, which had probably been exacerbated by the more efficient heating system. In twenty years it had probably undergone some 40–60 years' light damage, while repeated swelling and drying of the fibres threatened to cause the threads to become brittle. This was enough for Rochdale Arts & Heritage Service: local sensitivities were set aside and the banner was sent for storage in controlled conditions in Rochdale, where it remains.[19]

More recently, the banner has been seen in public once more. In 2009 the organisers of the march from Middleton to Manchester, part of the 190th-anniversary Peterloo commemoration, got permission

Figure 7: The Middleton Peterloo banner displayed alongside the new plaque on the former Free Trade Hall, 16 Aug. 2009. Phot Terry Wyke

to borrow the replica banner. Starting at the plaque marking the spot in Middleton where the march set off, it was taken up the hill to the Samuel Bamford memorial in Middleton churchyard, then down to Long Street, past the Conservative club which had lowered its blinds for Bamford's funeral, and down Rochdale Road. Carried in turn by the small band of marchers it followed the 1819 route exactly, taking the same detour along the narrow defile at Collyhurst where Bamford feared interception by troops, and was reunited with a replica of the notorious black Saddleworth and Lees banner on the outskirts of the city centre before going to the site of St Peter's Field and forming the backdrop as the names of the dead of 1819 were read out.

The original banner itself was allowed out under strictly controlled conditions in 2011 to form part of the 'Shelley's Ghost' exhibition at the Wordsworth Trust in Grasmere. Among the poems for which Shelley is most famous is 'The Mask of Anarchy', his deadly commentary on Peterloo, and additional funding was found to pay for secure, shock-proof transport for the banner from Rochdale to Grasmere. There, it was at last possible to see clearly every thread and letter of the banner, and to appreciate just how fine, and how fragile, it was. As a bonus Harry Johnson, living in the south Lakes, was able to visit the exhibition, so reuniting the banner with the great-great nephew of the young woman who had rescued it from St Peter's Field nearly two hundred years before.[20]

The use of silk with painted gold lettering places the Middleton banner in an older tradition from most of the other banners at Peterloo. The female reformers of Oldham 'bore a white silk banner, most elegantly displayed, inscribed *"Major Cartwright's Bill, Annual Parliaments, Universal Suffrage, and Vote by Ballot"*. In one compartment was Justice, holding the scales in one hand and a sword in the other; in another, a large eye, representing the eye of *Providence* equally watching over the rich and the poor.' There may have been other silk banners, such as the red banners of the Royton female reformers and the flag with an image of Britannia and William Wallace's slogan 'God Armeth the Patriot'.[21]

The most controversial banner was that from Lees and Saddleworth, however, whose piratical black colour, and alleged skull and crossbones and 'bloody dagger' appeared to give a threatening meaning to its slogan of 'liberty or death'. In fact the images were misread by panicky (or malicious) loyalist witnesses; they were in fact figures of justice, with a sword, and a pair of clasped hands, a common motif used on trade society banners.[22] It can be seen on the hustings in the silk handkerchief picture, its horizontal top pole prefiguring the common design of reform banners in 1831–2. A record of how it was made appears in the testimony of Robert Harrop, manager of the cotton-spinning factory at Lees.

> Remembered directions being given to buy some bleached cambric to make a flag for the Manchester meeting. The colour was white. No instructions were given to put any motto on it, but a number of persons engaged to put on certain devices and inscriptions. A young man engaged to do them in black. This was done, and it did not answer. When he begun, the letters went through, so as to intercept the reading. It was then agreed, as they had no other paint, that the flag should be painted black; this was done, and the letters, &c. were painted white.

'The fringe was supplied by the women', Harrop added. He denied that the black colour was intended to be offensive although the organiser of the Lees and Saddleworth contingent, 'Doctor' Joseph Healey, claimed that of the possible dark colours '*black was finally preferred, that the flag might appear in mourning for the expiring liberties of our country.*'[23] A modern reproduction of the banner, kept in Saddleworth Museum and allowed out for the annual Peterloo commemoration, faithfully reproduces the original, including its Roman-style central pole. The Middleton banners, associated with caps of liberty, shared the symbolism of Roman citizenship.[24]

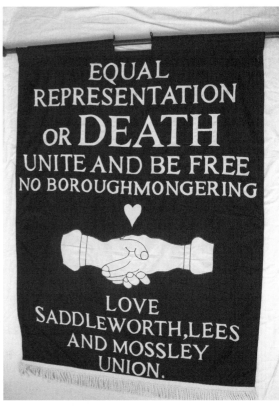

Figure 9: A modern replica of the controversial Saddleworth Peterloo banne Photo: Dave McGealy

The provocative black-and-white slogans of the Lees cotton banner contrast with the more restrained silk banner from Middleton. Its positive messages of 'Liberty and Fraternity' and 'Unity and Strength', picked out in gold lettering on dyed silk, place the Middleton banner firmly in the eighteenth-century friendly-society and trade-society traditions. The use of locally-woven silk was itself a statement of occupational community pride, similar to that on display at the annual parish rushbearing processions which the march to Peterloo also resembled. It was also in the tradition of military colours, which were also made of silk and associated with marching bands and used to mark the position of locally-recruited contingents just like the Middleton banner. The claim that radicals were the true patriots, loyal to the uncorrupted constitution, was an essential part of the radical position in this period. In separating the Middleton banner from the mass of waving flags near the hustings, Bamford was (perhaps unconsciously) acknowledging a difference of approach.[25]

The Middleton banner turns out to be distinctive in other ways. The then National Museum of Labour History's 1998–9 National Banner Survey turned up very few early-nineteenth-century banners, and only five which appear to be from the period 1815–20, including the Middleton banner. Two of these, the Carlile 'Liberty or Death' banners and the Skelmanthorpe banner, are from post-Peterloo protests, as is the Trowbridge Queen Caroline banner from 1820. The Galston

Figure 10: The date of Peterloo commemorated on a Chartist banner from Galston. Photo: Nick Mansfield/ People's History Museum, Manchester

reform banner dated 1819 appears to be later as it also advertizes 'The People's Charter'; nineteenth-century flags and banners often bore the dates of earlier campaigns to give historical force to their claims for representation. Older flags and banners do survive: there are one or two trade-society banners, the earliest from 1797, which may possibly have been carried on reform demonstrations. There are a number of election banners expressing support for both Whig and Tory candidates, but these are creations of the gentry. A Scottish covenanting flag dated 1745 survives as the only older British protest flag. This makes the Middleton banner England's oldest banner of political protest, and the most important surviving artefact from what has been called 'the heroic age of popular radicalism.'[26] How good it would be to see it on public display once more in time for the Peterloo bicentenary on 16 August 2019.

*I am grateful to Jeff Cowton, Harry Johnson, Vivian Lochhead, Nick Mansfield, and the staff at Middleton Local Studies Library and Rochdale Arts and Heritage for help with this article.*

# The poetry of Peterloo[1]

John
Gardner,
Alison
Morgan
and
Robert
Poole

## Anon, 'A new song'

From the *Medusa*, 1 (9 October 1819), 'In commemoration of the invincible courage of the Manchester Yeomanry Cavalry, displayed in St. Peter's Field, on 16th August, in the year 1819'.

> In these times so notorious,
> So *happy*, so *glorious*,
> What man is there would not rejoice, O?
> When for courage renown'd,
> And with *laurels* are crown'd
> Our Manchester cavalry boys, O!

> Thou thousands appear'd
> And their standards they rear'd
> Our Yeomanry then show'd no fear, O!
> But with sabre so bright,
> They burn'd for the fight,
> And resolv'd not to let fall a tear, O!

> Tho' their fathers or brothers,
> Or sisters or mothers,
> With innocence all should come arm'd, O!
> They had courage enough,
> To contend with stuff,
> For with that their hearts never were charm'd, O!

> So now each on his steed,
> Gallop'd off at full speed
> While with sabre he wounded the air, O!
> And on massacre bent
> To Saint Peter's Field went
> Nor man, woman, or child would be spare, O!

'Tis true, tho' not armed
Their cause might have charmed
E'en the devil himself to give ear, O!
But these lads of true fire,
Held their characters higher,
And cry'd 'Damn it, what is there to fear, O!'

A woman and child,
In their way ran so wild;
The woman cried – 'spare, spare my child, O!'
But these true sons of Mars,
Exclaim'd 'now for the wars,
Our glory must never be spoil'd, O!'

Of courage so vast
In times present or past,
None sure ever heard of the like, O!
For man, woman or child,
Or they frown'd or they smil'd,
These man had the boldness to strike, O!

Of their conduct so bold,
None too oft can be told,
So proverbially always declare, O!
(When of courage you speak,
In the strong or the weak)
'He's as BOLD AS A MANCHESTER HERO!'

## H. Morton, 'The sword king'

From the *Black Dwarf*, 3 (22 September 1819).

Who is it that flies in the tumult so fast
When the yeomanry bugles are mingling their blast?
The mother who folds her dear child to her breast,
And screams, as around her expire the oppress'd;
'Oh! hush my darling! Relinquish they fear,'
'My mother! My mother! The sword king is near!
The sword king with sabre so bloody and bright,
Ah! Shade my young eyes from the horrible sight!'

'Base brat of reform, shall thy cries bar my way,
To the laurels that bloom for the loyal today?
Shalt thou live to rear banner, white, emerald, or blue?
No! this is our yeomanry's own Waterloo.'
'My mother! My mother! And dost thou not hear
What curses the yeomanry shout in thine ear?'
'Oh! hush thee my child, let the murderers come!
There is vengeance in heaven for the base who strike home!'

'A curse on your standards so flaunting and fine,
Surrender or perish! – die rebel – 'tis mine!'
'My mother! My mother! Oh! hold me now fast,
The sword king and steed will o'ertake us at last!'
The mother she trembled, she doubled her speed,
But dark on her path swept the black yeoman's steed;
And ere she arrived at her own cottage door,
Life throbb'd in her poor baby's bosom no more.

## Percy Bysshe Shelley, 'The ballad of the starving mother'

From Kelvin Everest, Jack Donovan, Michael Rossington and Cian Duffy
(eds.), *The Poems of Percy Bysshe Shelley* (3 vols, London, 2011), vol. 3,
pp. 489–93.

Young Parson Richards stood at his gate
Feeding his hound with bread;
Hunch after hunch, the mere beast ate
Moving his tail and his head.

A woman came up with a babe at her breast
Which was flaccid with toil and hunger –
She cried – 'Give me food and give me rest;
We die if I wait much longer. –

'The poor thing sucks and no milk will come;
He would cry, but his strength is gone, –
His wasting weakness has left him dumb –
Ye can hardly hear him moan.

'The skin round his eyes is pale and blue –
His eyes are glazed – not with tears –
I wish for a little moment that you
Could know what a mother fears.

'Give me a piece of that fine white bread;
I would give you some blood for it –
Before I faint and my infant is dead –
O give me a little bit.

'Alas it was sold, that trinket of gold
Which my ruiner gave to me –
All the winter nights on my bosom, as cold
It lay, as his heart might be.

'And the single blanket of threadbare woof
Under which we both cried to sleep,
Is gone – the rain drenches us through the roof –
And I moan, but no longer weep.

'What would it avail me to prostitute
This lean body squalid and wild? –
And yet by the God who made me I'd do it
If I could but save my child.

'Perhaps you would like – but alas you are
A staid and holy man, –
And if you were not – would anyone care
For these limbs so meagre and wan? –

'Aye, aye, – one as rich and as grave as you
Once found them a dear delight, –
I scarce think he would be as cruel now
If he saw them in this sad plight.

'Give me bread – my hot bowels gnaw –
I'll tear down the garden gate;
I'll fight with the dog, – I'll tear from his maw
The crust which he just has ate –

'Priest, consider that God who created us
Meant this for a world of love –
Remember the story of Lazarus
You preach to the people of –

'And upon my soul I begin to think
'Twere a joy beyond all pleasure
To sit up in Heaven, and see you drink
In Hell, of your own bad measure.

'Will you say God said this to frighten the rich?
He will only damn the poor?
That the deadly sins are alone those which
There are many temptations for? –

'We doubt, the great Power has made us each
Such as we were to be –
And then to damn us; – the thing would impeach
His justice and charity.

'And yet I cannot imagine how we
Can call *him* just and good;
When he sends a wretched woman like me
To a man like you, for food.

'O God! This poor dear child did I
At thy command bear and cherish –
Thou bad'st us increase and multiply –
And our tyrants bid us perish, –

'Water! Water! and bread and beer!
A little morsel of bread! –
My own dear baby is dying, I fear! –
And I – I hope – am dead."

The man of God with a surly frown
To the garden wicket paced,
And he saw the woman had fallen down
With her face below her waist.

The child lay stiff as a frozen straw
In the woman's white cold breast –
And the parson in its dead features saw
His own to the truth expressed.

He turned form the bosom whose heart was broke;
Once it pillowed him as he slept. –
He turned from the lips that no longer spoke,
From the eyes that no longer wept. –

## Samuel Bamford, 'Ode to a plotting parson'

Bamford's 'Ode to a plotting parson' is about the
notorious magistrate, the Revd William Hay. It was
published in the radical *Manchester Observer* on 26
February 1820, dated 12 January and signed simply
'B'. The first five verses only were reprinted in his 1864
anthology *Homely Rhymes*. As Bamford struggled to
raise the means to defend himself and his fellow
reformers from serious criminal charges, relieve the
victims of Peterloo, and bring its perpetrators to
justice, Hay was rewarded for his role at Peterloo
by promotion to become Rector of Rochdale, one of
the richest livings in the country. Like Shelley, he
adopts a relentless, simple metre and his angers swells
with every stanza, culminating in a terrible ritual
excommunication. For sheer power it rivals Shelley's
'Masque of anarchy'.

Come over the hills out of York, parson Hay;
Thy living is goodly, thy mansion is gay;
Thy flock will be scattered, if longer thou stay,
Our shepherd, our vicar – the good parson Hay.

Oh, fear not, for thou shalt have plenty indeed,
Far more than a shepherd so humble will need;
Thy wage shall be ample - two thousand or more,
Which tithes and exactions will bring to thy store.

And if thou *shouldst* wish for a little increase,
The lambs thou may'st *sell*, and the flock thou mayst fleece;
The market is good, and the prices are high,
And butchers are ready with money to buy.

Thy dwelling it stands on the ridge on the hill,
And the town lies below it, so quiet and so still;
With a church at thy elbow for preaching and prayer,
And a rich congregation to slaver and stare.

And here, like a good loyal priest shalt thou reign,
The cause of thy patrons with zeal to maintain;
And the poor, and the hungry, shall faint at thy word,
As thou doomst them to hell in the name of the Lord.

And here is a Barrack with soldiers enow,
The deed which thou willest all ready to do;
They will rush on the people in martial array,
If thou but thy blood-dripping cassock display.

And Meacher shall ever be close by thy side,
With a brave troop of Yeomanry ready to ride;
For the steed shall be saddled, the sword shall be bare,
And there shall be none the defenceless to spare!

Then the joys which thou felt upon St Peter's Field,
Each week, or each month some new outrage shall yield;
And thine eye which is failing shall brighten again,
And pitiless gaze on the wounded and slain.

Then thy Prince too shall thank thee and add to thy wealth,
Thou shalt preach down sedition, and pray for his health;
And Sidmouth, and Canning, and sweet Castlereagh,
Shall write pleasant letters to dear cousin Hay.

Each dungeon now silent shall sound with a groan,
For the captive shall mourn in its darkness alone;
And the chain shall be polish'd which now hangs in rust,
And brighten'd the bar which is mouldering to dust.

And the tears of the virgin in torrents shall flow,
Unheeded her tears, and unpitied her woe;
The blush of her cheek like a rose-bud shall fade,
For the youth whom thy villainous arts have betrayed.

For thy spies they shall lurk by the window at night,
Like blood-hounds, to smell out the prey of thy spite;
And the laugh shall be hush'd, and the townsmen shall meet,
But none, e'en his neighbour shall venture to greet.

And now, gloomy famine shall stalk thro' the land,
No comfort the poor shall receive at thy hand;
And the widow shall curse thee while life doth remain,
And the orphan shall lisp back her curses again.

And the night wind shall sound like a scream in thine ear,
And the tempest shall shake thee with terrible fear,
And the zephyr, which fans thee, shall bring thee no cure:
It will whisper a tale which thou canst not endure.

And the day shall arise but its joys shall be fled,
And the season of darkness shall add to thy dread;
And a mark of affliction thou ever shalt be,
And none shall partake of thy troubles with thee.

## Anon, 'St Ethelstone's Day'

### ECCE HOMO.

To the Immortal memory of the
    Rev.ᵈ William H⸱⸱⸱ R⸱⸱⸱⸱⸱ of &c &c
Who, on the fatal, but ever memorable
        16.ᵗʰ of August, 1819,
was translated, from this Life to a better .

"The Ashes of the Just
"Smell sweet, and blossom in the dust. !

Erratum. for Life, read LIVING.                    Justitia scripsit.

Figure 2: A sketch of William Hay. Courtesy of Chetham's Library

Bamford's 'Ode to a Plotting Parson' shares a metre and a theme with this slightly earlier poem, and may have been inspired by it. The subject is another high Tory clerical magistrate, Charles Wicksted Ethelston (1767–1830) of Longsight, long active against reformers and responsible (he claimed) for reading out the Riot Act at Peterloo. George Cruikshank's satirical caricature of him as a Janus-faced clergyman and hanging judge has come to stand for the whole class of clerical magistrates. This poem was published in the *Theological Comet, or Freethinking Englishman* on 6 November 1819, with this note.

The following little song is from the last new, deep, and affecting tragedy, called, 'The Peterloo Massacre', as performed at Manchester, on the 16th of August, or, 'Saint Ethelstone's Day', 1819, with unbounded applause; and, it is conjectured, from the high patronage with which this tragedy has met, that it will be repeated during the present season! Indeed, some are so sanguine in their expectations, that they think it probable it may have a run during the Christmas holidays, instead of 'George Barnwell'!! But, be that as it may, I here present you with the song, which is to the Prince's favourite tune of – 'Gee-ip Dobbin'. – A.D.

A Manchester parson, to church and king staunch,
Much fam'd in the pulpit, but more on the bench,
Resolv'd to be *sainted* without more delay;
And, the SIXTEENTH OF AUGUST was fixed for the day.

To contrive the best means, all his genius was bent,
How to celebrate such an auspicious event;
When he saw the reformers, in marching array,
Move onto the field on SAINT ETHELSTONE'S DAY.

The, the oath of his office, inform'd him 'twas good,
That the vest of a saint should be sprinkl'd with blood;
When his Counsellors whispered, ''Twill be the best way,
The Reformers to crush on SAINT ETHELSTONE'S DAY.

He took the advice, and, to make all things sure,
Read the riot act o'er, on the step of his door;
When the Yeomanry Butchers all galloped away,
To do some great exploit on SAINT ETHELSTONE'S DAY.

They hack'd off the breasts of the women, and then,
They cut off the ears and the noses of men;
In every direction they slaughtered away,
'Till drunken with blood on SAINT ETHELSTONE'S DAY.

'Cut away, my brave fellows, you see how they faint,
They are BLACKGUARD REFORMERS', exclaimed the new *Saint*;
'Send them to the Devil, my lads, your own way,
And, no doubt they'll remember SAINT ETHELSTONE'S DAY.'

Figure 3:
The Revd
C.W. Ethelstone
of Manchester,
as depicted
by George
Cruikshank,
from William
Hone's *The
Political House
that Jack Built*
(1819)

THE CLERICAL MAGISTRATE.

# Dickens on Peterloo

Charles
Dickens

## Introduction

This account of Peterloo appeared in Charles Dickens's magazine *All the Year Round* on 8 June 1867, and was reproduced in the *Manchester Weekly Times* on 15 June.* Dickens knew Manchester quite well. He had first visited the town early in his career, in 1838, with letters of introduction from his Lancashire-born friend the novelist Harrison Ainsworth, and had returned a number of times to give speeches and public readings; one visit in the autumn of 1843 to raise funds for the Athenaeum provided the inspiration for *A Christmas Carol*. Most recently, he had given public readings at the Free Trade Hall in February 1867, on the very site of Peterloo.

Dickens had no personal knowledge of the events of 1819 (he was seven years old at the time). He also used jobbing writers to produce material for *All the Year Round*, but he supervised the magazine closely and the sentiments as well as the context suggest that there is a great deal of Dickens in this piece. He relies on other printed accounts, particularly that of John Tyas of *The Times*, who had been present, and above all on Samuel Bamford's *Passages in the Life of a Radical* (1844). Bamford saw Dickens at a meeting in Manchester on 3 July 1847 to raise money for

\* *A note on sources:* The text is taken from the *Manchester Weekly Times Supplement*, 15 July 1867, checked against the text in *All the Year Round*, 8 July 1967, available online at The Internet Archive. The differences are few, and typographical; the error of 'Seaton' for 'Saxton' is in the original. Manchester Central Library has two unpublished typescripts entitled 'Dickens in Manchester', by W.E.A. Axon and L.M. Angus-Butterworth. See also volumes 4–7 of the Pilgrim edition of *The letters of Charles Dickens* (particularly vol. 4 (1977), p. 457 and note; and vol. 6 (1988), p. 447); Malcolm Andrews, *Charles Dickens and his performing selves* (Oxford, 2006), appendix; D.G. Paz, *Dickens and Barnaby Rudge* (Woodbridge, 2006), esp. ch. 5, 'Dickens and Chartism'; Michael Slater, *Charles Dickens* (New Haven, CT; 2009); and the *Daily News*, iss. 1, 21 Jan. 1846.

Dickens's friend Leigh Hunt, and may possibly have been introduced to him. In 1851, after coming to live in London, Bamford was recommended to Dickens as a possible writer for *Household Words* by Thomas Carlyle, who described him as 'the brave Bamford' – a comment which Dickens seems to have remembered in his commendation of Bamford here. Dickens's wider framework of events in Manchester seems to be taken from Archibald Prentice's *Historical Sketches and Personal Recollections of Manchester* (1851), and Prentice in turn draws heavily on other writers, including Bamford. Dickens's content therefore is second- or third-hand, and cannot be relied upon; his casualty figures are far too low, for example. And when he claims that 'the reformers were growing violent and seditious' or 'the manufacturing classes grew more determined and revengeful', Dickens is operating in fictional mode.

Dickens's account of Peterloo is perhaps most interesting as a little-known example of his otherwise much-studied writing about crowds and popular politics. He had written about the destructive Gordon riots of 1780 in London in his novel *Barnaby Rudge* (1841), with the Chartist disturbances of the period very much in mind, and about the Preston cotton strike (or, rather, lockout) in a journalistic piece called 'On Strike' published in *Household Words* on 11 February 1854. He briefly visited Preston to attend strike meetings, and the episode formed the background to his next novel *Hard Times.* He had also been present at the Chartist meeting on Kennington Common in south London in April 1848. He refused to enlist as a special constable and instead attended as an observer, apparently not sharing in the widespread alarm at the prospect of riot or even revolution. The newspaper he founded in 1846, the *Daily News,* stood for 'the Principles of Progress and Improvement; of Education, Civil and Religious Liberty, and Equal Legislation', and aimed for 'a calm and moderate tone'. Mixing with the Manchester's progressive and literary elite on his visits, Dickens would have absorbed their attitudes in contrast to the aggressive and rigid high Toryism of the generation before.

Dickens shared the common belief of the time that crowds of any kind were dangerous and unstable, and was easily swayed by demagogues such as Hunt. He sympathized imaginatively with the sufferings of the poor, believing that poverty led decent people to desperate acts, but had little faith in the ability of even skilled artisans to think for themselves politically. His fiercest criticism was of the propertied classes who failed to understand the problems of the poor and who responded to unrest born of distress with harshness and prejudice, inflaming social tensions which it was their responsibility to alleviate. All these caricatures are visible in Dickens's version of Peterloo.

But whatever his beliefs about working-class unrest in general, at Peterloo Dickens is wholly on the side of the people. He completely accepts Bamford's innocent explanation for the use of military drilling and insists that there was nothing at all to fear from the crowd; the yeomanry would have been quite safe if they had stayed put after getting stuck. Whilst having little truck with Hunt as a politician, he reproduces his whole speech to show that he gave no provocation. He attacks the magistrates for prejudice, repressiveness, and sheer panic, and the troops – yeomanry and hussars alike – for violent conduct. Nowhere else in his writing does Dickens so unequivocally take the side of the workers. For Dickens, Peterloo became the supreme example of one of his most heartfelt themes: the alienation of rich and poor.

*Robert Poole*

## Old stories re-told
## Peterloo

On Saturday, the 31st of July, 1819, the Manchester reformers, wishing to appoint Orator Hunt 'legislatorial attorney' for their city, issued an advertisement in the *Manchester Observer* inviting their friends to meet on the 9th of August in the area near St. Peter's Church; the alarmed magistrates pronounced the meeting illegal, and warned the citizens on their peril to abstain from attending it. Meanwhile, as the magistrates had refused to attend to the petition from the reformers for a meeting, the original promoters gave notice that a meeting would take place in St. Peter's Field on Monday, the 16th of August; Mr. Hunt in the chair.

Before we proceed, let us look back a little. There can be no doubt that the Spa Fields riots of 1816, trifling as they were (for the thirty thousand rioters did nothing but plunder a baker or two and a gun-shop), had very much alarmed the Tory party and Lord Sidmouth, as they showed a restless discontent and an angry impatience for reform – very natural, as it seems to us now, but very irritating to the Chinese politicians then. It must, indeed, be allowed, that about this time the frequent arrests of supposed conspirators had converted many violent men into dangerous plotters; but broken-down swindlers like Thistlewood were not the men by whom our modern reforms were really originated. The pressure of the old war still lay like a heavy nightmare on the industry of England. Firm after firm went down like card-houses in 1818 and 1819. The cotton-spinners who had traded during high prices were ruined in great numbers, and their workmen suffered with them. On the 13th of July, 1819, when the Prince Regent (a man at the head of the country, but at the tail of the age) prorogued parliament, he spoke of the disaffection in the manufacturing districts, and propounded that great axiom still so popular with the Anglo-Chinese politician, that no disaffected persons, meeting under the pretence of reform, had in reality any other object than the subversion of the constitution. It was this notion, highly convenient to all opposers of progress, that set the unreasoning sabres going at Peterloo. The proclaiming political opponents as seditious and dangerous persons is one of the most ingenious stratagems ever adopted by the opponents of progress, and is a trick by no means yet played out.

The manufacturing labourer is by no means so stupid as the agricultural labourer, and he is not so patient of his political deprivations and of starvation. In July, 1818, the Manchester spinners, restless under their distress, had begun to realise the necessity of organisation and of united action. Unable to resist the oppressions of greedy wealth, hunger had driven them to union. They met daily; they subscribed to support each other during strikes; they chose delegates. These meetings sometimes led to dangerous collisions. In September, 1818, the spinners, pelting the windows of Messrs. Gray's factory, near Ancoats-street, were fired at by the inmates, and several were dangerously wounded. Dragoons then dispersed the mob. About the same time, a riot at Barnsley was put down, after the rioters had broken open the town prison and rescued a rioter who had been seized.

In 1819 several irritating events had happened. In January, Hunt had been beaten in the Manchester theatre by some Hussar officers, under the pretence that he had hissed when 'God save the King' was called for. Later in the year, some reform speakers at Glasgow had proposed to march to London, and present a petition in person to the Prince Regent. On the 19th of July, Sir Charles Wolseley, a violent politician, was arrested. He had been elected legislatorial attorney and representative of Birmingham. On the 22nd, a constable named Buck was shot by some workmen at Stockport, in their efforts to secure a reform orator who was in the constable's custody.

Both sides were going too far. The law was becoming illegal, the reformers were growing violent and seditious. The word 'Radical' was now first used to indicate reformers who struck at the root of political abuses. Female reform societies were founded at Blackburn. The reformers began also to practise systematic drilling. Among the honest and quiet men there was no mischief meant by this drilling, whatever the younger and more fanatical might secretly plan. The Tory press had, with the insolence peculiar to that age, derided the oppressed working men with their rags and dirt, and the confusion and scramble of their mobs. The opprobrious epithet, 'swinish multitude', got into vogue. The drill was introduced to preserve order and peace. It was adopted first solely with a view to the great Manchester meeting. It was practised at Bury, Bolton, and Rochdale. The pent-up weavers and spinners liked the exercise. That frank, honest man, Bamford, who was often present at these drills, says, in his fresh, pleasant way: 'When dusk came, and we could no longer see to work, we jumped from our looms, rushed to the sweet cool air of the fields, or the waste lands, or the green lane-sides; or, in the grey of a fine Sunday morn, we would saunter through the mists, fragrant with the night odour of flowers or new hay, and, ascending the Tandle hills, salute the broad sun as he climbed from behind the high moors of Saddleworth.'

There were no arms used; there was no concealment; there was no midnight muster; there was, to the bulk, no double-dealing at all in the matter. Sometimes a youngster would brag and talk violently, or as the men clapped their hands when they stood at ease, some would call it 'firing;' that was all; but that was sufficient for spies.

The long wished-for Monday came at last. Many a fly-shuttle ceased for that day to dart across the loom. Bamford has left us, in his 'History of a Radical', a vivid description of the spirit in which the workmen from the villages round Manchester joined the procession, and the almost solemn manner in which the march was conducted. By eight o'clock in the morning (he says) the whole town of Middleton was on the alert. Even those who would not or could not go to Manchester came out to see their friends and relations start. The people, marching five abreast, were headed by twelve young men, two deep, each holding in his hand a bunch of laurel, 'as a token of amity and peace'. Above the men who walked five abreast waved two silk flags, one blue and the other green, inscribed, in gilt letters, with the mottoes: 'Unity and Strength', 'Liberty and Fraternity', 'Parliaments Annual', 'Suffrage Universal'.

And between these flags was carried, on a pole, a cap of liberty, of crimson velvet, and a branch of laurel. To every hundred men there was a leader, who wore a sprig of laurel in his hat; and over these captains there were superior officers, also decorated. Bamford, the leader of the whole, walked at the head of his column of 3,000, with a bugler by his side to sound the orders for advancing, halting, and retiring. Before setting forth, Bamford formed the Middleton men into a hollow square, and addressed them in his own forcible, sensible manner. He expressed a hope that their conduct would that day be marked by the steadiness and seriousness befitting so important an occasion. He requested them to offer no insult or provocation to any by word or deed, nor to retaliate in any way, lest even the smallest disturbance might serve as a pretext for dispersing the meeting. If the peace-officers came to arrest himself or any other person, they were to be peaceable and not to offer any resistance. He lastly told them that, in conformity with a rule laid down by the committee, no sticks nor weapons were to be carried in the ranks, and those who had them, were requested to leave them behind. This was accordingly done, and only the old and infirm retained their walking-sticks.

Bamford, always a truthful and careful observer, says his men were most decently though humbly attired. There was not one who did not exhibit a white Sunday's shirt, a neckcloth, or other apparel, in clean though homely condition. Having cheered their leader, the Middleton men resumed their marching order; the music struck up gaily, and the column moved forward. About 3,000 Rochdale people soon joined them. A couple of hundred young married women preceded the column, and many girls danced to the music or sang snatches of songs. Some children also went with them, and several hundred stragglers walked by their side. The column increased in number at every hamlet it passed through.

At Newtown, the partner of a firm for which Bamford had lately worked came up, took him by the hand, and said, kindly though earnestly, that he hoped no harm was intended by all those people that were coming in; Bamford replied that he would pledge his life for their perfect peaceableness.

'Look at them,' said Bamford. 'Do they look like persons wishing to outrage the law? They are heads of decent working families. No, no, my dear sir and respected master, if any wrong or violence takes place, it will be committed by men of a different stamp from these.'

The master replied he was glad to hear it, and was happy he had seen Bamford; and, in reply to Bamford's inquiry, he said 'he did not believe they would be interrupted at the meeting'.

'Then,' said Bamford, 'all will be well', and shook hands with his master and left him. As they entered Manchester, Bamford heard that Dr. Healey, a quack doctor, had led the Lees and Saddleworth union, following a coal-black flag, inscribed, in ghastly white letters: 'Equal Representation or Death'; and above this, 'Love' – with a heart and two hands joined.

Even at that thoughtful moment, Bamford confesses he could not help smiling at the notion of his little friend heading a funeral procession of his own patients. The Middleton men reached St. Peter's Field about half-past eleven.

The Jacobite [i.e. Jacobin] emblems were eminently unwise. The Tories of Manchester were already quite enough astounded at the form and precision of the marching, and at the great number of the visitors. A contemporary writer says, with almost ludicrous horror:

Half an hour ago I met in Oldham-street an immense mass of men, marching in common time, five abreast, with two white flags, and a very respectable band of music, consisting of not less than 30 performers. I counted these files until about two thousand men had passed, when the crowd became so great that I could no longer pursue my reckoning, but I conceive that the whole party drawn up and marching in order could not be less than 4,000 or 5,000. Very shortly afterwards a party of about eight thousand passed the Exchange. These also were in military array, preceded by flags, red and black, with the cap of Jacobinism. The former of the two parties came from Bury, the latter from Royton. Similar parties came in from Stockport and the other towns in the neighbourhood. I have just been at the spot appointed for the meeting; about fifteen thousand persons are already there, men and women.

St. Peter's Field, then a large open space of two or three acres, is now nearly in the centre of that great metropolis of industry, Manchester. The Free-Trade Hall stands on its site, and a theatre, a museum, and numerous palatial warehouses skirt the ground. In the centre of the space on this unlucky August day stood two carts with a sort of stage formed upon them. Around the carts were planted five banners, two red, two white, and one black. Upon one side of the latter was a hand holding the scales of justice, with the inscription, 'Taxation without representation is unjust and tyrannical.' On the other side was at the top 'Love'; beneath, 'Unite and be free', 'Equal representation or Death'. On some of the other flags were, 'No Corn Laws', 'Let's die like men, and not be sold like Slaves'.

That heavy sullen oppression of dread suspense and alarm that precedes a thunderstorm hung over Manchester. The shop-windows in Market-place, Market-street, and the body of the town, were closed, and from an early hour in the forenoon all business was suspended – not from a dread of the harmless reformers, but from fear of some violence being used against them. In the principal streets an immense number of country people were strolling about. The more retired parts of the town were silent as death. The scene, says an eye-witness, excited an impression at once melancholy and awful. The wildest rumours were current. It was said that Hunt was to be arrested on the hustings, and it was known that the Manchester and Salford yeomanry cavalry, one hundred and forty in number (nearly all master manufacturers), were concealed in Messrs. Pickford's yard. Capital had grown cruel in its angry alarm. About two hundred special constables had been sworn in. The Cheshire yeomanry, nearly four hundred strong, and the 1st Dragoon Guards were near the city. The magistrates could also rely promptly on six troops of the 15th Hussars, nearly the whole of the 31st and 88th Foot, and two companies of Horse Artillery. They could not help being afraid, property is always timid; but, with such an overwhelming force, they need scarcely have been cruel, for there were soldiers enough to have swept the streets and to have sacked the city. We all know what a single file of grenadiers can do against even an armed and infuriated rabble. Witness those terrible Lord George Gordon riots; witness the Bristol riots. Remember the French in Madrid; remember even that savage outbreak of the Reds, when Cavaignac mowed them down in heaps. What riot has there been in England since Jack Cade struck London Stone with his dripping sword, that twenty dragoons could not have trampled down, right or wrong?

The special constables and the local yeomanry the magistrates held in their own leash. The soldiers were under the command of Colonel Guy L'Estrange, of the 31st Regiment, who was senior officer in the absence of Sir John Byng (afterwards Earl of Strafford), the general of the district, who was then at Pontefract, and to whom no intimation of the intended movements had been sent. Early on the forenoon of the 16th, half the constables, whose presence was by no means necessary except to irritate the people and move the more desperate to some overt act, were posted close to the hustings, in the centre of St. Peter's Field; the rest in a line of communication with a private house on the south side of the irregular square space, to which the mischievous magistrates had repaired about eleven o'clock from the Star Inn, where they had at first assembled. This house was about three hundred yards from the hustings. A committee of fevered county magistrates had been constantly sitting since the Saturday morning taking depositions, listening to petitions and remonstrances against the meeting, and trying to settle what to do in the imaginary crisis, which existed only in their own fears. It was at last decided, after much flurried talking, not to attempt to prevent the meeting, but to arrest Hunt and the other leaders publicly and ignominiously when the speaking had commenced. The troops were to wait till it was seen how the meeting went on, and what might arise. In the meantime, two squadrons (340 men) of the 15th Hussars having been marched into the town from the barracks in the suburbs about ten o'clock, were dismounted in a wide street a quarter of a mile to the north of St. Peter's Field. The Cheshire yeomanry were formed to the left of the same street. The rest of the hussars were with the artillery between the cavalry barracks and the town. The Manchester yeomanry, quite ready for work, were stationed in a street to the east of the field.

The infantry were also in readiness. An eye-witness, writing from Manchester before the meeting, said: 'In short, here is military force enough to crush ten such mobs.' If large armies are unmanageable, how still more helpless is a vast unarmed crowd!

A little before one, an unknown man began to address the (nearly) eighty thousand peaceable artisans and country people now assembled in the field. The faces turned expectantly towards the hustings and the banners. The man spoke calmly enough. He said: 'If we are mad, as our enemies call us, it is the most pleasant loss of senses I ever experienced, and I hope it will never be extinct but with death. At this important crisis it behoves every free-born Englishman to abstain from violence. We only desire our fair and just rights; let us demand them with steadiness and perseverance, and victory will be the certain result.'*

A few minutes to one o'clock a rolling shout proclaimed the arrival of the great demagogue, and eighty thousand voices shouted welcome to the vain and empty man they delighted to honour. There he was, a handsome broad-shouldered man, with the restless face. He wore, as usual, his theatrical country squire dress, blue coat and brass buttons, top-boots, and impudent white hat, then the badge of the Radical party. He was preceded by a noisy band of music and by flags, while above the crowd rose a board, inscribed 'Order'. It was said that Wooler, the dreaded and hideous editor of the *Black Dwarf* paper, was with him; this

---

* The unknown man was George Swift, one of the ten York defendants, author of one of the three new accounts of Peterloo in this volume. Dickens is adapting the account of his words given by Henry Horton at the York trial: 'we are not mad as they call us; if we are mad, it is the most pleasant sensibility I ever felt in my life': *The Trial of Henry Hunt and Others* (1820), pp. 41–5.

was not true. There sat in the carriage his allies, Johnson, Moorhouse, Seaton [Saxton], and Swift. Hunt stood up in the barouche, eyeing the enormous multitude with astonishment and satisfaction. On the box sat an Amazon named Mary Waterworth, bearing the standard of the Stockport Female Reformers, and waving a white handkerchief. She had just been lifted into the carriage, probably out of compassion, as it passed through the crowd.

Hunt's band struck up 'Rule Britannia' and 'God save the King'. The people generally took their hats off. As soon as the orator mounted the hustings the music ceased. It was proposed that Mr. Hunt should take the chair; the motion was seconded and carried by acclamation. The orator, removing his white hat, advanced to the front of the hustings, and addressed the great hushed multitude.

'Gentlemen,' he said, 'I crave your indulgence while I proceed to state the nature and object of this meeting, and I particularly request that no gentleman will call silence, as it produces more disorder than any other circumstance, and perhaps will give our enemies the opportunity of causing a further encroachment on our rights and liberties. Gentlemen, for the honour you have done me in electing me chairman on this important occasion I return you my sincere and heartfelt thanks. I am happy to see such an immense concourse of people assembled, and I fearfully regret that I shall not be able to make myself heard by all of you, but those who are able to hear me will, I hope, do so peaceably and quietly. It is useless to attempt to relate the proceedings that have occurred in your town during the last ten days, or to state to you the cause of the meeting on Monday being postponed; you are all acquainted with it. Those wise magistrates, who were the cause of preventing the meeting on Monday last, fancied they had achieved a glorious victory; but their pusillanimous conduct since, and the presence of such an immense and respectable assembly as now stands before me, prove the contrary. A placard which nobody could understand had been posted up all over the town, signed by Tom Long and Jack Short, and some such contemptible beings. If any one is riotous, put him down, and keep him down.' He was about to proceed, when the appearance of cavalry in the distance stopped him for the moment.

In the meantime, Nadin, the chief constable, had informed Mr. Hulton, the chairman of the bench of magistrates, that he could not execute the warrant for the arrest of Hunt and his colleagues without military aid. Mr. Hulton instantly wrote to the commander of the Manchester yeomanry, and to Colonel L'Estrange, to bring up the regular troops to the house where the magistrates were.

The yeomanry came first, being nearest. Their blue and white uniforms were almost instantly seen as the troopers galloped down Mosely-street and Peter-street, and ranged themselves, sword in hand, in front of the 'Cottage', a well-known building on the south side of Peter's Field, near where the magistrates were at the windows. Hunt, seeing the yeomen, to save the people breaking on that side nearest the horses, cried out that it was only some trick to frighten the meeting, and called to the people round the hustings to stand firm, and give three cheers of good will. The yeomanry remained under the wall about five minutes, during which time, it is said, the Riot Act was read. They then waved their swords and dashed at once into the crowd. They were soon brought to a stand: the crowd was dense, and now held firm. The yeomanry ranks were broken, the troopers separated, got wedged in the mob, powerless alike to retire or advance. There was no great harm in this dilemma; there they could have remained till the meeting was over, and as the crowd dispersed have arrested the speakers. No overt act had been committed; no yeoman was pulled from his horse, struck, or pelted.

At this moment – so immediately that the closest observers describe it as simultaneously – two squadrons of hussars cantered up round the west side of the field. They had only been a quarter of a mile off. Mr. Hulton sees the Manchester yeomanry, his own friends, as he thinks, in danger. Colonel L'Estrange asks him what he is to do. The magistrate, in an agony of frenzied, but quite irrational alarm, cries:

'Good God, sir, do you not see how they are attacking the yeomanry? Disperse the crowd.'

Fatal and foolish words! The officer is a mere agent of the civil power; it is not for him to reflect or decide. The men look along the line waiting for his cry. He shouts, 'Forward!' the trumpet sounds, and the three hundred and seventy men dash down on the eighty thousand close-packed and harmless people. Mr. Hulton (imbecile!) leaves the window, 'because he would rather not see any advance of the military'. We all remember the fool in the Proverbs, who flung about firebrands and called it sport. The charge swept the people down in heaps. Yeomen and constables were trampled back by their too zealous friends; men, women, and children were piled in struggling masses. An eye-witness says:

'The troops instantly dashed off at full gallop amongst the people, actually hacking their way up to the hustings. A cordon of special constables was drawn from the house occupied by the magistrates towards the stage, and fared as ill from the attacks of the soldiers as the people at large. A comparatively undisciplined body, led on by officers who had never had any experience in military affairs, and probably all under the influence both of personal fear and considerable political feelings of hostility, could not be expected to act either with coolness or discrimination; and, accordingly, men, women, and children, constables and reformers, were all equally exposed to their attacks; numbers were trampled down, and numbers were cut down. When they arrived at the hustings, sixteen banners and a cap of liberty were torn or cut from the hands of those who held them, and Hunt, Johnston, and Seaton [Saxton], with several other persons, including three or four women, were taken into custody. Hunt was hurried along by the constables to the house where the magistrates were sitting, crying out 'Murder!' as he was every instant struck by the bludgeons of numbers of constables who surrounded him. An attempt was made to knock his hat off, but unsuccessfully; and just as he was going up the steps a person struck him on the head with both fists.'

But the dreadful scene of slaughter and uncalled-for cruelty had eye-witnesses of a far more observant and thoughtful description than the one whose letter we have just quoted. Bamford, a man honest and true to the core, watched it all with a beating heart and with burning eyes.

When he first saw the troops launched at the unoffending people, he called out to those near him – he, perhaps, scarcely knew why – 'They are riding upon us; stand fast.' The cry rang through the ranks of the Middleton men. 'Stand fast!' The cavalry got confused. 'They evidently,' he says, 'could not, with all the weight of man and horse, penetrate that compact mass of human beings; and their sabres were plied to hew a way through naked held-up hands and defenceless heads; and then chopped limbs and wound-gaping skulls were seen; and groans and cries were mingled with the din of that horrid confusion. 'Ah! ah!' 'For shame! for shame!' was shouted. Then 'Break! break! They are killing them in front, and they cannot get away'; and there was a general cry of 'Break! break!' For a moment the crowd held back as in a pause; then was a rush, heavy and resistless as a headlong sea, and a sound like low thunder, with screams, prayers, and imprecations from the crowd, moiled and sabre-doomed, who could not escape. ... In ten minutes from the commencement of the havoc, the field was an open and almost deserted space. The sun looked down through a sultry and motionless air. ... The hustings remained, with a few broken and hewed flag-staves erect, and a torn and gashed banner or two dropping; whilst over the whole field were strewed caps, bonnets, hats, shawls, and shoes, and other parts of male and female dress, trampled, torn, and Bloody. ... Several mounds of human beings still remained where they had fallen, crushed down and smothered. Some of these still groaning, others with staring eyes, were gasping for breath; and others would never breathe more. All was silent save those low sounds, and the occasional snorting and pawing of steeds. Persons might sometimes be noticed peeping from attics and over the tall ridgings of houses, but they quickly withdrew, as if fearful of being observed, or unable to sustain the full gaze of a scene so hideous and abhorrent.'

Another eye-witness says: 'The shrieks of women and the groans of men were to be heard at some distance. Every person who attended out of curiosity immediately fled. The crush was so great in one part of the field that it knocked down some outbuildings at the end of a row of houses, on which there were at least twenty or thirty persons, with an immense crash. As I was carried along by the crowd, I saw several almost buried in the ruins. Others, in their anxiety to escape, had fallen down, and had been trampled on by the populace.' The frightened people, helpless as scared sheep, were pursued at lull gallop by the sabres through all the avenues leading to St. Peter's Field; and even the distant parts of the town rang with the echoes of the hoofs of the pursuers' horses. It was a cruel and brutal carnage.

That night the infirmary was crowded with wounded and dying persons, gashed, trampled, crushed, and bruised, their limbs fractured by sabre blows or by the feet of the hussar horses. Five or six were dead; thirty dangerously wounded; forty much injured. A special constable, Mr. Ashworth, landlord of the Bull's Head, was killed; one of the Manchester yeomen was beaten off his horse by a brickbat, and had his skull fractured. No soldier appears to have been even bruised, and only this one yeoman, who, some said, was really injured by a fall from his horse. About thirty of the unfortunate wounded persons had been slashed with sabres on the heads, hands, and shoulders.

That night, even though roused by this cruelty, the Manchester people broke out into no considerable riot. At half-past four the mob again assembled at St. Peter's Church, and was soon dispersed. They then gathered at New Cross, a place inhabited by the lower Irish, and broke open a shop. The military fired, killed one man, and dangerously wounded several others. The soldiers paraded the streets all that night. All the roads leading from that town to Middleton, Leigh, Royton, presented a distressing spectacle of men, women, and children, all hurrying homeward in the greatest disorder, some with their clothes torn, others lamed by the wounds they had received in the affray. On Tuesday morning several hundreds of persons were seen within fourteen miles of Manchester still lying in the fields by the roadside, overcome with fatigue, or unable, from the injuries they had received, to reach their homes.

Hunt and his friends were brought up before the magistrates on the Friday following, but were remanded till that day week, by which time Bamford, Moorhouse, and others were arrested. They were then again brought up, and informed that government had, for the present, abandoned the charge of high treason, and that they would be only detained till they should find bail to be tried for the misdemeanour of having conspired to alter the law by force and threats.

The Tories tried very hard to appear still alarmed. The grand jury of the county of Lancaster threw out all the bills against individual Manchester yeomen for cutting and maiming. An inquest sat at Oldham for nine days on one of the sufferers, but the proceedings at last grew confused and irregular, and were quashed by the Court of King's Bench. The more violent Tories even affected great satisfaction at 'the decisive and effective measures to preserve public tranquillity' taken by the Manchester magistrates. These were Lord Sidmouth's own words in his letters to the lord-lieutenants of Lancashire and Cheshire. The attorney and solicitor-general thought the conduct completely justified. Lord Eldon was blandly delighted. He pronounced the meeting an overt act of treason, as 'numbers constituted force, force terror, and terror illegality'. He pressed very hard to arraign Hunt for high treason, but was overruled. The orator was eventually sent to Ilchester jail for two years and a half. Sympathisers with the sufferers were sharply rebuked. The Regent himself majestically reproved the common council of London for their address to him upon the subject. Westminster, Norwich, York, Bristol, Liverpool, and Nottingham, undaunted by this awful reproof, sent in addresses, however, condemning the magistrates and the weak but coercive government. For attending a meeting at York of twenty thousand persons, and signing a requisition to the high sheriff, Earl Fitzwilliam was deprived of the office of lord-lieutenant of the West Riding. Sir Francis Burdett, for fervently protesting, was proceeded against for libel. The Duke of Hamilton, lord-lieutenant of the county of Lanark, nevertheless sent fifty pounds for the relief of the Manchester sufferers.

Many of the Tories loudly insisted that the magistrates had acted rightly, and talked of 'the necessary ardour' of the troops. Lord Redesdale even stupidly contended that all reform meetings were overt acts of treasonable conspiracy. Lord Eldon cried aloud for more stringent acts of parliament, as there was 'nothing to be done now' but to let the meetings take place, and reading the Riot Act if there was a riot at any of them. That warm-hearted and wise father (or rather stepfather) of his people, the Regent, was also charmed with the Manchester magistrates. He expressed his 'approbation and high commendation of the conduct of the magistrates and civil authorities at Manchester, as well as the officers and troops, both regular and yeomanry cavalry, whose firmness and effectual support of the civil power preserved the peace of the town on that most critical occasion'.

Calmly, it must be allowed that the magistrates had done nothing illegal. But the wicked folly was to send forty yeomen to break through from fifty to eighty thousand people; the cruelty was, before even a stone was thrown, to proclaim the meeting a riot, and to launch soldiers on a helpless mob, packed together too close to be dangerous, even if it had shown the slightest wish to be so. The ground could have been occupied beforehand, the meeting prevented by turning back the country levies before they entered the town. The arrests should have been made before or after the meeting. The arrests once made, the meeting could no longer have been mischievous. Rage at their own blunders, mingled with fear, led the magistrates to give orders for a charge that ended in the death of at least six people, the wounding of some eighty others, and innumerable secret casualties that never came to light. The overt act was clearly wanting, and that alone would have been a pretence for the cruelty shown.

That same year the tyrannical Six Acts were passed by that timid but oppressive statesman, Lord Sidmouth. That very autumn, the manufacturing classes grew more determined and revengeful. In September there were three days' riot at Paisley and Glasgow; in November there were rumours of a general rising; and early the next year the Cato-street conspiracy was organised.

In bitter parody of the name of Wellington's great victory, the scene of that cruel sabring of the inoffensive Manchester workmen was christened by the name of Peterloo.

Figure 1: A line drawing of Richard Carlile's print 'To Henry Hunt' was used to illustrate Dickens's Peterloo piece in the *Manchester Evening News*, having featured in a recent exhibition on 'Old Manchester and Salford'. The paper noted: 'Amongst the many interesting events representing the past events and aspects of Manchester shown at the Exhibition few attracted more notice than the representations of Peterloo. ... Portraits of Henry Hunt, Revd W.D. Hay, Joseph Nadin, Samuel Bamford – all actors in the Peterloo tragedy – were also to be seen at the Exhibition'

# Remembering Peterloo
# in the twenty-first century

Paul
Fitzgerald

The campaign to ensure an appropriate memorial to the Peterloo massacre in Manchester began for me in 2007 with a cartoon about the Tiananmen Square massacre of 1989 – one which made the penny drop. Looking at it, an obvious question occurred: we know why there isn't a memorial to Tiananmen in Beijing, but how come there isn't one to Peterloo in Manchester?

A quick hunt revealed that the only existing commemoration was strikingly inappropriate: a blue plaque on the side of the Free Trade Hall with the following euphemistic wording.

> THE SITE OF ST PETER'S FIELDS
> WHERE ON 16TH AUGUST 1819
> HENRY HUNT, RADICAL ORATOR
> ADDRESSED AN ASSEMBLY OF
> ABOUT 60,000 PEOPLE
> THEIR SUBSEQUENT DISPERSAL
> BY THE MILITARY IS
> REMEMBERED AS
> 'PETERLOO'

Demanding that this plaque be replaced became the obvious start to a campaign to ensure a memorial was created. After asking both the Radisson Hotel (the leisure chain who now own the Free Trade Hall) and council officers (the department responsible for commemoration plaques) to install a new version, and being told no, a group of local political activists decided to take matters into their own hands for the 2007 anniversary.[1]

At the same time, we were contacted by the *Guardian* newspaper in response to our press releases, and included in a two-page article by Martin Wainwright about the commemoration of Peterloo – or rather the lack of it.[2]

The *Guardian* article led to a phone call to us from Richard Leese, the leader of the City Council. Having seen the article upon returning from holiday he wanted to assure us a memorial plan was in hand, as a result of his having been approached by pupils from Moorside High School in Swinton. They had studied the massacre in class and were asking why there was no monument to it. After a discussion about whether or not their plans were for something realistic, rather than symbolic, the action went ahead, and in front of a strong media presence activists climbed a ladder and taped a new red plaque, with appropriate wording, on top of the old one. The same plaque was then nailed into the pavement in St Peter's Square and surrounded by flowers. We were astonished by how long it lasted in this location.

In December 2007 the Council put in place a new red plaque, based upon the campaign's wording but modified as a result of advice to the council from historian Robert Poole. The plaque was unveiled on 10 December 2007 by the Lord Mayor of Manchester and local historian Sheila Lemoigne, a descendant of a Peterloo veteran. This plaque has now become the focus of the Council's annual wreath-laying on 16 August.

---

**Geoff Bridson, former Labour councillor for Didsbury, writes:**

In 2006 I was a delegate at the Labour Party spring conference, the first to be held at the new conference centre at G-Mex. We were on the edge of St Peter's Field so we looked for some commemoration of Peterloo, but it was hard to find – a small blue plaque high on the wall of the Radisson Hotel. Independently of this, Tristram Hunt wrote a feature article in the *Guardian* (G2, 24 July 2006) calling for more public memorials for events from radical history, leading with the example of Peterloo. Back in Didsbury I spoke with Gareth Tidman of the *South Manchester Reporter* which printed an article (3 August 2006, at http://www.manchestereveningnews.co.uk/news/local-news/time-to-pay-tribuite-to-victims-of-peterloo-1040329). This was a year before Martin Wainwright's piece in the *Guardian* (17 August 2007) which also mentioned the conference. I raised the issue at meetings of the Manchester Labour Party, and around the same time some members, including Tony Lloyd MP and councillors Jim Battle and Mike Amesbury, began Peterloo day commemorations, arranging a wreath-laying in St Peter's Square for the 2009 anniversary. When Paul Fitzgerald's Manchester group staged its action for a new plaque in 2007, Harriet Monkhouse from Didsbury and I joined it. When in September 2013 the Tory Party conference came to Manchester and were greeted by a 50,000-strong demonstration, I was there with a 'Remember Peterloo' placard. It attracted a lot of interest.

Figure 1: Three plaques: the old one from 1972; the Peterloo Memorial Campaign's 2007 suggestion; and the new plaque installed in 2007

For the next anniversary the group, which was now meeting regularly, arrived at the site of the massacre with replica banners, and glued fifteen metallic horses' hooves onto the paving to symbolize both the charge of the yeomanry, and the number of casualties. This reflected some of the ideas for a memorial that had been mooted at a well-attended design day earlier in the same year.

The 190th anniversary in 2009 proved hugely successful, with approximately 200 people arriving at the G-Mex plaza to raise liberty caps on poles, with various groups marching in along the routes originally used by the Peterloo protesters. The march from Oldham was organized by Dave McGealy of Oldham community radio, while the small contingent from Middleton was led by Martin Gittins, who performed. This year's event was no doubt given a boost by Peterloo featuring in Jeremy Deller's high-profile art event 'Procession' at the Manchester International Festival earlier that summer. Tony Lloyd MP spoke to support the plan

Figure 2: Councillor Jim Battle and Tony Lloyd MP lay a wreath to the victims of Peterloo in the Peace Gardens, St Peter's Square, 16 August 2009. Photo: Robert Poole

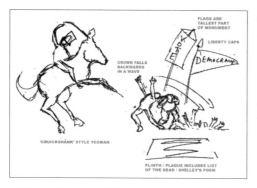
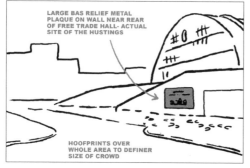

for a memorial and councillor Jim Battle read part of Shelley's 'Mask of Anarchy', getting the crowd to join in with the line 'Ye are many, they are few'.

Along the way, we had been informed that the council's Director of Culture would be leading the project, and after a brief informal meeting with her we attended a larger minuted one in the Town Hall, on 19 August 2009. At this it was stated that the memorial would be decided by an open design competition, subject to EU procurement rules, and that the memorial would be part of a redesign of St Peter's Square itself (rather than at the centre of the protest, the G-Mex plaza, as we had proposed.) A budget of £1 million was indicated. This would involve first issuing a design brief, which would obviously be an important document. There was discussion of a place for the campaign on the commissioning team, and of having a stakeholder panel as part of the design process, but nothing came of this.

In the summer of 2010 designs went on public display for the new look of St Peter's Square itself. Despite assurances that the monument would be designed separately these models and drawings included a range of memorial designs, with some that ironically came very close to our spoof suggestions of fifteen metal pillars or a block of concrete. We objected to these designs in writing and happily all were rejected, although it was unclear what had happened to the idea of a separate international design competition for the memorial.

Figure 3: Two suggestions from the 2008 Design Day (left), and the most popular option from the 2013 Design Day (right). Photos: Paul Fitzgerald/ Peterloo Memorial Campaign

## The Middleton March

As a life long 'dabbler' in local history, it struck me as significant early in 2009, that the 190th anniversary of the Peterloo Massacre was imminent. I decided it was memorable enough to mark it in some way.

I had dipped into Sam Bamford's 'Passages in The Life of a Radical' from time to time and read his account of his involvement in the event. As a keen walker it seemed logical that I should re-create the walk from Barrowfields in Middleton to St Peter's Field (or as near as possible to the site thereof) in Manchester. This walk was originally a personal 'homage' to the great man and his beliefs. However, my wife was happy to come along for company and a friend who lives in Middleton, Bob Ashworth (no relation to either of the Ashworths killed at Peterloo) was also keen to join in.

Around that time I became aware of the walk organized by Oldham community radio from Oldham to Manchester. I spoke to my friend, station manager Dave McGealy, and he offered to promote 'our' walk as an alternative to the somewhat longer, and more demanding, Oldham march. I appeared on the radio, gave details of the itinerary, and waited. Another contact, at the *Middleton Guardian* newspaper ran an article a week or two before, and I had high hopes of a good turnout.

In the meantime I managed to find a transcript of Sam Bamford's words before the start of the Middleton march and Bob agreed to play the part and read the words to the assembled masses at a few minutes before 9 o'clock. On the day we duly arrived, bright and early at 8.30am. By 8.45 it was clear that my high hopes may have been a little optimistic! By 8.55 we numbered five and, after a rousing speech from 'Mr Bamford' we set off. (See Fig. 6, p. 128).

We had been fortunate to arrange the loan of a replica banner from Middleton Library for the occasion and we stopped at Bamford's memorial in St Leonard's churchyard. We followed the original route exactly, including the unscheduled diversion the group made (against Bamford's better judgement) towards Collyhurst to rendezvous with the Hunt contingent. We had arranged to meet with the Oldham contingent at the end of Oldham Road, and we duly joined forces with their grand parade for the final stage of the walk across town.

On the steps of G-Mex in Manchester a short ceremony was held (organized by the Peterloo Memorial Campaign) and Bob and I gave a rendition of a well known song about the Massacre. In subsequent years I have tried to promote the walk to a wider audience and, indeed, numbers have increased (a little). Our biggest turnout to date has been twelve brave souls.

*Martin Gittins*

Figure 4: Paul Fitzgerald addresses the 2010 anniversary rally outside G-Mex, watched by Captain Birley of the Manchester yeomanry (Geoff Bridson). Photo: Robert Poole

Figure 5: The campaign's design outside the People's History Museum, August 2011. Photo: Robert Poole

In the absence of a design brief from the council we decided to promote our own favoured option. At another well-attended anniversary commemoration in 2011 we made a seven-foot tall reproduction of Cruickshank's 1819 memorial 'design' showing a yeoman cutting down an unarmed woman and child, and paraded it through the streets from the People's History Museum to St Peter's Field.

We waited until 2012 for our next meeting, this time with the Public-Private Partnership Unit which had now taken over the task of the memorial design from the director of Culture. The meeting confirmed a suggestion that we had first heard informally from the leader of the council: the memorial was now going to be a set of gates, closing one end of Library Walk as part of the St Peter's Square revamp. This was, we were officially told, the 'strongly favoured option'. This caused outrage in the group, since no public design process had been followed. Others commented that a set of gates to close off a public space was hardly the most appropriate way to commemorate a rally for democracy.

On 6 July 2012, shortly after a report ridiculing the idea of the gates had been

published in *Private Eye* magazine, we learned from the council that the scheme was dead. We were also informed that the memorial would definitely no longer be in St Peter's Square and that three councillors would now be choosing a design between them, in order to avoid a 'horse designed by a committee'. The campaign group then offered the council a list of locations that it felt would be appropriate. When no official statement about the cancellation appeared we decided to announce to the press that the gates were no more on the August 2012 anniversary. After raising a giant 15-foot liberty cap statue at the site of the Peterloo speakers' cart, we made a compromise suggestion: that the new design process should offer a shortlist of three options, chosen by the three councillors, to be put to an indicative but non-binding public vote.

2013 has proved to be decisive year with several Peterloo-related theatre events raising its public profile, the most prominent being actress Maxine Peake's reading of Shelley's 'The Masque of Anarchy' for the Manchester International Festival. The campaign subsequently saw a steep rise in the number of people joining its facebook page and twitter feed, and a record number, approximately 200, attending the annual commemoration wreath-laying, at which Maxine read the names of the fifteen who died. It did finally bring a clear and encouraging written statement from the council: 'A commissioning group of senior councillors and the city's director of galleries will be appointing an artist who has a proven track record of working with, and consulting, a wider range of people and organizations to create a memorial of which Manchester can be proud. We intend to make an announcement before the end of the year. Neither the form nor the location of the monument are being prescribed by the council and there will be plenty of room for public involvement. We will work with the Memorial Group and anyone else in the city who shares our interest in creating a fitting and high quality memorial to the Peterloo Massacre.'

A memorial design day, open to the public and held on 18 August at the People's History Museum, attracted over thirty designs, with a strong consensus that the massacre itself, the attack on the crowd by troops, needed to be included. The designs and their voting scores (there was one clear winner) will be presented to the council soon, but as I write new ideas are emerging from several quarters and the campaign, at last, is taking on a momentum of its own, independent of the group who have been carrying it for the last six years. It's with much excitement that we wait to see what happens next ...

*The Peterloo Memorial Campaign website is at http://www. peterloomassacre.org/*

# Notes

## What don't we know about Peterloo?    *Robert Poole*

1. E.P. Thompson, *The making of the English working class* (London, 1968), p. 660 and ch. 15; Paul Mason, 'The fearless and the free', programme note to *The masque of anarchy*, Manchester International Festival, July 2013; John Foster, *Class struggle in the industrial revolution* (London, 1974), pp. 3–7, 140–9.

2. The exception is Robert Walmsley, *Peterloo: the case reopened* (Manchester, 1969), a wholly unsuccessful attempt to exonerate the authorities in general and his magistrate ancestor William Hutton in particular. For E.P. Thompson's devastating review of this 'sustained exercise in special pleading' see 'Thompson on Peterloo', *Manchester Region History Review*, 3 (1989), pp. 67–72.

3. The Peterloo Witness Project, undertaken at the University of Cumbria and further supported by the University of Central Lancashire, has succeeded in identifying, collecting and digitizing or transcribing most of the surviving eye-witness accounts of the events of 16 Aug. 1819. Volunteers at the 2012 Manchester Histories Festival assisted with transcription, and thanks are due to Geoff Barlow, Nigel Barlow, Martin Gittins, Mike Jenkinson, Yvonne Jez, Ryan Jones, Lee Kendall, Dave McGealy, Roy Read, Claire Robinson, Peter Trumper, Chris Westhead, Becky Wright and several anonymous participants.

4. The National Archives [hereafter TNA], TS11/1051, TS11/1125 and TS36/2.

5. *The Times*, 19, 20 Aug. 1819; *Leeds Mercury*, 21, 24 Aug. 1819; *Liverpool Mercury*, 20 Aug. 1819; [anon.], *Peterloo Massacre* (Manchester, 1819), pp. 56–62; Manchester Central Library, [hereafter MCL], *The Courier*, in *Report of the Manchester meeting* (Manchester, 1819); *Bury and Norwich Post*, 25 Aug. 1819.

6. *Manchester Observer*, 21 Aug. 1819; *Manchester Gazette*, 21 Aug. 1819; *Manchester Mercury*, 21 Aug. 1819; *Manchester Herald*, 29 Aug. 1819; Jeremiah Garnett's account for the *Manchester Courier*, in [anon.], *Peterloo Massacre*, pp. 56–62.

7. *Sherwin's Weekly Political Register*, 18 Aug. 1819; *The Republican*, 27 Aug. 1819; *Black Dwarf*, 1–29 Sep. 1819.

8. *Memoirs of Henry Hunt*, vol. 3 (1822), available online from Project Gutenberg at http://www.gutenberg.org/dirs/ etext05/8hnt310.txt; MCL, MSC 1920, Memoir of George Swift; 'The Account of Joseph Healey of Lees', *Black Dwarf*, 29 Sep. 1819; Samuel Bamford, *Passages in the life of a radical* (Manchester, 1839–42), ed. W.H. Chaloner (London, 1967), book 1, ch. 39.

9. Robert Mutrie's account is in Philip Lawson, 'Reassessing Peterloo', *History Today*, 38 (1988), and 'Peterloo: A constable's eye-view reassessed', *Manchester Region History Review*, 3 (1989), pp. 39–42, from Bute MSS. 373, Mountstuart, Scotland. For other accounts by Mutrie see TNA HO42/16 fol. 299, HO42/196 fol. 28; and *The Whole Proceedings before the Coroner's Inquest at Oldham on the Body of John Lees* (1820) [hereafter *John Lees Inquest*], pp. 411–40.

10. TNA TS11/4763/1055–6, Letters of Major Dyneley.

11. F.A. Bruton, *Three accounts of Peterloo by eyewitnesses* (Manchester, 1921).

12. Francis Philips, *An exposure of the calumnies ... against the magistrates and the yeomanry cavalry of Manchester & Salford* (London, 2nd edn, 1819).

13. Greater Manchester County Record Office, Memoir of Joseph Barrett, Q41, pp. 16–25; Bruton, *Three accounts* for Smith and Stanley; James Weatherley, *Recollections of Manchester* (at Chetham's Library, Manchester), with thanks to Michael

Powell; Robert Walmsley Papers, Working Class Movement Library, Salford, Memoir of John Galloway, transcript.

14. Bruton, *Three accounts*, p. 53.
15. *John Lees Inquest*, pp. 161–3, 177–8, 521–32.
16. *John Lees Inquest*, p. 566.
17. *John Lees Inquest*, pp. 73–80.
18. G.H.H. Glasgow, 'The John Lees inquest of 1819 and the Peterloo massacre', *Transactions of the Historic Society of Lancashire and Cheshire*, 148 (1998).
19. Robert Poole, 'By the law or the sword: Peterloo revisited', *History*, 91 (2006), pp. 272–5.
20. Walmsley, *Peterloo*, pp. 553–5.
21. TNA HO40/11 fol. 266, Maule to Hobhouse, 24 Mar. 1820.
22. *The trial of Henry Hunt and others* (Manchester, 1820), pp. 49–56.
23. *Report of the proceedings in the cause of Redford vs Birley and others* (Manchester, 1822).
24. J. McDonnell (ed.), *Reports of state trials* (London, 1888), vol. 1, p. 1071.
25. Thompson, 'Thompson on Peterloo', pp. 70–1.
26. The material is to be found spread across TNA HO42/192, 195, 196 and 198, with much of the later material in HO40/16. Large PDFs of these boxes are available on the TNA website but the images are neither searchable nor catalogued. Subscribers to the Gale Nineteenth-Century Collections Online can access the same material but complicated by garbled and error-ridden catalogue entries. A 2013–14 British Academy pilot project at the Universities of Central Lancashire and Hertfordshire, 'Understanding the Home Office Disturbances papers', seeks to test ways of making this material more accessible.
27. TNA HO40/11 fol. 259, Maule to Hobhouse, 23 Mar. 1820.
28. Long ago Donald Read noted that the majority of the prosecution witnesses at York and Lancaster who testified to their alarm were compromised in some way: Read, *Peterloo: the massacre and its background* (Manchester, 1958), pp. 179–80.
29. Devon Record Office, Addington Papers, 152M C1818 OH14.
30. The originals are in the Home Office papers, TNA HO42 196 and 198 and HO40/16. The Treasury Solicitor's papers (n. 4 above) summarize the evidence.
31. John Ryland's Library [hereafter JRL], English MS 1197 12. The actual wording inadvertently warned people to 'abstain at their peril', but the threat was clear enough.
32. TNA HO79/3 part 3, fol. 447, Hobhouse to Hay, 23 July 1819.
33. TNA HO41/4 pp. 431, 434, Hobhouse to Norris, 3, 4 Aug. 1819. See also HO79/3 part 3, pp. 478–83, Hobhouse to Byng, 3, 4 Aug. 1819 and Hobhouse to Norris, 4 Aug. 1819.
34. TNA HO41/4 p. 358, Hobhouse to Norris, 17 July 1819. The magistrates' copy of this letter is in JRL English MS 1197, item 6.
35. TNA HO79/3 part 3, p. 457, Hobhouse to Norris, 26 July 1817. This evidence is rehearsed at greater length in Poole, 'By the law or the sword'.
36. Walmsley, *Peterloo*, pp. 553–5; *Report of the proceedings in the cause of Redford vs Birley*, pp. 360–81.
37. Yeomanry statement, JRL English MS 1197, item 26.
38. See for example the account of Joseph Barrett, one of the 'Three new accounts of Peterloo' in this volume.
39. Reworking the article for the *Manchester Region History Review*, Lawson moderated his claims, arguing merely that Mutrie's evidence showed that sections of the crowd were not helpless victims: Lawson, 'Reassessing Peterloo', and 'Peterloo: A constable's eye-view reassessed'.
40. TNA HO42/196 fol. 28, Statement of Robert Mutrie, Nov. 1819; HO42/198 fols. 592–3, Norris to Sidmouth, 10 Nov. 1819; cutting on reverse of JRL English MS 1197, item 27; *John Lees Inquest*, pp. 411–40.
41. Bamford, *Passages in the life of a radical*, book 2, ch. 12.
42. *The trial of Henry Hunt and others*, pp. 104–7.

43. Addington Papers, Devon Record Office, C1819 152M OH11, Sidmouth to Hay, 13 Nov. 1819.

44. R. Poole, 'French revolution or peasants' revolt? Petitioners and rebels from the Blanketeers to the Chartists', *Labour History Review*, 74 (2009), and sources cited therein.

45. Katrina Navickas, *Loyalism and radicalism in Lancashire 1798–1815* (Oxford, 2009).

46. John Belchem, *Orator Hunt: Henry Hunt and working-class radicalism* (Oxford, 1988); Belchem, 'Radical language and ideology in early nineteenth-century England: the challenge of the mass platform', *Albion*, 20 (1988).

47. Michael Bush, *The casualties of Peterloo* (Lancaster, 2005).

48. Robert Glen, *Urban workers in the early industrial revolution* (London, 1984), chs. 9–10.

49. Dorothy Thompson, 'Women and nineteenth-century radical politics: a lost dimension', in her *Outsiders* (London, 1993), ch. 3; Linda Colley, *Britons: forging the nation, 1707–1837* (New Haven, CT; 1992), ch. 6; Anna Clark, *The struggle for the breeches: gender and the making of the British working class* (London, 1995); Paul A. Custer, 'Refiguring Jemima: gender, work and politics in Lancashire, 1770–1820', *Past and Present*, 195 (2007).

50. James Epstein, 'Understanding the Cap of Liberty: symbolic practice and social conflict in early nineteenth-century England', *Past and Present*, 122 (1989).

## Manchester loyalism in the 1790s  *Frank O'Gorman*

1. Notably E.P. Thompson, *The making of the English working class* (London, 1963); G. Williams, *Artisans and Sans Culottes* (London, 1968); A. Goodwin, *The Friends of Liberty: The English democratic movement in the age of the French Revolution* (London, 1979). As T.S. Ashton once remarked, Manchester by the end of the eighteenth century had acquired 'quasi-metropolitan functions', in his *Economic History of England* (London, 1955), p. 96.

2. Thompson, *The making of the English working class*, pp. 122–3.

3. E.C. Black, *The Association: British extra-parliamentary organisation, 1763–93* (Cambridge, MA; 1963). Black's view may be summarized (p. 272) when he remarks that the political contest between the reformers and the loyalists was a contest between the poor and the rich. D.G. Ginter, 'The Loyalist Association movement of 1792–3 and British public opinion', *Historical Journal*, 9 (1966).

4. H. Dickinson, 'Popular conservatism and militant loyalism, 1789–1815' in H. Dickinson (ed.), *Britain and the French Revolution, 1789–1815* (Basingstoke, 1989), pp. 11–20, 123–5; R. Dozier, *For king, constitution and country: the English*

loyalists and the French Revolution (Lexington, KY; 1983), pp. 55–102.

5. N. Rogers, *Crowds, culture and politics in Georgian Britain* (Oxford, 1998), p. 207.

6. D. Eastwood, *Governing rural England: tradition and transformation in local government* (Oxford, 1994). See also M. Philp, 'Vulgar conservatism, 1792–3', *English Historical Review*, 110 (1995), pp. 44, 67–8; J.E. Cookson, *The British armed nation, 1793–1815* (Oxford, 1997), pp. 212, 228, 238–41, 252–3.

7. Rogers, *Crowds, culture and politics*, p. 187.

8. It petitioned against reform and continued in existence until 1804.

9. George Phillips, *The Necessity for a Speedy and Effectual Reform of Parliament* (Manchester, 1792). There is evidence that the leading reform society, the Manchester Constitutional Society, officially commissioned this work: Neil Strange, 'Manchester loyalism, 1792–8' (MPhil dissertation, Manchester University, 1990), p. 56. I am indebted to Neil Strange's thesis in several sections of this work.

10. *Manchester Chronicle*, 9 June 1792.

11. *Manchester Mercury*, 5 June 1792.

12. *Manchester Chronicle*, 9 June 1792. The latest account of the St Ann's Square riot

is quick to depict it as a planned attack on dissenters but no evidence is presented to justify this view. See K. Navickas, *Loyalism and radicalism in Lancashire, 1798–1815* (Oxford, 2009), p. 39.

13. *Manchester Mercury*, 26 June 1792.
14. *Manchester Chronicle*, 15 Dec. 1792.
15. *Manchester Mercury*, 20 Nov. 1792.
16. *Manchester Mercury*, 4 Dec. 1792.
17. *Manchester Mercury*, 25 Dec. 1792.
18. *Manchester Mercury*, 18 Dec. 1792.
19. *Manchester Mercury*, 18 Dec. 1792; T. Walker, *A Review of Events which have Occurred in Manchester During the Last Five Years* (London, 1794), pp. 54–64, 70–4, 81–4.
20. Manchester is exceptionally fortunate to possess the most detailed original records of any Loyal Association in the country. The minutes of the committee of this, the premier organisation of loyalism in Manchester, have survived and are to be found in Chetham's Library.
21. *Manchester Mercury*, 25 Dec. 1792; 11 Jan., 12 Feb., 26 Feb., 26 Apr. 1793.
22. For details of the personnel of the Bull's Head committee I am indebted to the researches of Neil Strange, see above n. 9.
23. A. Mitchell, 'The Association movement of 1792–3', *Historical Journal*, 4 (1961).
24. See Dozier, *For king, constitution and country*, p. 9; Ginter, 'Loyalist Association movement', p. 189; Black, *The Association*, p. 272; Mitchell, 'The Association movement', p. 66.
25. The 'Tory-Landowner' view of loyalism stubbornly persists. The latest discussion of loyalism announces, without evidence, that 'The middle classes aspired to the gentry level of estates' (Navickas, *Loyalism and radicalism*, p. 23) and that 'middle-class members of loyalist elites were aspirants to gentry status' (p. 87). Were they? Some may have done but the statistical connection between the loyalist middle classes and the middle classes who did so aspire is never drawn.
26. Navickas, *Loyalism and radicalism*, p. 197.
27. Both Dozier, *For king, constitution and country;* and Ginter, 'The Loyalist Association movement' in their different ways are keen rescue loyalism from the charge of extremist reaction. Dozier (p. 81) argues that 'in their emphasis upon efficiency, equality, and moderation there is no anti-reform bias whatever' and described as 'the largest sustained vote of confidence ever given by the English public to their constitution' (p. 100).
28. See my paper 'The Paine burnings of 1792–3', *Past and Present*, 193 (2006), pp. 111–55.
29. *Manchester Mercury*, 1 Jan. 1793.
30. M. Harrison, *Crowds and history: mass phenomena in English towns, 1790–1835* (Cambridge, 1988), p. 141.
31. Rogers, *Crowds, culture and politics* p. 202–9.
32. *Manchester Mercury*, 9 June 1795.
33. Strange, 'Manchester loyalism', pp. 123–5.
34. This was more even than in 1803 when something over £21,000 was subscribed from 1,300 individuals: Navickas, *Loyalism and radicalism*, p. 48.
35. J. Cookson, *The British armed nation* (Oxford, 1997), pp. 15, 24–6, 37, 211–12.
36. Navickas, *Loyalism and radicalism*, pp. 50–2.
37. *Ibid.*, p. 49.
38. Philp, 'Vulgar conservatism'.

### Lancashire Britishness: Patriotism in the Manchester region during the Napoleonic Wars    Katrina Navickas

1. Linda Colley, *Britons: forging the nation, 1707–1837* (New Haven, CT; 1992); Linda Colley, 'The apotheosis of George III: loyalty, royalty and the British nation, 1760–1820', *Past and Present*, 102 (1984), pp. 94–129. The present article expands on material discussed in Katrina Navickas, *Loyalism and radicalism in Lancashire, 1798–1815* (Oxford, 2009).
2. Alexandra Franklin, 'John Bull in a dream: fear and fantasy in the visual satires of 1803', in Mark Philp (ed.), *Resisting*

*Napoleon: the British response to the threat of invasion, 1793–1815* (Oxford, 2006), pp. 125–40; Miles Taylor, 'John Bull and the iconography of public opinion in England, c.1712–1929', *Past and Present*, 134 (1992), pp. 93–128; K.D.M. Snell, *The regional novel in Britain and Ireland, 1800–1900* (Cambridge, 1998), p. 46; *The prose works of William Wordsworth* (Cirencester, 2005), p. 190.

3. Tameside Archives, DD 41/1, manuscript of the ballad written by Mr William Hampson; The National Archives [hereafter TNA], PC1/3118, papers relating to United Irishmen and United Englishmen, 1798; Roger Wells, *Insurrection: the British experience, 1795–1803* (Gloucester, 1983), p. 200; Alan Booth, 'The United Englishmen and radical politics in the industrial north-west of England, 1795–1803', *International Review of Social History*, 31 (1986), p. 276; Navickas, *Loyalism and radicalism*, pp. 141–2.

4. Parliamentary Papers, 1803–4, 10 (XI), Returns of Yeomanry and Volunteer Corps; TNA HO50/76, Internal Defence, Lancaster District, Volunteer lists, 3 Sep. 1803; J. Fortescue, *County lieuten-ancies and the army, 1803–14* (London, 1909), p. 66.

5. Manchester Archives and Local Studies, BR 356 M12, Accounts of the treasurers to the Committee for General Defence, 1803.

6. *Blackburn Mail*, 21 Dec. 1803.

7. Chetham's Library, A.6.30, autobiography of James Weatherley, transcript.

8. Warrington Library, 'A new song in praise of the Warrington Volunteers' by J.B., 'One of the Corps', 1803; MS 11, Warrington Volunteers muster roll, 1807; Warrington poor rates 1802; *Blackburn Mail*, 24 Aug. 1803.

9. J.E. Cookson, *The British armed nation, 1793–1815* (Oxford, 1997), p. 236.

10. Broadside printed by J. Harrop, Manchester, Oct. 1798.

11. Timothy Jenks, 'Contesting the hero: the funeral of Admiral Lord Nelson', *Journal of British Studies*, 39 (2000), p. 423; Gerald Jordan and Nicholas Rogers, 'Admirals as heroes: patriotism and liberty in Hanoverian England', *Journal of British Studies*, 28 (1989), p. 222.

12. Stuart Semmel, *Napoleon and the British* (New Haven, CT; 2003), p. 58.

13. Robert Walker, 'Tim Bobbin the Second', *Plebeian Politics, or, the principles and practices of certain mole-eyed maniacs vulgarly called warrites* (Manchester, 1803), p. 33. Dukinfield Lodge near Audenshaw was the seat of Francis Dukinfield Astley, mine-owner and later high sheriff of Cheshire; nearby Shepley Hall was owned at the time by John Lowe, partner in an extensive calico printing works. Edwin Butterworth, *An historical account of the towns of Ashton-under-Lyne, Stalybridge, and Dukinfield* (Ashton, 1842), pp. 123, 162. For more on Robert Walker, see Katrina Navickas, '"Theaw Kon Ekspect No Mooar Eawt ov a Pig Thin a Grunt": searching for the radical dialect voice in industrial Lancashire and the West Riding, 1798–1819', in Michael Brown, John Kirk and Andrew Noble, *United islands? The languages of resistance* (London, 2012).

14. Craig Horner, 'The rise and fall of Manchester's "set of infernal miscreants": radicalism in 1790s Manchester', *Manchester Region History Review*, 12 (1998), p. 21; Cookson, *The British armed nation*.

15. Philip Harling, 'Rethinking old corruption', *Past and Present*, 147 (1995), pp. 127–58.

16. Stuart Semmel, 'Radicals, loyalists, and the royal jubilee of 1809', *Journal of British Studies*, 46 (2007), pp. 544–5, 554; Philip Harling, 'The Duke of York affair, 1809, and the complexities of war-time patriotism', *Historical Journal*, 39 (1996), pp. 963–84.

17. *Manchester Mercury*, 31 Oct. 1809; Donald Read, *Peterloo: the massacre and its background* (Manchester, 1958), p. 76; William Hone depicted Ethelston as 'the clerical magistrate' in his radical satirical pamphlet, *The Political House that Jack Built* (London, 1820).

18. *Blackburn Mail*, 28 Sep. 1803; *The Times*,

20 Sep. 1803; Navickas, *Loyalism and radicalism*, p. 57.

19. *Manchester Mercury*, 31 Oct. 1809; Bolton Archives, ZZ530/1, diaries of John Holden; 'A Lady', *An account of the celebration of the jubilee on the 25th October, 1809* (Birmingham, n.d.), p. 96.

20. Katrina Honeyman, *The origins of enterprise: business leadership in the industrial revolution* (Manchester, 1982), p. 102; John Aikin, *A description of the country from thirty to forty miles round Manchester* (Manchester, 1795), p. 468; Henry Taylor, *Old halls of Lancashire and Cheshire* (Manchester, 1884).

21. 'A Lady', *An account*, p. 101.

22. 'A Lady', *An account*, p. 94; *Manchester Mercury*, 31 Oct. 1809.

23. Malcolm Chase, 'From millennium to anniversary: the concept of Jubilee in late-eighteenth and early-nineteenth-century England', *Past and Present*, 129 (1990), pp. 141–2, 144.

24. Semmel, 'Radicals, loyalists, and the royal jubilee', p. 558.

25. Brian Lewis, *The middlemost and the milltowns: bourgeois culture and politics in early industrial England* (Stanford, CA; 2001), p. 290.

26. Arthur Aspinall, *The early English trade unions: documents from the Home Office papers in the Public Record Office* (London, 1949), pp. 102–3; Navickas, *Loyalism and radicalism*, p. 187; Malcolm Chase, *Early trade unionism: fraternity, skill and the politics of labour* (Aldershot, 2000), p. 66.

27. Paul Monod, *Jacobitism and the English people, 1688–1788* (Cambridge, 1989); Daniel Szechi, *The Jacobites: Britain and Europe, 1688–1788* (Manchester, 1994); J. Aston, *Manchester Guide* (Manchester, 1804), p. 136; H. Broxap, *The later nonjurors* (Cambridge, 1924), p. 288; R.A. Burrows and H.S. Kershaw, *The Ancient and Loyal Corporation of Ardwick* (Ardwick, 1954), p. 1; Manchester Archives and Local Studies, BR F 369.242.A.3, Ancient and Loyal Corporation of Ardwick

MS; Frederick Stancliffe, *John Shaw's, 1738–1938* (Manchester, 1939), p. 26.

28. Monod, *English Jacobitism*, p. 209; George Atkinson Ward (ed.), *Journals and letters of the late Samuel Curwen* (New York, 1842), pp. 137, 241; P. Marshall, 'Manchester and the American Revolution', *Bulletin of the John Rylands Library*, 62 (1979), p. 173.

29. Manchester Archives and Local Studies, M62/1/2–3, Ledgers of William and Thomas Wood of Didsbury; Bolton Archives, Bolton vestry ledgers; Peter Nockles, *The Oxford movement in context: Anglican high churchmanship, 1760–1857* (Cambridge, 1994), p. 51.

30. Lewis, *The middlemost and the milltowns*, p. 19.

31. Navickas, *Loyalism and radicalism*, p. 123; 'A Lady', *An account*, p. 99; Oldham Local Studies, William Rowbottom, 'Annals of Oldham', typescript; Bolton Archives, diaries of John Holden.

32. J.C. Scholes, *History of Bolton* (Bolton, 1892), p. 432.

33. M. Busteed and R. Hodgson, 'Irish migrant responses to urban life in early nineteenth-century Manchester', *Geographical Journal*, 162 (1996); *Liverpool Chronicle*, 12 Aug. 1807; *Manchester Mercury*, 21 July 1807; Oldham Archives, Rowbottom diaries.

34. Frank Neal, 'Manchester origins of the Orange Order', *Manchester Region History Review*, 4 (1990–1); *Cowdroy's Manchester Gazette*, 25 Apr. 1807; *Manchester Mercury*, 21 July 1807; Frank O. Darvall, *Popular disturbances and public order in Regency England* (London, 1969), p. 256; Navickas, *Loyalism and radicalism*, p. 121.

35. Navickas, *Loyalism and radicalism*, pp. 126–7; William Nuttall, *Orange miscellany* (Huddersfield, 1815), p. 200; H. Senior, *Orangeism in Ireland and Britain, 1795–1836* (London, 1966); Bernadette Turner, 'A loyal Englishman? John Lloyd and aspects of oath-taking in 1812', in M.T. Davis, *Radicalism and revolution in Britain, 1775–1848* (Basingstoke, 2000), pp. 133–42.

'These Lancashire women are witches in politics': Female reform societies and the theatre of radicalism, 1819–1820     *Ruth Mather*

1. *Morning Chronicle*, 1 July 1819.
2. *Morning Post*, 13 July 1819; *Trewman's Exeter Flying Post or Plymouth and Cornish Advertiser*, 15 July 1819.
3. Anna Clark, *The struggle for the breeches* (London, 1995), p. 161; Paul Custer, 'Refiguring Jemima: gender, work and politics in Lancashire, 1770–1820', *Past and Present*, 195 (2007), p. 155.
4. Address of the female reformers of Blackburn published in *Black Dwarf*, 14 July 1819, reprinted in Ruth and Edmund Frow (eds), *Political women, 1800–1850* (London, 1989), p. 21; *Manchester Observer*, 31 July 1819.
5. Clark, *The struggle for the breeches*, pp. 159–60.
6. Clark, *The struggle for the breeches*, pp. 122–40; for an example of women engaging in Luddite protest see Samuel Bamford, *Early days (Manchester, 1848)*, ed. W.H. Chaloner (London, 1967), ch. 27, p. 304; for an example of food riots see William Rowbottom, '*The Most Dismal Times': William Rowbottom's Diary*, Part 1, 1787–1799, trans and ann. Alan Peat (Oldham, 1996), p. 74.
7. The National Archives [hereafter TNA] HO33/2/17 f. 64–8, Elizabeth Salt, 'To all persons desirous of, and friendly to, establishing an union on legal principles, for the purpose of supporting the innocent mothers, wives & children, of such persons as are, or may hereafter be suffering, under want of a just remuneration for their Labours' (1818).
8. Samuel Bamford was sheltered by an unnamed female reformer during the suspension of Habeas Corpus in 1817. He also took credit for the introduction of female voting: see Samuel Bamford, *Passages in the life of a radical* (Manchester, 1839–42), ed. W.H. Chaloner (London, 1967), book 1, ch. 6, p. 39.
9. TNA HO42/176 f. 399, Account of meeting at Besses o'th' Barn, 20 Apr. 1819.
10. Manchester female reformers' address published in *Manchester Observer*, 31 July 1819, repr. in Frow and Frow (eds), *Political women*, pp. 24–5.
11. Blackburn female reformers' address, in Frow and Frow (eds), *Political women*, p. 23.
12. Letter from the female reformers of Bolton-le-Moors, in *Cobbett's Weekly Political Register*, 29 Dec. 1819.
13. Stockport female reformers' address in *Manchester Observer*, 31 July 1819.
14. Manchester female reformers' address in Frow and Frow (eds), *Political women*, p. 25.
15. Joanne Bailey, '"Think wot a mother must feel": Parenting in English pauper letters, c.1760–1834', *Family and Community History*, 13 (2010), pp. 13–14.
16. Clark, *The struggle for the breeches*, p. 161, citing 'The Village Disputants' in Hannah More, *Cheap Repository Tracts suited to the Present Times* (1819), p. 114, in which a radical man 'must own that since our Debby has turned speechmaker, the children are all in rags, and I can't get a clean shirt'.
17. TNA HO42/189 f. 5, Handbill, 'To the Women of England'.
18. *Morning Post*, 4 Aug. 1819.
19. For comments on male inadequacy, see Michael Bush, 'The women at Peterloo: The impact of female reform at the Manchester meeting of 16 August 1819', *History*, 89 (2004), pp. 216–17, 220–3. James Epstein also recognizes the contradiction between modest language and the use of the revolutionary Cap of Liberty in *Radical expression: political language, ritual and symbol in England, 1790–1850* (Oxford, 1994), p. 88.
20. *Morning Post*, 13 July 1819; TNA HO42/190 f. 205–6, Anonymous report from Middleton to Sidmouth, 26 July 1819.
21. *Manchester Observer*, 31 July 1819, in Frow and Frow (eds), *Political women*, p. 26.
22. Epstein, *Radical expression*, p. 91; *Cobbett's Weekly Political Register*, 23 Oct. 1819.

23. Tameside Local Studies and Archives, Ashton-under-Lyne, DO41/1, Papers relating to the Ashton volunteers, William Hampson, 'The Standards of Loyalty, Sung on July 10th 1799, the day which the Colours, given by Lady Stamford to the Ashton Under Lyne Volunteers'.

24. See TNA HO42/191 f. 79–80 for Charles Wrigley's report to Sidmouth, 9 Aug. 1819, in which he describes 'men, women (with children in their arms) and a vast multitude of boys, of all ages, marching … in defiance of all authority, and with countenances expressive of mischief, and a bold determination to advance in their work of destruction.'

25. Bush, 'The women at Peterloo', p. 220.

26. Blackburn female reformers' address, Frow and Frow (eds), *Political women*, p. 22.

27. TNA HO42/178 f. 434–4, John Livesey's account of a meeting at Failsworth, 13 July 1819; TNA HO42/177 f. 543, Livesey's Report of meeting at Lydgate Church, Saddleworth, 4 May 1818. The latter is the same meeting at which Bamford advocated female voting.

28. 'An Old Spartan', *Literary Chronicle*, 28 Aug. 1819.

29. Hannah More, 'The Ploughman's Ditty; Being an Answer to that Foolish Question, What have the POOR to lose? A Question frequently asked during the Alarm of Invasion', quoted in Matthew McCormack, *The independent man: citizenship and gender politics in Georgian England* (Manchester, 2005), p. 146.

30. Clark gives the excellent example of an 1803 broadsheet in which French soldiers declared that they would happily rape both men and women in the event of a successful invasion: see *The struggle for the breeches*, p. 154.

31. Clark again offers examples, including Thomas Paine's depiction as a wife-beater and the gleeful capitalization on Godwin's revelations of Mary Wollstonecraft's pre-marital affairs: *The struggle for the breeches*, p. 152.

32. Resolutions of a meeting of the Association for Preserving Liberty and Property Against Republicans and Levellers, printed in the *Observer*, 16 Dec. 1792.

33. Blackburn female reformers' address, in Frow and Frow (eds), *Political women*, pp. 22–3.

34. Manchester female reformers' address, in Frow and Frow (eds), *Political women*, pp. 25–6.

35. *The Republican, vol. 2*, 21 Jan. 1820, p. 71.

36. Custer, 'Refiguring Jemima', p. 128. Colonel Ralph Fletcher used the phrase in a letter to the Home Office in 1818: see TNA HO42/179 f. 135, quoted in 'Refiguring Jemima', p. 143.

37. TNA H042/191 f. 41–2, Information of Charles Wrigley regarding a reform meeting at Leigh, 11 Aug. 1819.

38. Helen Rogers, *Women and the people: authority, authorship and the radical tradition in nineteenth-century England* (Farnham, 2000), p. 21.

39. Bamford, *Early days*, ch. 1, p. 5; ch. 5, p. 52.

40. Bamford, *Early days*, ch. 26.

41. Letter from David Whitehead to Betty Wood, 4 Feb. 1818, quoted in Steve King, 'Love, religion and power in the making of marriages in early nineteenth-century rural industrial Lancashire', *Rural History*, 21 (2010), p. 11.

42. Letter from Betty Wood to David Whitehead, 16 Feb. 1818, quoted in King, 'Love, religion and power in the making of marriages', p. 12, and see also p. 17. E.P. Thompson also notes that economic independence could benefit unmarried women, although it could restrict them in other ways, in *The making of the English working class* (London, 2nd edn., 1968), p. 452.

43. See David Vincent, *Bread, knowledge and freedom: a study of nineteenth-century working-class autobiography* (London, 1981), p. 54.

44. Vincent, *Bread, knowledge and freedom*, p. 55.

45. For the response to Malthusianism in Chartist discourse, see Anna Clark, 'The rhetoric of chartist domesticity: gender, language, and class in the 1830s and 1840

*Journal of British Studies*, 31 (1992), p. 66. Clark's conclusions are equally relevant to the radical movement in 1819.

46. Salt, *To all persons desirous of, and friendly to, establishing an union on legal principles*, pp. 4–5.

47. Bamford, *Passages in the life of a radical*, book 1, ch. 7.

48. *Black Dwarf*, 24 Nov. 1819.

49. See Robert Poole, 'The march to Peterloo: politics and festivity in late Georgian England', *Past and Present*, 192 (2006) for an analysis of the competing presentations of the march.

50. *The trial of Henry Hunt and others* (Manchester, 1820), pp. 17, 111–12, 130–1.

51 Manchester Archives and Local Studies, Broadsides Collection, GB127, 'The Answer to Peterloo' (1819).

52. Bush, 'The women at Peterloo', pp. 226–7.

53. Henry Hunt, quoted in Bush, 'The women at Peterloo', p. 225.

54. George Cruikshank, 'Manchester Heroes' (London, 1819).

55. *Cap of Liberty*, 20 Oct. 1819, reprinted

in Frow and Frow (eds), *Political women*, pp. 27–30.

56. Donald Read, *Peterloo: the massacre and its background* (Manchester, 1958), pp. 171–2.

57. Diana Donald, 'The power of print: graphic images of Peterloo', *Manchester Region History Review*, 3 (1989), pp. 26–7.

58. *Cobbett's Weekly Political Register*, 29 Dec. 1819.

59. TNA HO42/198 f. 673, evidence of Mary Slater of Great Lever Hall, 7 Nov. 1819.

60. Bush, 'The women at Peterloo', pp. 222–3.

61. *Address to Henry Hunt from the female reformers of Manchester* (1820), quoted in Bush, 'The women at Peterloo', p. 221.

62. TNA HO48/24, 25 July 1820, quoted in Nicholas Rogers, *Crowds, culture and politics in Georgian Britain* (Oxford, 1998), p. 257.

63. From the address of 'The Ladies of Edinburgh', quoted in Clark, *The struggle for the breeches*, p. 171.

64. *Manchester Observer*, 23 Sep. 1820.

65. Clark, *The struggle for the breeches*, p. 166.

66. *Manchester Observer*, 11 Nov. 1820.

**Starving mothers and murdered children in cultural representations of Peterloo**     *Alison Morgan*

1. In 2007 a red plaque commemorating Peterloo replaced a blue plaque on the wall of the Radisson hotel (once the Free Trade Hall) in Manchester. The new plaque states that fifteen were killed and more than 600 injured.

2. Joyce Marlow, *The Peterloo massacre* (London, 1969), pp. 150–1; Michael Bush, *The casualties of Peterloo* (Lancaster, 2005), p. 90.

3. Bush, *The casualties of Peterloo*, p. 31.

4. James Chandler, *England in 1819: the politics of literary culture and the case of romantic historicism* (Chicago, 1998), p. xvi.

5. It is widely believed that, in 1820, Shelley wished to publish the poems he wrote after Peterloo in a 'little volume of *popular songs*', although there is debate regarding the contents of this intended volume. Due to the repressive political climate at the

time, the collection was never published. See Shelley's letter to Leigh Hunt in F.L. Jones (ed.), *The letters of Percy Bysshe Shelley* (2 vols, Oxford, 1964), vol. 2, p. 191.

6. John Gardner, *Poetry and popular protest: Peterloo, Cato Street and the Queen Caroline controversy* (Hampshire, 2011), p. 77.

7. Whilst in Italy, Shelley appears to have received regular parcels of periodicals from Peacock, including 'Cobbett's ... Examiners ... Edinburgh and Quarterly Reviews'. He would have learned about Peterloo from letters and the *Examiner*: Thomas Love Peacock, *The works of Thomas Love Peacock: essays, memoirs, letters and unfinished novels*, eds, H.F.B. Brett-Smith and C.E. Jones (10 vols, New York, 1967), vol. 8, p. 196. However, I disagree with Gardner that Peacock could have sent Shelley copies of the *Black Dwarf*, given

that post was regularly intercepted: Gardner, *Poetry and popular protest*, p. 77.

8. John Tyas, 'Express from Manchester', *The Times*, 19 Aug. 1819, p. 2.

9. Ian Haywood, 'Shelley's *Mask of Anarchy* and the visual iconography of female distress', in Phil Connell and Nigel Leask (eds), *Romanticism and popular culture in Britain and Ireland* (Cambridge, 2009), pp. 148–73, at p. 150.

10. John Tyas, 'Dispersal of the reform meeting', *Examiner*, 608, 22 Aug. 1819, p. 529. Shelley first mentions Peterloo on 6 Sep. in a letter to Charles Ollier, in Jones, *The letters of Percy Bysshe Shelley*, vol. 2, p. 117. Letters between England and Italy routinely took two weeks, hence the delay in Shelley hearing the news.

11. Elizabeth Farren, 'Further information regarding the late Manchester disturbances', *Examiner*, 612, 19 Sep. 1819, p. 597.

12. 'Manchester reform meeting', *Leeds Mercury*, 21 Aug. 1819, p. 3.

13. 'Manchester Meeting', *Gentleman's Magazine and Historical Chronicle*, 89 (Aug. 1819), p. 171.

14. *Ibid.*, p. 173.

15. 'State of public affairs', *Quarterly Review*, 22 (Jan. 1820), p. 502.

16. E.P. Thompson, *The making of the English working class* (London, 1980), p. 750.

17. 'From the *Black Dwarf* in London', *Black Dwarf*, 3, 25 Aug. 1819, p. 551. Original emphases.

18. Sir Francis Burdett, 'Address to the electors of Westminster', *Black Dwarf*, 3, 25 Aug. 1819, p. 550. Original emphases.

19. Ashley Cross, '"What a world we make the oppressor and the oppressed": George Cruikshank, Percy Shelley and the gendering of revolution in 1819', *Journal of English Literary History*, 71 (2004), pp. 167–207.

20. Eric Taplin, 'Peterloo Artefacts', *Manchester Region History Review*, 3 (1989), pp. 91–5, at p. 93.

21. One of these handkerchiefs is part of the collection of Peterloo artefacts at the Working Class Movement Library at Salford. The People's History Museum

in Manchester also has a handkerchief bearing this image.

22. Julie Kipp, *Romanticism, maternity and the body politic* (Cambridge, 2003); Stephen C. Behrendt, '"A few harmless numbers": British women poets and the climate of war, 1793–1825', in Philip Shaw (ed.), *Romantic wars: studies in culture and conflict, 1793–1822* (Hampshire, 2000), pp. 13–36, at p. 14.

23. Gardner, *Poetry and popular protest*, p. 33.

24. William Hone and George Cruikshank, *The Political House that Jack Built* (London, 1821); Marcus Wood, *Radical satire and print culture, 1790–1822* (Oxford, 1994), p. 215.

25. See note 17.

26. Diana Donald, 'The power of print: graphic images of Peterloo', *Manchester Region History Review*, 3 (1989), pp. 21–30, at pp. 22–3.

27. Anna Clark discusses the graphic satire employed by the anti-radicals, in which the women protestors at Peterloo were portrayed as unfeminine and grotesque: Anna Clark, *The struggle for the breeches: gender and the making of the British working class* (London, 1995), p. 161.

28. Diana Donald, *The age of caricature: satirical prints in the reign of George III* (London, 1996), p. 192.

29. 'The Manchester yeoman', *Examiner*, 610, 5 Sep. 1819, p. 567, lines 1–4.

30. *Ibid*, lines 19–22.

31. 'From Mr. Batty, Clerk To — Milne, Esq. Coroner, To His Friend in London', *Black Dwarf*, 3, 15 Sep. 1819, pp. 610–11. Coroner Milne was in charge of the inquest relating to Peterloo victims.

32. *Ibid*, p. 611.

33. 'A new song', *Medusa*, 1, 9 Oct. 1819, in Paul Keen (ed.), *The popular radical press in Britain 1817–21* (6 vols, London, 2003), vol. 5, p. 279.

34. *Ibid*, lines 31–6.

35. H. Morton, 'The sword king', *Black Dwarf*, 3, 22 Sep. 1819, p. 627, line 7.

36. *Ibid*, lines 9–12.

37. *Ibid*, lines 21–4.

38. Percy Bysshe Shelley, 'Peter Bell the third', in Jack Donovan, Cian Duffy, Kelvin Everest and Michael Rossington (eds), *The poems of Percy Bysshe Shelley* (3 vols, London, 2011), vol. 3, p. 144, lines 647–9. John Gardner writes in more detail on the links between Peterloo and 'Peter Bell the third' in *Poetry and popular protest*, pp. 92–100.

39. Haywood, 'Shelley's *Mask of Anarchy*', p. 153.

40. Shelley, 'The ballad of the starving mother', p. 45, lines 98–101.

41. Carlene Adamson (ed.), *The Bodleian Shelley manuscripts: The witch of atlas notebook* (New York, 1997), p. xxxvii.

42. Shelley, 'The ballad of the starving mother', p. 493, lines 77–80.

43. Shelley, 'The ballad of the starving mother', p. 490, line 5.

44. Kipp, *Romanticism, maternity and the body politic*, p. 156.

45. Shelley, 'The ballad of the starving mother', p. 492, lines 53–6.

46. Shelley, 'The ballad of the starving mother', p. 492, lines 65–9.

47. Richard Holmes, *Shelley: the pursuit* (New York, 1994), p. 562.

48. In *The Mask of Anarchy*, Shelley (p. 45, lines 86–9) writes:

> When one fled past, a Maniac maid,
> And her name was Hope, she said:
> But she looked more like Despair,
> And she cried out in the air.

49. I have written elsewhere on Shelley's Irish poems written in 1812–13 and the way in which he uses tropes central to Irish nationalism: Alison Morgan, 'Shelley in 1819: radical, nationalist and balladeer' (PhD thesis, University of Salford, 2012).

## William Hone and Peterloo    *John Gardner*

1. For a fuller account of this see John Gardner, *Poetry and popular protest: Peterloo, Cato Street and the Queen Caroline Controversy* (Basingstoke and New York, 2011).

2. See Kyle Grimes, 'William Hone', in Gary Kelly and Edd [*sic*] Applegate (eds), *British reform writers: dictionary of literary biography* (Detroit, 1996), vol. 158, p. 163.

3. Although these pamphlets are mainly to be found in copyright libraries, they can also be accessed at Chetham's public library in Manchester and online at http://honearchive.org.

4. Marcus Wood, *Radical satire and print culture, 1790–1822* (Oxford, 1994), p. 269.

5. Hyder Edward Rollins (ed.), *The letters of John Keats* (2 vols, Cambridge, 1958), vol. 1, p. 19.

6. Letter from Dorothy Wordsworth to T. Monkhouse, Jan. 1818, in Ernest De Selincourt (ed.), *The letters of Dorothy and William Wordsworth; the middle years* (2 vols, Oxford, 1937), vol. 2, p. 804.

7. Thomas Davison first published cantos 1 and 2 of Byron's *Don Juan* on 15 July 1819.

8. Hugh J. Luke, Jr. 'The publishing of Byron's "Don Juan"', *Proceedings of the Modern Language Association*, 80 (1965), p. 209.

9. Cited by Hone in his preface to *Wat Tyler: A Dramatic Poem* (London, 1817), p. v.

10. See Robert Poole, 'French Revolution or Peasants' Revolt?', *Labour History Review*, (2009), pp. 13–14.

11. Robert Southey, *The poetical works of Robert Southey* (2 vols, London, 1837–8), vol. 2, p. 22.

12. William Hazlitt in an unsigned review of *Wat Tyler* featured in the *Examiner* on 9 Mar. 1817 calls Southey, 'a literary prostitute [...] The author of *Wat Tyler* was an Ultra-Jacobin; the author of Parliamentary Reform is an Ultra-royalist; the one was a frantic demagogue; the other is a servile court-fool.'

13. Kenneth Curry (ed.), *New letters of Robert Southey* (2 vols, New York, 1965), vol. 2, p. 210.

14. John Wardroper, *The caricatures of George Cruikshank* (Boston, 1978), p. 84.

15. From William Hone, *The Political House that Jack Built* (London, 1820).

16. For more on conservative publications see Kevin Gilmartin, *Writing against*

revolution: literary conservatism in Britain, 1790–1832 (Cambridge, 2007).

17. M. Adams, The True Political House that Jack Built: being a parody on [William Hone's] 'The Political House that Jack Built' (London, 1820).

18. Wood, Radical satire and print culture, p. 263.

19. The Loyalist; or, Anti-Radical; Consisting of Three Departments: Satyrical, Miscellaneous, and Historical (London, 1820), p. v.

20. Cited in James Chandler, England in 1819: the politics of literary culture and the case of romantic historicism (Chicago, 1998), p. 21.

21. Hone may well have been aware of Shelley's poem. Richard Holmes claims that in April of 1816 Shelley was in communication with Hone about the printing of some of his political works. See Richard Holmes, Shelley: the pursuit (London, 1995), p. 366.

22. For a fuller account of advertising in the period see Wood, Radical satire and print culture, pp. 155–214.

23. Wood, Radical satire and print culture, p. 212.

24. Ibid., p. 211.

25. William Hone, A Slap at Slop and the Bridge-Street Gang (London, 1821), p. 35.

26. Summary of the Report of a Select Committee Appointed to Enquire Into the Causes which have Led to the Extensive Depreciation or Reduction in the Remuneration for Labour in Great Britain and the Extreme Privation and Calamitous Distress Consequent Thereupon (London, 1823), p. 16.

27. Ibid., p. 17.

28. William Thackeray, An essay on the genius of George Cruikshank with numerous illustrations of his works (London, 1840), pp. 6–7.

29. Kyle Grimes, 'William Hone's liturgical parodies' in Michael T. Davis (ed.), Radicalism and revolution in Britain, 1775–1848: essays in honour of Michael I. Thomis (London, 2000), p. 149.

30. Samuel Bamford, Passages in the life of a radical (Manchester, 1839–42), ed. W.H. Chaloner (London, 1967), book 1, ch. 5.

31. Gary Dyer, British satire and the politics of style, 1789–1832 (Cambridge, 1997), p. 141.

## Radical banners from Peterloo to Chartism    Matthew Roberts

1. Northern Star, 24 Aug. 1839; The National Archives [hereafter TNA], Home Office [hereafter HO] 40/36, Reginald Hyde Clarke to Home Office, 16 Nov. 1838; TNA, Treasury Solicitor's Papers, 11/815, Case respecting a torchlight meeting at Hyde.

2. Northern Star, 17 Nov. 1838.

3. Paul Pickering's exemplary local study of Chartism in Manchester and Salford pointed to the rich potential of banners as sources for studying the ideology of the rank and file, but his research was limited to an analysis of just forty-four banners carried by Chartists in 'six major parades' between 1838 and 1842. It is not clear from Pickering's account how representative these six major parades were of the region, let alone elsewhere in Britain, nor whether Chartist use of banners changed over the ten-year period of their agitation: Paul

A. Pickering, Chartism and the Chartists in Manchester and Salford (Basingstoke, 1995), pp. 159–65, 214–16.

4. John Barrell, 'Radicalism, visual culture and spectacle in the 1790s', Romanticism on the web, 46 (2007), http://www.erudit. org/revue/ron/2007/v/n46/016131ar.html [accessed 29 Oct. 2012].

5. James Epstein, The lion of freedom: Feargus O'Connor and the Chartist movement, 1832–1842 (London, 1982), pp. 60, 66.

6. I have found only two such instances between 1838 and 1843: a meeting at Salcoats in Oct. 1840 and Markinch in Nov. 1840, though there must have been others: Scottish Patriot, 17 Oct. 1840, 7 Nov. 1840.

7. Stephen Connolly, '"Under the banners of death": iconoclasm, iconophobia and the scopic vocabularies of English popular

politics, 1789–1821' (PhD thesis, University of Manchester, 2009), pp. 38–9.

8. TNA, HO 42/158, Major Chippendale to Home Office, 29 Dec. 1816.

9. TNA, HO 42/164, Deposition of 'No. 2 of Manchester', 4 Apr. 1817.

10. *Lancaster Gazette*, 21 June 1817; *Liverpool Mercury*, 23 May 1817.

11. It is worth noting, however, that, contrary to the claims of the authorities, there were no banners bearing images of skull and crossbones (or bloody daggers) at Peterloo. Thanks to Robert Poole for drawing my attention to this.

12. E.P. Thompson, 'Thompson on Peterloo', *Manchester Region History Review*, 3 (1989), p. 73.

13. Samuel Bamford, *Passages in the life of a radical* (Manchester, 1839–42), ed. W.H. Chaloner (London, 1967), book 1, ch. 33, p. 197.

14. *The trial of Henry Hunt and others* (Manchester, 1820), p. 150.

15. *Black Dwarf*, 6 Oct. 1819, p. 659.

16. *The Trial of Henry Hunt and others*, pp. 134–6.

17. *Parliamentary Debates* [hereafter *PD*], House of Commons [hereafter HC], 24 Nov. 1819, col. 293.

18. *PD*, HC, 24 Nov. 1819, col. 209.

19. Sidmouth quoted in George Pellew, *The life and correspondence of the first viscount Sidmouth* (3 vols, London, 1847), vol. 3, p. 286.

20. *PD*, HC, 24 Nov. 1819, col. 159.

21. *The Trial of Henry Hunt and others*, p. 26.

22. *PD*, House of Lords, 27 Dec. 1819, col. 1588.

23. *PD*, HC, 24 Nov. 1819, col. 190.

24. *PD*, House of Lords, 30 Nov. 1819, col. 430.

25. Michael Lobban, 'From seditious libel to unlawful assembly: Peterloo and the changing face of political crime, c.1770–1820', *Oxford Journal of Legal Studies*, 10 (1990), pp. 307–52.

26. Quoted in James Epstein, 'Understanding the Cap of Liberty: symbolic practice and social conflict in early nineteenth-century England', *Past and Present*, 122 (1989), pp. 75–118, at p. 114.

27. Epstein, 'The Cap of Liberty', p. 115.

28. *Manchester Times*, 14 May 1831; James Wheeler, *Manchester: its political, social and commercial history* (London, 1836), p. 131.

29. *Manchester Times*, 9 Apr., 7 May, 20 Aug. 1831.

30. *Manchester Courier*, 21 Aug. 1830.

31. *Manchester Times*, 19 May 1832.

32. *Manchester Times*, 1 Sep. 1832; *Manchester Courier*, 1 Sep. 1832.

33. Epstein, 'The Cap of Liberty', p. 116.

34. R.G. Gammage, *History of the Chartist movement, 1837–1854* (1894; London, 1969), p. 61.

35. Neil Pye, 'The Home Office and the suppression of Chartism in the West Riding, c.1838–1848' (PhD thesis, University of Huddersfield, 2011), pp. 76, 96.

36. TNA, HO 40/36, Hyde Clarke to Home Office, 16 Nov. 1838; TNA, HO 40/37, James Partington to Home Office, 3 Apr. 1839; TNA, HO 40/37, Deposition of Robert Newton of Ashton, 29 Apr. 1839; TNA, HO 40/43, Jas. Brown Brooke to Home Office, 2 Apr. 1839.

37. James Epstein, *In practice: studies in the language and culture of popular politics in modern Britain* (Stanford, CA; 2003), p. 21.

38. TNA, 11/815, Treasury Solicitor's Papers.

39. *Northern Star*, 24 Aug. 1839.

40. Edward Wise, *The law relating to riots and unlawful assemblies* (London, 1848), p. 94.

41. On this point see Nick Mansfield, 'Radical banners as sites of memory: the National Banner Survey', in Paul A. Pickering and Alex Tyrrell (eds), *Contested sites: commemoration, memorial and popular politics in nineteenth-century Britain* (Aldershot, 2004), pp. 93–4.

42. John Saville, *1848: the British state and the Chartist movement* (Cambridge, 1987), p. 22.

43. Elaine A. Reynolds, *Before the Bobbies: the night watch and police reform in metropolitan London, 1720–1830* (Stanford, CA; 1998), p. 110.

44. W. Napier, *The life and opinions of General Sir Charles Napier* (4 vols, London, 1857), vol. 2, pp. 39, 57, 63–6, 146.

45. Napier, *The life and opinions of General Sir Charles Napier*, pp. 37, 69.
46. Pye, 'The Home Office and the suppression of Chartism', pp. 62–3.
47. *Champion*, 25 Aug. 1839.
48. Pye, 'The Home Office and the suppression of Chartism'; Saville, *1848: the British state and the Chartist movement*.
49. Bamford, *Passages in the life of a radical*, book 2, ch. 14, p. 67.
50. TNA, HO 40/37, James Woods to Home Office, 29 Dec. 1838. For similar statements see TNA, HO 40/37, Clement Royds to Home Office, 24 Dec. 1838, Hyde Magistrates to Home Office, 23 Apr. 1839.
51. The banner is on display at the Tolson Museum, Halifax. For the history of the flag see the accompanying caption, reproduced at: http://www.kirklees.gov.uk/leisure/museums/tolson/topten/skelman-thorpe.shtml [accessed 29 Oct. 2012].
52. Michael Sanders, *Chartist poetry: aesthetics, politics, history* (Cambridge, 2009), p. 21.
53. *Brighton Patriot*, 1 Jan. 1839.
54. Malcolm Chase, *Chartism: a new history* (Manchester, 2007), p. 159.
55. Martin Hewitt, *The emergence of stability in the industrial city: Manchester, 1832–67* (Aldershot, 1996), p. 240.
56. *Manchester Times*, 25 Mar. 1848; *Manchester and Salford Advertiser*, 25 Mar. 1848.
57. *Manchester Times*, 8 Apr. 1848 (meeting at Bolton and in Stevenson Square, though, interestingly, at another meeting held in Stevenson Square to protest against oakum picking, tricolour flags were present, though this meeting was not organized by the Chartists); 11 Apr. 1848 (meeting in Stevenson Square and camp meeting at Haughton Green corroborated by report in *Manchester and Salford Advertiser*, 15 Apr. 1848); 15 Apr. 1848 (meeting in Smithfield Market, corroborated by report in *Manchester and Salford Advertiser*, 15 Apr. 1848); 18 Apr. 1848 (meetings in Stevenson Square); 9 May 1848 (camp meeting at Stalybridge).
58. *Manchester and Salford Advertiser*, 11 Mar., 19 Aug. 1848; *Manchester Times*, 22 Aug. 1848.
59. *Manchester and Salford Advertiser*, 8 Apr. 1848.
60. *Manchester and Salford Advertiser*, 22 Apr. 1848.
61. *Manchester Times*, 3 June 1848; *Manchester Courier*, 30 Aug. 1848; *Manchester and Salford Advertiser*, 3 June 1848.
62. *Manchester and Salford Advertiser*, 17 June 1848.
63. Hewitt, *The emergence of stability*, pp. 239–41.
64. Quoted in Mansfield, 'Radical banners as sites of memory', p. 94.
65. William Lovett, *The life and struggles of William Lovett in his pursuit of bread, knowledge and freedom* (1876; London, 1976), p. 204.
66. *Manchester Times*, 22 Aug. 1840; Paul A. Pickering and Alex Tyrrell, *The people's bread: a history of the Anti-Corn Law League* (London, 2000), p. 195.
67. *Northern Star*, 22 Sep. 1838.
68. For this interpretation of popular politics see James Vernon, *Politics and the people: a study in English political culture, c.1815–1867* (Cambridge, 1993).
69. Pickering, *Chartism and the Chartists in Manchester and Salford*, pp. 160–1.
70. *Northern Star*, 10 July 1841; *Manchester Times*, 5 June 1841.
71. Hewitt, *The emergence of stability*, p. 242.
72. John Brewer, 'Commercialisation and politics', in Neil McKendrick, John Brewer and J.H. Plumb (eds), *The birth of a consumer society: the commercialisation of eighteenth-century England* (London, 1982) pp. 235–62.
73. Epstein, *In practice*, pp. 60–1.
74. Robert Poole, 'The march to Peterloo: politics and festivity in late Georgian England', *Past and Present*, 192 (2006), p. 151.

1. There is no modern bibliography of Peterloo. Margaret E. Leighton's *Peterloo. Monday, 16th August 1819: a bibliography* (Manchester, 1969) remains a useful starting point, especially for printed primary sources.

2. M.L. Bush, *The casualties of Peterloo* (Lancaster, 2005).

3. Some artefacts have found their way into public collections. See the incomplete list in Eric Taplin, 'Peterloo Artefacts', *Manchester Region History Review*, 3 (1989), pp. 91–4.

4. 'Scaitcliffe Armoury and Trophies of Antiquity' (n.p., 7 vols, n.d.), vol. 2, p. 168. John Crossley (1778–1830) resided at Scaitcliffe Hall, Todmorden. The history of the collection requires further research but no sale catalogue has been traced. A seven-volume manuscript catalogue detailing the collection remained in the family. It includes original Peterloo documents, broadsides and an especially fine example of a Peterloo handkerchief sold to raise money for the victims, as well as letters of provenance. These volumes were sold at auction by Hartleys in Ilkley, 14 Sep. 2011 (Lots 757–63). Frustratingly, they were not sold as a single lot and no public institution made a bid. I am most grateful to John Worthy for allowing me to consult vols 2 and 4.

5. 'Scaitcliffe Armoury', vol. 2, pp. 164–8.

6. Sworn statement dated 19 Nov. 1819, 'Scaitcliffe Armoury', vol. 2, p. 160.

7. 'Scaitcliffe Armoury', vol. 2, p. 238. Ogden was found guilty of illegal drilling in Jan. 1820. The weapon with its nine-inch blade was said to have been found in Ogden's house and shown to the court by a constable after he had been sentenced.

8. J. Epstein, *Radical expression: political language, ritual, and symbol in England, 1790–1850* (Oxford, 1994), pp. 163–4. The best known is the Middleton banner, now in Rochdale, formerly in the Liberal Club and public library in Middleton.

9. T. Swindells, *Manchester streets and Manchester men* (Manchester, 1906), pp. 253–4. The chapel floorboards were sold when the building was taken down in 1829. Advert from Richard Lane in *Manchester Guardian*, 21 Feb. 1829, p. 1.

10. Letter from Francis Place to John C. Hobhouse quoted in Ben Ainley, *Marxism Today*, Aug. 1969, p. 253.

11. S.G. Checkland, *The Gladstones: a family biography, 1764–1851* (Cambridge, 1971), p. 112.

12. F. and K. Wood (eds), *A Lancashire gentleman: the letters and journals of Richard Hodgkinson, 1763–1847* (Stroud, 1992), p. 4. See Manchester Central Library, L302/1, 'Manchester Pitt Club. Songs and Glees to be sung on the anniversary', but on the limitations of the printed record, note Archibald Prentice's comment that 'the greater part of the toasts at the anniversary dinners were too grossly indelicate to be printed at the present day', *Historical Sketches and Personal Reminiscences of Manchester* (London and Manchester, 1851; 1970), p. 429.

13. The Leeds volunteer cavalry and the Huddersfield and Oldham yeomanry cavalry explained attending dinners on the anniversary of Peterloo as a coincidence. See *Leeds Mercury*, 25 Aug. 1821, p. 3.

14. J.R.M. Albrecht, 'Hugh Hornby Birley', *Transactions of Lancashire and Cheshire Antiquarian Society*, 40 (1922–3), p. 197; *Manchester Mercury*, 3 June 1820, p. 3.

15. *Manchester Guardian*, 27 Apr. 1822, p. 2. The Manchester yeomanry were in the words of the *Manchester Guardian* 'very discourtesly greeted by the populace' when they took part in Manchester's coronation celebrations in 1821.

16. W. Brimelow, *Political and parliamentary history of Bolton* (Bolton, 1882), pp. 41–2.

17. *Manchester Guardian*, 18 Aug. 1821, p. 3; J. Epstein, 'Radical dining, toasting and symbolic expression in early nineteenth-century Lancashire: rituals of solidarity', *Albion*, 20 (1988), pp. 271–91.

18. Report in *Morning Post*, 22 Aug. 1826, p. 2.

19. *Poor Man's Guardian*, 19 May 1832, pp. 395–6.

20. *Manchester Guardian*, 1 Sep. 1832, p. 3.

21. Report in *Manchester Guardian*, 20 Aug. 1836, p. 3.

22. There is no close study of land ownership, public usage and access, and later developments on and around St Peter's Field, either before or after 1819, a surprising omission given that Richard Cobden presented part of the site for the building of the Free Trade Hall.

23. For instance, Richard Baron Howard, when investigating Manchester's public health for Chadwick's 1842 Report observed that 'The year 1819 is notorious as that in which the great Radical meeting, commonly called "Peterloo", was held, the immediate result of which was necessarily much misery': House of Commons Parliamentary Papers, Edwin Chadwick, *Local reports on the Sanitary Condition of the Labouring Population of Great Britain.*, vol. 27 (1842), p. 328.

24. T. Carlyle, *Past and present* (London, 1843).

25. James Epstein has provided a nuanced examination of the rituals associated with these commemorative occasions: *Radical expression*, ch. 5.

26. John Belchem, *'Orator Hunt': Henry Hunt and English working-class radicalism* (Oxford, 1985), pp. 276–7; P.A. Pickering, *Chartism and the Chartists in Manchester and Salford* (Basingstoke, 1995), pp. 35–6; Pickering, *Feargus O'Connor: a political life* (Monmouth, 2008).

27. *Manchester Guardian*, 26 Mar. 1842, p. 2.

28. P.A. Pickering and A. Tyrrell, 'In the thickest of the fight: the Reverend James Scholefield (1790–1855) and the Bible Christians of Manchester and Salford', *Albion*, 26 (1994), pp. 461–82; entry in Keith Gildart, David Howell and Neville Kirk (eds), *Dictionary of labour biography*, vol. 11 (Basingstoke, 2003), pp. 251–3.

29. *Northern Star*, 2 Apr. 1842, p. 6.

30. The *Northern Star*'s issue for Saturday 20 Aug. included engravings of Hunt's Monument and of the 'horrible Manchester Massacre', and a list of the names of the Manchester yeomanry 'who dyed their drunken hands in the blood of an unarmed people'.

31. M. Jenkins, *The General Strike of 1842* (London, 1980), pp. 81–8, 223–5.

32. V.I. Tomlinson, 'Postscript to Peterloo', *Manchester Region History Review*, 3 (1989), pp. 51–9.

33. *Manchester Guardian*, 1 Jan. 1863, p. 3.

34. *The Tories and their punishment of the people at the Peterloo meeting: a few words addressed to working men, the electors of Manchester and elsewhere, as to their duty* (Manchester, 1868); James R. Moore, *The transformation of urban Liberalism* (Aldershot, 2006), p. 87.

35. G.M. Trevelyan, *The life of John Bright* (London, 1913), p. 20.

36. *Manchester Guardian*, 3 Dec. 1889, pp. 7, 9.

37. *Manchester Guardian*, 1 Feb. 1869, p. 3; *Manchester Courier*, 1 Feb. 1863, p. 3.

38. See also Tony Taylor, 'Commemoration, memorialisation and political memory in post-Chartist radicalism: The 1885 Halifax Chartist reunion in context', in Owen Ashton, Robert Fyson and Stephen Roberts (eds), *The Chartist legacy* (Woodbridge, 1999), pp. 255–85.

39. *Manchester Times*, 8 June 1867, p. 7.

40. Photo of Peterloo veterans in 1884 reproduced in J. Liddington and J. Norris, *One hand tied behind us* (London, 1978), facing p. 128, referencing Percival Percival [*sic*], *Failsworth folk and Failsworth memories* (Manchester, 1901).

41. *Manchester Guardian*, 16 Apr. 1872, p. 6.

42. *Manchester Weekly Times*, 27 Apr. 1872, p. 7.

43. T. Wyke and H. Cocks, *Public sculpture in Greater Manchester* (Liverpool, 2004), p. 311. A stone tablet was placed on his cottage in Union Street, Middleton in 190( the inscription reading: 'Samuel Bamford, Reformer, resided & was arrested in this house, Aug 26, 1819'.

44. J. Treuherz, 'Ford Madox Brown and the Manchester murals', in J.H.G. Archer (ed.), *Art and architecture in Victorian Manchester* (Manchester, 1985), p. 172; Mary Bennett, *Ford Madox Brown: a*

catalogue raisonné (New Haven, CT; 2010), vol. 2, pp. 342–5.

45. S. Cunniffe and T. Wyke, 'Memorialising its hero: Liberal Manchester's statue of Oliver Cromwell', Bulletin of the John Rylands Library, 89 (2012–13), pp. 179–206.

46. James Haslam, 'Where first I heard of Peterloo', Manchester Guardian, 13 Aug. 1919.

47. J.R. Green, A short history of the English people (London, 1903), ch. 10.

48. W.E.A. Axon, Annals of Manchester (Manchester, 1886), p. 157; Manchester Courier, 1 Nov. 1886, p. 8.

49. John Ashton, Social England under the Regency (London, 2 vols, 1884), vol. 2, p. 204; H. Gibbins, Industry in England (London, 1897), p. 377, n. 1.

50. Mrs G. Linnaeus Banks recalled as a young girl living in Oldham Road watching the anniversary procession, including a large banner (painted by Henry Whaite) depicting the massacre: The Manchester Man (Manchester, 1895), p. 476. Extracts from contemporary sources about Peterloo were included in the novel but she regretted not being able to reproduce particular images of the massacre in the illustrated edition of 1896.

51. The Pioneer: A Political Handy-Sheet for Men and Women, 63, 27 Oct. 1888.

52. Unveiled 29 June 1908, reports in Manchester City News, 4 July 1908; Manchester Courier, 3 July 1908, p. 14; Manchester Guardian, 30 June 1908, pp. 6, 7. At the same time, the Reform Club was presented with a collection of contemporary Peterloo prints and publications.

53. Following the closure of the Reform Club it was purchased by the Greater Manchester Museum of Science and Industry at auction in 1987. Currently displayed in the 'Making of Manchester' Gallery at MOSI.

54. Liddington and Norris, One hand tied behind us, quoting Estelle Pankhurst, 'Battle of Peterloo' in Votes for Women, Oct. 1907. Goulden family discussed in Paula Bartley, Emmeline Pankhurst (London, 2002), pp. 18–19.

55. On the holiday mood of those attending Peterloo see R. Poole, 'The march to Peterloo: politics and festivity in late Georgian England', Past and Present, 192 (2006), pp. 109–53.

56. Manchester City News, 23 Aug. 1919, p. 2; Manchester Evening News, 16 Aug. 1919, p. 3. Adam R. Seipp, The ordeal of peace: demobilization and the urban experience in Britain and Germany 1917–1921 (Farnham, 2009), pp. 153–4.

57. Manchester Guardian, 18 Aug. 1919.

58. J.H. Hudson, Peterloo: a history of the Massacre and the conditions which preceded it (Manchester, [1919]). Hudson was from Swinton. J. Bruce Glasier contributed a preface to the pamphlet in which he lamented the failure of the working class 'to fulfil the hopes for which the martyrs of Peterloo were slain'.

59. For example, article by the Labour journalist, A.W. Humphrey on Peterloo, Cotton Factory Times, 15 Aug. 1919, p. 1.

60. Charles Glyde's The centenary of the massacre of British workers: Peterloo, Manchester, Monday, August 16th, 1819 (Bradford, 1919) was a notable exception but little read outside socialist circles. Glyde was a socialist councillor in Bradford but had Lancashire roots, having been a member of Bolton SDF in the 1880s. The pamphlet opened with Bamford's 'Patriot Hymn' and quoted extensively from his writings.

61. A short report of the anniversary under the heading 'Old unhappy far-off things and battles long ago' was one of the few references in the Manchester Evening Chronicle, 16 Aug. 1919, p. 2.

62. 'Library notes and news', Bulletin of the John Rylands Library, 5 (1919), p. 192.

63. Clare Griffiths, 'Remembering Tolpuddle: rural history and commemoration in the inter-war labour movement', History Workshop Journal, 44 (1997), pp. 144–9.

64. Published as a booklet by Manchester University Press in 1919, and also in Bulletin of the John Rylands Library, 5 (1919).

65. G.M. Trevelyan, 'The number of casualties at Peterloo', History, 7 (1922), pp. 200–5.

66. Caroline Trevelyan's father was Robert Needham Philips, Liberal MP for Bury; her uncle, Mark Philips was one of Manchester's first MPs in 1832.

67. J.L. and B. Hammond, *The town labourer, 1760–1832* (London, 1917), pp. 89–92.

68. [The Communist Party of Great Britain], *Peterloo: the story of the terrible massacre of the Lancashire workers at St. Peter's Fields, Manchester on August 16th, 1819, and the lessons of Peterloo* (London, 1928).

69. Mark Starr, *A worker looks at history* (Sheffield, 1925). Starr's industrial history was first published in 1917. Poem signed J.B. This was sent by Eddie Frow for inclusion in the *Manchester Region History Review* Peterloo number but not published.

70. *Historical Pageant of Manchester: Heaton Park, October 2nd and 9th 1926* (Manchester, 1926).

71. Wadsworth's collection of posters, letters and other documents relating to Peterloo was presented to the John Rylands Library after his death.

72. M. Anderson (ed.), *Lancashire Cotton Pageant. 25 June to 9 July 1932. Official Programme* ([1932]), pp. 33–7. The playwright and broadcaster Edward P. Gee, and Matthew Anderson, were experienced pageant organisers in Lancashire: see Mick Wallis, 'Delving the levels of memory and dressing up in the past', in Clive Barker and Maggie B. Gale (eds), *British theatre between the wars, 1918–1939* (Cambridge, 2000), p. 201.

73. Reviews in *Manchester City News*, 25 June 1932, p. 9; *Manchester Evening News*, 25 June 1932, p. 1; *The Times*, 27 June 1932, p. 9.

74. The popular local writer and public speaker, Sidney F. Wicks, writing in the *Manchester City News*, 2 July 1938.

75. *Manchester Guardian*, 8 Jan. 1938, p. 14.

76. *Manchester Guardian*, 9 Apr. 1938, p. 15, includes a letter criticizing the pageant committee's misrepresentation of the city's history by choosing events such as the visit of Queen Victoria in preference to 'Peterloo, the building of the Free Trade Hall as a monument to an important social victory, the Chartist movement, and the first Trades Union Congress'. One of the authors was the young Rodney H. Hilton, who was born in Middleton and whose Marxist sympathies shaped his work as a medieval historian.

77. *Manchester Evening News*, 7 Apr. 1938, p. 8.

78. *Manchester City News*, 18 June 1938, p. 8; *Manchester Evening Chronicle*, 27 June 1938, p. 5; *Manchester Historical Pageant, June 27 to July 2 1938: Book of Words* ([1938]), p. 83.

79. *Manchester Evening News*, 24 June 1938, p. 15.

80. Articles by Grierson and Mould on 'They Build a City' in *Manchester Evening News*, 28 Feb. – 2 Mar. 1938. The three-act play, *They build a city. The story of those who have made Manchester great* [1938] was reviewed in *Manchester Guardian*, 14 June 1938.

81. *Manchester Historical Pageant June 27th to July 2nd … Official souvenir and programme* ([1938]). Reports in *Manchester Guardian*, 20 June 1938, p. 13; *The Times*, 1, 13 June 1938; *Manchester Guardian*, 12 July 1937, p. 11; Report of pageant and Peterloo banner, *Daily Worker*, 12 July 1938, p. 1.

82. *Daily Worker*, 25 Feb. 1939, p. 5.

83. Humphry House's 'Peterloo' in the *News Chronicle*, 16 Aug. 1939 (reprinted in his posthumous *All in due time* [London, 1955], pp. 46–9) was something of an exception, at least if we accept the results from those London papers that currently can be searched electronically.

84. *Howard Spring, Fame is the Spur* (London, 1940) sold well, though one suspects wide regional variations; advert in *Observer*, 14 July 1940, claims 15,000 copies sold in the first week.

85. The film version (1947) was made by the Boulting brothers. The released film was very heavily cut by the studio. For an insightful examination of the differences between the novel and the film see Anthony Aldgate and Jeffrey Richards, *Best of British: cinema and society from*

*1930* (London, 2002) pp. 95–108. The novel was also serialized on radio (1949) and television (BBC, 1982).

86. Talk by Howitt to Manchester Luncheon Club, *Manchester Guardian*, 20 Dec. 1952, p. 3.

87. *Manchester Guardian*, 17 Oct. 1951, p. 5.

88. Ellis Smith, *The story of Peterloo* ([1952]).

89. N. Kirk, 'Commonsense, commitment and objectivity: themes in the recent historiography of Peterloo', *Manchester Region History Review*, 3 (1989), pp. 61–6.

90. *Oldham Chronicle*, 23 Oct. 1954, p. 5.

91. Eric Hobsbawm, 'History and the "dark satanic mills"', *Marxism Today* (May 1959), pp. 132–9. But note that Chaloner was one of academics responsible for reprinting Bamford's works: *The autobiography of Samuel Bamford. Volume one: Early days, together with an account of the arrest* (London, 1967); *Volume Two: Passages in the life of a radical* (London, 1967).

92. Working Class Movement Library, Salford, Peterloo File (92), Letter from Chaloner to Walmsley, dated 3 Sep. 1969.

93. Michael Kennedy's review in the *Daily Telegraph*, 18 July 1969, p. 16, was extremely positive, praising Walmsley for correcting the lies that encrusted Peterloo and discrediting witnesses such as Bamford who had 'muddied the stream of history'. Other reviewers such as W.G. Hoskins in the *New Statesman*, 29 Aug. 1969, pp. 279–80, did not accept the whitewashing of the magistrates.

94. *Times Literary Supplement*, 11 Dec. 1969. Walmsley was permitted only a short reply on 15 Jan. 1970. He prepared a much longer rebuttal of Thompson's argument but was unable to find a publisher for 'The Peterloo Reopener and his critics' (Manchester Archives and Local Studies Library, typescript, 1970). Pressures of time and cost prevented reprinting this in the Peterloo edition of the *Manchester Region History Review* in 1989. It should be made available on a Peterloo website.

5. Review in *Evening Standard*, 19 Aug. 1969.

5. Joyce Marlow recalls shooting scenes on the Pennine moors: see http://www.joycemarlow.co.uk. 'The Peterloo Massacre' was broadcast by Granada on 27 July 1970 at 11.00 pm. No copy has been located. A radio documentary, 'Peaceably if we may: The Massacre of Peterloo' was broadcast on BBC Radio 4, 19 Aug. 1969.

97. 'Peterloo. August 16th 1819. A commemoration at the Free Trade Hall Manchester on 16th August 1969' ([1969]). An address by Michael Foot MP was part of the entertainment.

98. *Guardian*, 28 Mar. 1969, p. 22.

99. Opposition to the resurgence of fascism in the early 1960s had led to calls to change the name of Mosley Street (named after the Mosley family who had been one of the leading families in Manchester up to the nineteenth century) to Peterloo Street. Oswald Mosley, leader of the BUF, was a descendant: see *Guardian*, 3 Aug. 1962, p. 14.

100. *Daily Telegraph*, 6 Nov. 1969; *Guardian*, 6 Nov. 1969, p. 24. The majority was larger than that in 1949 when Labour councillors had proposed that a new ward in the city centre be named Peterloo rather than St Peter's: see reports in *Manchester Guardian*, 10 Nov. 1948; 3 Feb. 1949, p. 6.

101. *Peterloo* ([1969]), pub. by Lancashire and Cheshire District of the Communist Party; E. and R. Frow, 'Peterloo: August 1819', *Comment*, Aug. 1969, pp. 519–23. The exhibition at Belle Vue was on 12 Oct. 1969.

102. The Hallé Orchestra had previously performed the music written for the 1947 film by John Wooldridge, described as 'a somewhat moody composition' in a review in *Manchester Evening News*, 9 May 1949, p. 6. On the commissioning of work by the TUC see A. Meredith and P. Harris, *Malcolm Arnold, rogue genius: the life and music of Britain's most misunderstood composer* (Norwich, 2004), pp. 272–4.

103. *Manchester Evening News*, 7 Sep. 1972, p. 9.

104. Report in *Guardian*, 7 Sep. 1972, p. 1; *Manchester Evening News*, 7 Sep. 1972, p. 9.

105. The inscription on the blue plaque read: 'The site of St Peter's Fields/ where on 16th August 1819/ Henry Hunt, radical orator/

addressed an assembly of/ about 60,000 people/ Their subsequent dispersal/ by the military is/ remembered as/ "PETERLOO".

106. Jim Dobbin, MP for Heywood and Middleton, recalled Middleton as the place from which 'Samuel Bamford, one of the great political poets and reformers, led a contingent from Middleton to Manchester, where a number were murdered at Peterloo in 1819': *Hansard*, 30 July 1997.

107. This echoed the comment from John Mack, Labour MP for Newcastle-under-Lyme, in the debate on the Education Bill in 1943 that Chartism and the trade unions were absent from his school history lessons: 'I was not told, what I should have been told, about the slaughter at Peterloo, when Viscount Castlereagh's troops committed an atrocity at Manchester': *Hansard*, 30 July 1943.

108. Joseph O'Neill, *The Manchester Martyrs* (Blackrock, Ireland; 2012) on the history of annual march from the 1970s onwards.

109. Interviewed in *Tribune*, 19 July 1985, Stringer commented: 'There is an absence of Labour history in Manchester and of a recognition that a lot of important events in Labour history happened here. Naming things for symbolic purposes I do think is important'.

110. Wyke and Cocks, *Public sculpture in Greater Manchester*, p. 133. In an interview with the author in 1988 Henry Blachnicki, Manchester City Council, stated that that one of the sites considered for Jackson's sculpture was the space in front of the recently opened G-MEX centre, directly overlooking the actual site of the massacre.

111. *Manchester Evening News*, 7 June 1989; Catharine Rew, 'The Pump House People's History Museum', *Manchester Region History Review*, 14 (2000), pp. 124–8.gtf

112. National Heritage Select Committee: *Our heritage: preserving it, prospering from it.* [1993–4 HC 139, i to vi]. Evidence given in Jan. 1994.

113. *Guardian*, 17 Aug. 1979, p. 2.

114. E. Vallance, *A radical history of Britain: visionaries, rebels and revolutionaries,*

the men and women who fought for our freedoms (London, 2009), ch. 13.

115. J.C.D. Clark, *English society, 1688–1832: ideology, social structure and political practice during the Ancien Regime* (Cambridge, 1985).

116. D. Donald, *The age of caricature: satirical prints in the age of George III* (New Haven, CT; 1996).

117. Anna Clark, *The struggle for the breeches: gender and the making of the British working class* (London; 1995). Also M.L. Bush, '"Dear Sisters of the Earth": the public voice of Manchester women at the time of Peterloo', *Bulletin of North West Labour History*, 28 (2003), pp. 14–21; and 'The women at Peterloo: the impact of female reform on the Manchester meeting of 16 August 1819', *History*, 89 (2004), pp. 209–32.

118. 'The day before he died, Trevelyan had Macaulay's third chapter read to him. His last words were "Peterloo". The nurse asked: "What about Peterloo, Master?" He replied, "1819," and did not speak again', quoted in John Vincent, 'G.M. Trevelyan's two terrible things', *London Review of Books*, 19 June 1980, p. 5.

119. Bush, *The casualties of Peterloo.*

120. Philip McKeiver, *Peterloo Massacre 1819* (Manchester, 2009); Mark Krantz, *Rise like lions: the history and lessons of the Peterloo Massacre of 1819* (London, 2011).

121. It should be compared with the dramatization of Peterloo in 'An Affair of State' (BBC TV, 7 Aug. 1976).

122. 'The Peterloo Massacre', a modern dress version directed by Mike Harris, was staged in the Upper Campfield Market as part of the City of Drama Festival in Sep. 1994.

123 *Morning Star*, 23 Aug. 2007, p. 8; *Manchester Evening News*, 17 Aug. 2007, p. 24. The inscription on the new plaque reads: 'St Peter's Fields/ The Peterloo Massacre/On 16 August 1819 a peaceful rally/ of 60,000 pro-democracy reformers,/ men, women and children,/ was attacked by armed cavalry/ resulting in 15 deaths and/ over 600 injuries.'

124. See essay by Paul Fitzgerald in this volume.
125. Oct. 2008, flyer.
126. Manchester City Council, 'Report on Public Art', 12 Nov. 2008.
127. *Manchester Manifest. Towards a sense of place: mapping Manchester's histories* (2010), by independent cultural consultants for Manchester City Council and MLA Renaissance North West: vol. 1, p. 7. The cover carried a view of the St Peter's Field site at the present day.
128. Manchester City Council, 'Strategic plan for Manchester city centre, 2009–2012'.
129. In the family vault beneath St Peter's church in 1845, though Birley's burial and subsequent re-burial are almost as lightly researched as those who were killed at St Peter's Field: Walmsley, *Peterloo: the case reopened* (Manchester, 1969), p. 559.
130. *Private Eye*, No. 1317, 29 June–12 July 2012, p. 15.
131. In writing this essay I have found particularly useful the essays in Daniel J. Walkowitz and L.M. Knauer (eds), *Memory and the impact of political transformation in public space* (Durham and London, 2004); and Paul A. Pickering and Alex Tyrell (eds), *Contested sites: commemoration, memorial and popular politics in nineteenth-century Britain* (Aldershot, 2004).
132. *Manchester Evening News*, 16 July 2010, p. 21.
133. There is no study of the presentation of Peterloo in school history texts. It should include a discussion about the mounting of and responses to John Hipkin's play for schoolchildren, *The Massacre of Peterloo* (London, 1968).
134 Parliamentary Business, Scottish Parliament, 5 Sep. 2001: http://www.scottish.parliament.uk/parliamentarybusiness/28862.

**The objects of Peterloo**   *Chris Burgess*

1. G.M. Trevelyan, *British history in the nineteenth century (1782–1901)* (London, 1922), p. 190.
2. D. Donald, 'The power of print: graphic images of Peterloo', *Manchester Region History Review*, 3 (1989), p. 21.
3. R. Poole, 'The March to Peterloo: Politics and Festivity in Late Georgian England', *Past and Present*, 192 (2006), pp. 109–15.
4. Anonymous, 'Peterloo Artefacts', *Manchester Region History Review*, 3 (1989), p. 91.
5. *The trial of Henry Hunt and others* (Manchester, 1820), p. 53.
6. T. Swindells, *Manchester Streets and Manchester Men* (Manchester, 1907), p. 23.
7. See for example the temporary museum of the Tiananmen Square Massacre in Hong Kong, 'Tiananmen Square Massacre Relics Bring Back Powerful Memories': http://ntdtv.org/en/news/china/2013-05-14/tiananmen-square-massacre-relics-bring-back-powerful-memories.html (accessed 17 May 2013).
8. F.A. Bruton (ed.), *Three accounts of Peterloo* (Manchester, 1919), p. 76.
9. With thanks to Dr Miles Lambert, Senior Curator, Gallery of Costume, for information about the dress.
10. 'Peterloo Artefacts', p. 93.
11. Thanks to Tim Millett for passing on information about this discovery. See www.historicmedals.com.
12. See J. Vernon, *Politics and the people* (Cambridge, 1993), p. 109. See also http://www.arts.manchester.ac.uk/subjectareas/history/research/manchesterpapers/files/fileuploadmax10mb,125123,en.pdf, p. 13 (accessed 17 May 2013).

## The Middleton Peterloo banner      *Robert Poole*

1. Samuel Bamford, *Passages in the life of a radical* (Manchester, 1839–42), ed. W.H. Chaloner (London, 1967), book 1, ch. 33.
2. *The Times*, 19 Aug. 1819.
3. *The trial of Henry Hunt and others* (Manchester, 1820), p. 106. Bamford and Dyson had colluded over their evidence beforehand.
4. On this, see R. Poole, 'The march to Peterloo: politics and festivity in late Georgian England', *Past and Present*, 192 (2006).
5. The National Archives (hereafter TNA), Home Office Papers (hereafter HO), HO42/192 f. 73–5, Jas Garnett Manchester to HO, 16 Aug. 1819; Bamford, *Passages in the life of a radical*, book 1, ch. 30.
6. Bamford, *Passages in the life of a radical*, book 1, ch. 36.
7. Rochdale Museum Service Middleton banner file Accession no. 2211, notes; *Middleton Guardian*, 16 Nov. 1979; Harry Johnson, 'The Middleton Peterloo banner: a missing link?', *Middleton Memories* (Middleton, 2011); personal communication. Family history research identified a possible candidate: Mary, afterwards Mather, born in 1806, who would have been thirteen at the time of Peterloo.
8. TNA, HO42/198 fol. 683, Information of Joseph Fletcher of Blakeley, 9 Nov 1819.
9. Bamford, *Passages in the life of a radical*, book 1, ch. 30.
10. Bamford, *Passages in the life of a radical*, book 2, ch. 37.
11. *Oldham Evening Chronicle*, 29 Sep. 1884.
12. Sim Schofield and William Trevor, 'Introduction' to Ben Brierley, *Failsworth: My Native Village. With Incidents of the Struggles of its Early Reformers* (Oldham, 1884), pp. 3–4.
13. F.A. Bruton, *Three Accounts of Peterloo* (Manchester 1921), App. A, pp. 75–6.
14. Bruton, *Three Accounts*.
15. Librarian to J.H. Dawson, Middleton Liberal Club, 8 May 1937, in banner provenance file, Rochdale Arts and Heritage Store.
16. Johnson, 'The Middleton Peterloo Banner'; Morris Garratt, 'The Peterloo banner: a short history', in Rochdale Arts and Heritage file on the banner, item 2211; *Middleton Guardian*, 16 Nov. 1979; personal communication from Harry Johnson. The generations add up. Harry Johnson at the time of writing is in his eighties, and his father's generation fought in the First World War: his father was one of seven children, two of whom died in it. It was perfectly feasible for a great uncle to have married someone whose mother was a young woman in 1819. The dating of the conversation to 1975 seems likely as an estimate had been prepared for conservation work on the banner that year. The removal of the banner from Middleton would have been prompted by the local government reorganisation of 1974 which had placed Middleton under Rochdale.
17. 'North West Museums and Galleries Textile Conservation Unit report 1978–212: Rochdale Museum Peterloo Banner, by Vivian Lochhead, 25 Apr. 1979', in Rochdale Arts and Heritage Middleton Banner file 2211.
18. Letter from NW Museums Service to Bill Johnson, 23 Aug. 1994, in Rochdale banner file 2211; *Middleton Guardian*, 22 Aug. 1996; information from Bill Johnson, 2012. In 2009, inspired by a public talk about Peterloo, Bill Johnson repainted the rusting blue heritage plaque marking the site of the Middleton Peterloo rally. He aroused the interest of a passing policeman, who complimented him on a good job and took a photograph to mark the occasion.
19. D. Walker, report on Middleton banner, and Vivian Lochhead, report on Middleton banner, 20 Dec. 2001, Rochdale Arts and Heritage Middleton banner file 2211.
20. The book of the exhibition, *Shelley's ghost* by Stephen Hebron and Elizabeth C. Denlinger (Oxford, 2010) does not include the banner, which was included for the Grasmere leg of the exhibition only.
21. *The Times*, 19 Aug. 1819.

22. It survives on the Goosnargh Amicable Society banner in Goosnargh parish church, near Preston: Nicholas Mansfield, 'Radical Rhymes and union jacks: a search for evidence of ideologies in the symbolism of nineteenth-century banners', University of Manchester Working Paper in Economic and Social History, 45 (2000), p. 21, at: http://www.humanities.manchester.ac.uk/medialibrary/arts/history/workingpapers/wp_45.pdf.

23. *The trial of Henry Hunt and others*, pp. 128–9; 'The Account of Joseph Healey of Lees', *Black Dwarf*, 29 Sep. 1819.

24. James Epstein, 'Understanding the Cap of Liberty: symbolic practice and social conflict in early nineteenth-century England', *Past and Present*, 122 (1989), reprinted in his *Radical expression* (Oxford, 1994).

25. Mansfield, 'Radical Rhymes'; Nick Mansfield, 'Military radicals and the making of class, 1790–1860', in Catriona Kennedy and Matthew McCormack (eds), *Men of arms: soldiering in Britain and Ireland, 1750–1850* (London, 2012).

26. Mansfield, 'Radical Rhymes'; June Barnes, 'Liberty or Death', *Cumberland and Westmorland Antiquarian and Archaeology Society Transactions*, 84 (1984); E.P. Thompson, *The making of the English working class* (1963; Penguin edn, 1968), p. 660.

**The Poetry of Peterloo**    *John Gardner, Alison Morgan and Robert Poole*

1. For an essay on 'The Poems of Peterloo' by Jim Clayson see *Manchester Region History Review* 3, 1 (1993), pp. 31–8.

**Remembering Peterloo in the twenty-first century**    *Paul Fitzgerald*

1. For images and other material, see the campaign website www.peterloomassacre.org.

2. *Guardian*, 13 Aug. 2007, and subsequent correspondence up to 20 Aug.

# Long reviews

## John Gardner
*Poetry and popular protest: Peterloo, Cato Street and the Queen Caroline Controversy* (Basingstoke, 2011). 264pp. ISBN: 9780230280717.

John Gardner's book provides a detailed reading of a range of literary, and to a more limited extent, graphic responses to the three political events cited in the book's title, events that were acted out in the years between 1819 and 1821. He is concerned to establish that these events were known and knowable in the minds of the mass of the population as 'narratives', which were thus available to be retold in various literary forms aimed at complex cross-class readerships and drawing on both high and vernacular modes of cultural discourse. Gardner sees these years as a time of strange and complicated alliances and formal experimentation that created a 'distinct literary period characterized by the relationship between literature and popular protests that seemed to be leading towards a Revolution' (p. 3). He acknowledges that there has been a great deal of recent scholarship on separate elements of his overall discussion. The Hone/Cruikshank collaborative pamphlets, for example, have provided commentators from Edgell Rickword through to Marcus Wood and Kyle Grimes's 'William Hone Biotext' website with an endlessly fascinating negotiation between the visual and the verbal, between humour and outrage, and between the vernacular and the genteel to deconstruct and explain. But Gardner seeks to elaborate on these available discussions in a number of ways, principally by challenging the notion that well known poets were forced to occupy a disengaged space in order to maintain their creative energy and freedom to write what they wanted, and that their writing consequently was a response to, rather than an engagement in, political activism. Instead Gardner seeks to make a case for poetry as a crucial political force, indeed 'the most effective cross-class disseminator of ideas' due to its potential for cheap broadside production [...] subtlety, compression, memory and democratic transmission' (p. 3).

To make this case, Gardner constructs networks of interconnected publications and dialogues between volume publications aimed at sophisticated readers and more vernacular broadside and pamphlets for each of his chosen topics, prefacing each discussion with a brief but pointed summary of the political context and sequence of events that formed (to use his preferred term) the 'narrative' which became widely available for contestation and re-writing by a wide variety of interested authors and graphic artists. Gardner's sense of the cultural and commercial structures of interconnectedness and response allow for important re-evaluations of significant figures and their work. Samuel Bamford's radical early career is expounded in order to challenge his later more spectatorly accounts of his engagement with the political events around Peterloo, for which he was an important literary witness. Shelley's interest in newspaper, magazine and broadside verse, and the extent to which his well known political poetry addressed the interests of readers of such poetry, is firmly established. Alison Morgan's recent Salford University PhD has both underlined and extended this analysis of the extent to which Shelley was caught up in talking to and with the poetry and doggerel published outside volume form. Byron's play *Marino Faliero* is read by Gardner in biographical as well as political terms as a form of peace offering to his friend John Cam Hobhouse, and Shelley's *Swellfoot the Tyrant* is located within a broader literary debate about how support for Queen Caroline might be regarded as part of a programme for revolutionary change by bringing down the monarchy. All these close textual readings, and many others, do succeed in building a model of the complex discourses that literary political radicalism constructed in these few years, and the ways in which literary levels and audiences were being elided into wider discussions that undermined conventional genres and modes of address.

Gardner's conclusion is a cautious one, rightly given that the radical literary vivacity and energy of the years between 1819 and 1821 seemed to disperse rapidly thereafter. He sees a loss of direct political engagement in the literature produced after 1821, but points to a 'new kind of literature that co-opted much of what the radicals had discovered, but was not directly political, and still functioned powerfully to dissolve the differences between elite and plebeian cultures' (p. 222). Gardner cites Pierce Egan's illustrated serialized novel *Life in London* (1821) as evidence for a transmuted but nonetheless significant tradition of literary forms that negotiated between demotic and genteel. There is a slight sense of disappointment here over the loss of radical energy here, a feeling shared. This

may well undersell the legacy of the kind of activist literature that Gardner has elucidated so carefully, a legacy which John Marriott has anthologized and discussed so well in his six volume collection *Unknown London* (2000). Marriott suggests that it is the new genres of illustrated urban investigation (including urban theatrical melodrama) that seek to resist a loss of socio-political energy among a mass reading public. If Gardner's conclusions suggest a somewhat underwhelming outcome for the radical voices of the years between 1819 and 1821, nonetheless his careful and well contextualized discussions of literary works within their immediate historical 'narratives' continues to suggest the complexity and interconnectedness that inform the literature of political activism in the early nineteenth century.

*Brian Maidment*
*Liverpool John Moores University*

## Alan Shelston
*Brief lives: Elizabeth Gaskell* (London, 2010). Pb. 101pp.

This new life of the Victorian novelist Elizabeth Gaskell (1811–65), who lived and worked in Manchester for most of her married life, is a welcome addition to Hesperus Press's series of short biographies of major writers (the press also publishes some of Gaskell's lesser-known shorter fiction, such as *Lois the Witch*). Alan Shelston, President of The Gaskell Society and a well-known authority on the author, draws on his editing experience of both Gaskell's fiction and her letters to provide a fascinating insight into a contradictory figure who has always proved a conundrum to biographers. A married woman who, unlike many of her contemporaries such as the Brontës, George Eliot and Christina Rossetti, managed to combine raising four daughters, a lust for travel and a humanitarian drive with the steady production of novels, stories and articles, was certainly unusual within mid-Victorian culture. This lively account of her life, her writing and her literary legacy will be appealing to both Gaskell fans and to those curious about the figure behind *Cranford* and *North and South*.

Shelston makes excellent use of material

from Gaskell's letters here, reminding us that her talent for letter-writing means that she joins the group of writers 'whose correspondence can be said to equate in interest to their works' (p. 19). Her spirited views on a range of subjects from shopping for pantaloons to more serious questions of courtship and marriage are well represented, helping to bring alive the busy woman behind the novels. Letters to her family, friends and publishers are revealing of the way in which she developed as a writer and a woman. Some of this correspondence would have been unavailable to Jenny Uglow when she published the standard biography of Gaskell in 1993, which therefore allows Shelston to offer new insights into the author. Her reactions to the death of her infant son Willie, which inspired her writing of *Mary Barton*, and her interactions with other public figures such as Charlotte Brontë, Florence Nightingale and Charles Dickens, editor of *Household Words* and *All the Year Round*, the periodicals in which many of her stories appeared, forced her to reassess her own views on the supernatural, marriage, war, and women's work, and help to place her and her writing in the cultural context. Whilst the scarcity of references in this series is sometimes a bit frustrating for scholars, students of history and literature, as well as general readers, will particularly benefit from the brevity and clarity of this life, which is an excellent general introduction to the author.

The chapter on 'Writing and Recognition', which deals with the writing of Gaskell's first industrial novel *Mary Barton* and its links to stories set in Manchester such as 'Lizzie Leigh', clearly sets out the impact of the author's work on the literary marketplace and the reviewers' responses to a tale which dared to tackle the north/south divide, as well as to inspire sympathy for the poor. Shelston is right to emphasize that this was not to be the only occasion on which 'she would find herself at odds with what was expected of a minister's wife' (p. 39), a strand he returns to in the following chapter about her rise to fame. Surprisingly, *North and South*, her other industrial novel, considered by many to be her most accomplished work, is covered fairly quickly, though this is perhaps to leave more space to discuss other texts. There is more material on her biography of Charlotte Brontë, and her relationship with her fellow author, which may be more appealing to the general reader. As well as offering insights into her novels, Shelston is careful to incorporate some discussion of her stories, plus a full list of the periodicals in which they appeared, in line with recent developments in Gaskell criticism and renewed interest in short fiction. Her Gothic tales, some of which appeared in Dickens's journals and have recently been collected together in a new edition, are now attracting much more attention, showing her interest in the sensational and the paranormal. As Shelston argues, 'despite her prolific output she rarely repeated herself in her writing and was always prepared to explore new possibilities' (p. 78). The study also refers to recent adaptations of Gaskell's work, such as the successful TV series of *Wives and Daughters* (1999) and *Cranford* (2008–9), which have helped to produce the legacy of Mrs Gaskell. Whilst the rather sheltered, nostalgic vision of Knutsford life in the early nineteenth century recreated as Cranford may remain her most popular and best-loved story, this study reinforces the broad range of her achievements, as a writer who was not afraid to tackle contentious subjects such as the sanitary conditions of the poor, the position of the unmarried mother, witchcraft and the supernatural.

*Emma Liggins*
*Manchester Metropolitan University*

**Matthew Yeo**

*The acquisition of books by Chetham's Library, 1655–1700* (Leiden and Boston, 2011). xx+263pp. ISBN13: 9789004206656.

Manchester's, perhaps England's, most attractive library can be justly proud of the 'Designation Status' recently bestowed on it by the Museums, Libraries and Archives Council: recognition of an importance not just national, but international. As Matthew Yeo shows in his interesting and detailed study of its early acquisitioning and the wider implications of that for the burgeoning field(s) of book history, Chetham's Library has one of the best early modern collections of printed materials in the world. By the late seventeenth-century, lettered Mancunians could enjoy a more comprehensive scholarly resource than most of the nation's private libraries, most university college libraries included. Its riches, though, seem to have transcended the needs of any immediate local readership in areas such as natural philosophy – where, Yeo highlights, strength in holdings of contemporary experimental works was marked. (Small wonder that John Dalton was later drawn to Manchester.) Crucial here was its founder's 'future-oriented' philanthropy. Enviable three centuries later in a climate which finds another great Manchester library planning a draconian programme of de-acquisitioning, Humphrey Chetham's endowment resulted not only in the formation of a 'Great Library' from scratch, but the continuing accumulation of materials intended for future, not just current, readers: 'a publick Library for ever'.

Yeo gives Chetham due notice, but the first half of his book is more concerned with the subsequent role played in the Library's history by his trustees and their circle – above all the Calvinist preacher Richard Johnson, and to a lesser extent the warden of the Collegiate Church, Nicholas Stratford – especially the likely bearing of religio-political outlook on early acquisition policy. For it was the trustees, not the librarian, who were responsible for purchasing books. They engaged a key contact of Johnson's, London bookseller Robert Littlebury, to supply the vast majority during this period. Yeo is now *the* authority on Littlebury: the chapter on his business relations with the trustees, activities as a book importer and small-scale publisher, and arrangements for delivery to Manchester, is particularly well researched. Littlebury's connections with the 'Latin' (i.e. continental) book trade are fundamental to one of Yeo's broader contentions: that acquisitions made by Chetham's and comparable institutions must be viewed in a pan-European, not merely English, context. In contrast to a standard livery-centred model of bookselling, Littlebury's interaction with Chetham's shows the significance of second-hand dealing in the period too, and Yeo makes a convincing case for the major importance of that area of the book trade, one too long neglected by historians.

The book's second half is devoted largely to surveying the Library's acquisitions in three chapters treating theology; classics, history and law; and medicine and natural philosophy books respectively – broad and blending subject categories. While classics, history and law titles (some thousand odd) were easily outnumbered by the theological material that constituted over half of the purchases in the period, Yeo shows that outlay on them was relatively greater. Discussing classics titles, he demonstrates the trustees' keenness to acquire the best editions available, the most famous – and expensive – being a set of Plato's works formerly owned by Ben Jonson. (Here is a rare reference to a figure in the canon of English literature – a tangential one though, for the almost complete absence of English literature in the Library's holdings at this

time is striking, albeit more so from a twenty-first-century perspective than a seventeenth-century one.) Considering the wide-ranging stock of theology and history, he suggests ways in which acquisitioning stemmed from an eirenic, ecumenical agenda: the formation of a post-Civil War Anglican identity. (Chetham's extensive holdings on the Civil War and popery crises were not acquired during the seventeenth century.) Hence, for example, the book's argument that desire to justify episcopal authority underlay the building of a significant patristics collection. Acquisitioning of legal books is contrasted with that of theological ones. They were received in two main deliveries in 1665 and 1689, instead of being bought continuously over the period, and Yeo argues that this probably reflected canny shifting of unprofitable, outdated stock more than the needs of any regional legal community, all part of his wider argument about the place of second-hand dealing.

Yeo's research was undertaken while he was the Library's first AHRC collaborative doctoral student. (*MRHR* readers may recall the useful 'progress report' on his work and the new Chetham's OPAC he wrote for this journal in 2008.) The book under review is a revision of his resulting 2009 Manchester University dissertation. In places I felt that a longer interval between it and print publication could have been beneficial, not least for ironing out a fair bit of repetition and dissertation-type signposting. Fuller editorial checking should have resulted in correction of not just a quantity of typos but also some slips all the more unfortunate for occurring in a bibliographical study. For example, in a section about Chetham's reception of recently published 'scientific' titles, John Wilkins's 1668 *Essay Towards a Real Character and Philosophical Language* is cited as 'Essay Towards a Real Character of Language'. (Even allowing for a seventeenth-century broadness in the omitted 'philosophical', 'scientific' seems an uncomfortable categorization of an important text of theoretical universal language planning.) Later in the same paragraph, referring to the French astronomer Ismael Boulliau – here misspelled 'Bouillau' – we are told that his *Opus Novum ad Arithmeticam Infinitorum* was delivered to Chetham's in the year of its publication. But the *Opus Novum* was published in 1682, the Library acquiring it two years later. A quibble perhaps, but it matters because it slightly undermines a point Yeo is making about time between publication and acquisition; confusion has presumably crept in with Jacques Boileau's far from scientific *Historia Confessionis Auricularis*, published in 1684 and accessed by the Library that year. More generally, the quality of the illustrations is on the low side for a book of this expense. Such quibbles aside, though, I learned much from Yeo's study, which seems likely to be regularly drawn on by historians of Manchester, of books and of libraries in years to come.

*Timothy Underhill*
*University of Cambridge*

## David Walsh

*Making angels in marble: the Conservatives, the early industrial working class and attempts at political incorporation* (London, 2012). 268pp. ISBN: 9780957000506.

David Walsh seeks to chart two political developments in the first half of the nineteenth century. The first development is how party politics evolved and organized in northern industrial towns, especially after many boroughs gained representation as a result of the 1832 Reform Act. The second development is the rise of working-class movements for political and social reform. The main focus of the book is how the Conservative party 'incorporated' the 'early industrial working class' into their ranks. The rise of working-class conservatism is an under-studied topic, and Walsh is right to point out its significance in the making of Victorian England. The book does not however always succeed in drawing the different lines of analysis together in a coherent explanation of working-class politics in this period.

Chapter 1 is an extended historiographical discussion of the formation of party in the early nineteenth century, especially the re-emergence of Toryism, which Walsh argued was predominantly influenced by the tenets of Edmund Burke. Chapter 2 charts the development of the 'emergent working class' before the Reform Act. It has a somewhat confusing structure, jumping around between analyses of radicalism, Luddism, Toryism, Jacobitism, back to Luddism, Chartism and then back to the 1820s. Chapters 3 and 4 examine the reorganisation of the Conservative party after 1832, and the party's efforts to organize their new working-class constituents. These two chapters form the backbone of the argument and are well researched using a variety of local archives. Walsh demonstrates how Conservative Associations operated as a network for the region's landed and manufacturing elites. Operative Conservatism became a vital force in party politics in Leeds, Blackburn, and other northern towns. Chapter 5 is a case study of the three electoral boroughs of Lancaster, Chester and Clitheroe. It compares their electorates, voting patterns, and the continuities of influence and corruption after the 1832 Reform Act. In all three towns, the Conservatives were able to adapt to post-1832 politics more successfully than the Liberals. Chapter 6 examines the new boroughs of Blackburn, Manchester, Bolton and Oldham. Operative Conservatism made progress in all these industrial towns, forged in the heat of bitter conflicts over reform and trade unionism. An important feature of the conflict that enabled Conservatism to gain sway was the Tories' alliance with Radicals over factory reform and the new poor law, as well as the Conservative efforts to integrate the working classes into their party structure after 1832.

The central argument of the book about the Conservatives' turn to appeal to the industrial working classes is important and convincing. Walsh does not, however, always support all his assertions or suppositions with sufficient evidence, especially in the sections dealing with the rise of working-class political activity. For instance, he claims: 'In the five or so years after 1831–2, the high level of working-class consciousness began to fragment, never reaching a comparable level of intensity for the next fifty years' (p. 65). Here he appears to be conflating collective action with 'consciousness', and does not effectively interrogate the relationship between class identity, radicalism, and conservative politics. There are some factual or interpretative errors in the analysis which weaken the reader's confidence in his argument. To take just one example, he claims: 'Most if not all the Sunday Schools in Lancashire before 1832 were 'radical' or nonconformist, the Anglican Church did begin [sic] Sunday School for working-class children until the later 1830s' (p. 56). In fact, the Anglican church had educated working-class children in numerous Sunday Schools since the later eighteenth century. Inter-denominational rivalry and suspicion led to conflict over the running of the schools around the turn of the century in Manchester and Stockport, and the legacy of this disagreement were separate denominational schools and the 'Whit Walks' as a demonstration of Anglican strength from 1801.

The book also does not always take account of the new historiography since Walsh wrote his PhD thesis in the late 1980s. The book offers a good account of party politics on the local scale, but the story of the development of the working class is less convincing. Little account is taken of the recent developments in labour history, or the study of plebeian radicalism after Gareth Stedman Jones and the 'linguistic turn' debates of the late 1980s. There is no engagement with, for example, Mark Philp's important idea about how loyalist local elites developed 'vulgar conservatism' among the lower classes in the 1790s. Another missing reference that would add weight to Walsh's thesis is J.J. Sack's argument about the origins of the Conservative party in Pittite Toryism of the 1810s. This is a shame, as Walsh's book has much to offer as a corrective to historians' over-emphasis on plebeian radicalism.

*Katrina Navickas*
*University of Hertfordshire*

## Neil Pye

*The Home Office and the Chartists, 1838–48: Protest and repression in the West Riding of Yorkshire* (Pontypool, 2013). 156pp. ISBN: 9780850366341.

Neil Pye has produced an engaging study of the Home Office's attempts to control and suppress the Chartist movement for parliamentary reform from 1838 to 1848. The book focuses on the West Riding of Yorkshire, but its analysis of how the Home Office, local magistrates and the military dealt with disorder in industrial urban areas is also highly applicable to the Manchester region.

The introduction surveys the main debates among historians about the purposes and structure of Chartism, and notes that there has been very little research into the policing and repression of Chartism since F.C. Mather's *Public order in the age of the Chartists* published in 1959. Pye's book provides a detailed and thorough reappraisal of the policies and actions of both local and national government. Chapter 2 is a useful explanation of the functions of the Home Office and the mechanisms of maintaining law and order. Pye underlines the limitations and restrictions of the central

state, even after the Home Office gained more powers from the 1820s onwards. He argues that defensive magistrates, corrupt lord lieutenants and over-aggressive military hindered the Home Office's attempts to streamline and reform the system of policing.

The following chapters chart the ways in which each successive home secretary dealt with Chartist unrest in the West Riding. Pye's central argument supports Dorothy Thompson and Neville Kirk's interpretation of why Chartism ultimately failed. In their view, Chartism was crushed by the 'hardened' approach of government to the suppression of unrest, especially from 1842 onwards. The impact of new forms of policing and new legislation was more significant than the 'soft' effects of the social reforms of the 1840s that attempted to remove some of the grievances of the working classes. For Pye, the governments' introduction of defensive and detective policing, and the 1839 Rural Constabulary Act and the 184[

Parish Constables Act, provided the framework for a more centralized policing system which ultimately served to defeat Chartism in 1848. Pye nonetheless shows that this was not an inevitable or straightforward process, hindered not least by the different personalities and governing styles of the different home secretaries, and by clashes and mistrust among the Home Office, local magistrates and the military generals. Chartists therefore did not face a unified governing elite, but different and often conflicting groups of authorities. Pye also points to the important effects of the railways and electric telegraph in enabling the Home Office to centralize some of its operations, although again the transformation was not sudden or complete.

Pye gives the reader a vivid sense of the urgent problems of enforcing law and order during the three key periods of unrest, 1838–40, 1842 and 1848. As this is a detailed study of the Home Office records in The National Archives, his approach is somewhat top-down and government-focused, and perhaps could have made more of surviving archives from the local magistracy and Chartists. The book is nonetheless a valuable addition to the history of Chartism and government in the early Victorian period.

*Katrina Navickas*
*University of Hertfordshire*

# Short reviews

## Edited by Chris Makepeace

Livi Michael, *The whispering road* (London, 2005).

*The whispering road* is a vivid and compelling novel for children set in and around Manchester in the 1830s. It takes us inside the street gangs, the poorest lodging houses, the travelling shows and the hospital. The thirteen-year-old central character is adopted as a social experiment by a fictional but plausible philanthropist Sheridan Mosley. It is Mosley who meets Dr James Kay and the weaver-turned-hospital governor John Sanderson, and experiences the thrill of radical politics with the activist printer Abel Heywood who tells him of Peterloo. Schoolteachers, whether of history, literature or drama, will find much they can work with in this brilliantly characterized and gripping story. The content is strong, making it more for secondary than primary age children, but my ten-year-old loved it. It ranks alongside all the classic Manchester novels.

*[this review by Robert Poole, UCLan]*

Gary James, *The Manchester City years* (Halifax, 2012). £25

As Britain's most popular contemporary sporting activity it is not surprising that association football has attracted considerable media attention, not least in the field of publishing where the spectrum of outputs ranges from the scholarly monograph to the populist, relatively lightweight 'autobiographies' of leading players, often produced quite early in their careers. Situated at various points along this continuum lie histories of football clubs, normally written by lifelong supporters, which treat the subject chronologically and are generally uncritical in their reflections. Many such texts may prove useful for supporters' quiz nights and for resolving pub debates but they fail to appeal to a wider readership which might be interested in situating that particular club history within a broader sporting, social and cultural context. Scholars, in particular, are reluctant to engage with this kind of text given the often suspect nature of some of the 'research' presented and the tendency for the perpetuation of myths, legends, 'magic moments' and 'father figures'. None of these criticisms, however, can be levelled at Gary James's book on Manchester City which combines an impressive depth of research with a writing style that keeps it accessible to the wider footballing community.

While adhering to the traditional chronological approach, and not really extending consideration of the topic to the social and political context, the work does take the reader beyond the banal in providing some excellent insights into the world of modern football. The tensions between clubs, the impact of money and the role of the media, including the observation that comments emanating from the club over a player transfer took news precedence over the swearing-in of the first black president of the United States (p. 543), all feature within these pages. Inevitably, the book is most comprehensive in dealing with the history of the club in the post-war period, which makes up two-thirds of the text, and the author draws on a range of primary sources that would be familiar to any historian. Club archives, newspaper and other media reports, are supplemented by an impressive range of quotations gleaned from interviews conducted with key individuals and keen supporters. In synthesizing this material into a logical, descriptive narrative the author demonstrates a rare ability to produce a readable, 'flowing' text and, even though James notes early on in the work that he expects many readers to dip in and out of the book, the serious, dedicated reader is seamlessly taken through the relevant events. Throughout the work the numerous and well-chosen illustrations add significant value and it is here, perhaps, that books like this, which focus on public engagement with the topic, tend to make more of an impact than the many scholarly monographs that might themselves have been enhanced with some judicious use of pictures and figures.

Although the range of sources available to the author for the periods before 1939 are obviously much more restricted it is this early section of the work that tends to be much more scholarly in nature, both in terms of the presentation of material and the quality of the research needed to illuminate the club's story. In addition, James does in these early stages of the work allow himself to speculate and interpret, rather than merely describe, and this definitely adds to its value. The linking of FA cup success, for example, to an increasing Mancunian identity and a unity of confidence (pp. 100–1) is an interesting concept and one that deserves further consideration, as does the fifty-year period that preceded this event. While finding the relevant sources may be more difficult the author has clearly managed to research some aspects of the Victorian football scene in Manchester and the time is ripe for a much more detailed regional consideration of the sport than is presented here. Nevertheless, the author is to be congratulated on producing a volume in a manner that appeals to such a broad church of footballing readership, ranging from the avid fan to the more serious student of the game's history.

*[this review by Dave Day,*
*Manchester Metropolitan University]*

Chris Makepeace, *Manchester then and now* (Stroud, 2012). Hardback. 95 pp. £12.99. ISBN 9780752468716.

It is now forty years since the publication of the first title in Chris Makepeace's landmark series *Manchester as it was*. This combination of original photographs of Manchester streets and scenes and informative captions proved a winning formula and no one has contributed more to increasing public awareness of the photographic record of Manchester's past than the author of the volume under review here. This latest addition to his extensive portfolio of publications is part of a series by the publisher on British towns and cities contrasting historic photographs with current views of the same locations. It is aimed at the non-specialist and designed to invoke an interest in local history. Historic images are reproduced in sepia regardless of age, although some are as recent as the 1970s. New photographs (by David Brearley) are in colour. The book is attractively produced and reasonably priced although the author has been constrained by the publisher's format and a light editorial hand (proof-reading could have been better). It is a pity space could not be found for suggestions for further reading or a list of relevant archive and online collections. The inclusion of a map or maps would have assisted the reader in the interpretation of some of the scenes and locations (does the publisher realize that Chris has written the excellent text accompaniments to several of the inestimable Godfrey maps of the region?). None of this is a criticism of the author and the book is a useful entry point for those interested in exploring the pictorial record of Manchester's past. If you do not have any Makepeace books on your shelves then start with this one but find out what else he has published too – you won't be disappointed.

*[this review by Alan Kidd]*

S. Forrest and T. Wyke, *Zion 100: a history of a building in Hulme* (Manchester, 2011). Bibliog. Illus. 48pp. £5.

The Zion Institute on Stretford Road in Hulme was one of the few buildings to survive the area's redevelopment in the latter half of the twentieth century. Zion Chapel was built by the Congregational Church in 1841 and became involved in helping the local community and providing facilities for residents. By 1911, the original chapel was unsuitable for the work that was being undertaken so the original building was replaced by the present building. With the redevelopment of Hulme, the congregation declined resulting in a merger with Tatton Street United Reformed Church in 1974. The former church was not demolished, but acquired by Manchester City Council to provide community facilities for the area as well as accommodation where artistic organisations could rehearse. The result has been the creation of a vibrant venue at the centre of regenerated community. The re-use of the building is a good example of what can be done with an old building that was a local landmark and remains so today.

This book traces the history of this church and the work it did during the nineteenth and twentieth centuries and includes a brief history of the development of Hulme so that the church's role can be put in its historical context. What is clear is that the community activities carried on at Zion today are a continuation of the community work that was started back in the nineteenth century, although today it is no longer under the auspices of the church.

It is a well written, well illustrated and informative book that should appeal to all those interested not only in the history of Hulme, especially the more recent history of this district, but also to those interested in the history of religion in the area and the Congregational Church itself.

M. Rose with K. Falconer and J. Holder, *Ancoats: cradle of industrialisation* (Swindon, 2011). Illus. Maps. Bibliog. 98pp. £9.99. ISBN: 9781848020276.

To the east of central Manchester lies the district of Ancoats which began to expand rapidly in the late eighteenth century as industry began to change from water to steam as a means of power for machinery. The use of steam power encouraged industry to move from water-powered sites to areas that were more accessible, where there were good transport facilities and where there were people to work in the mills and factories. During the early nineteenth century, the growth in the size of Ancoats was unremitting so that by the middle of the century it was larger than many independent towns.

As Ancoats was part of Manchester, its history has tended to be overshadowed by that of Manchester yet it is an area that has always attracted attention as shown by the demand for the special issue of the *Manchester Region History Review* devoted to aspects of its history in 1993. This new publication traces the history

of Ancoats and the many aspects of life that went to make it such an important manufacturing and residential area for many thousands of people. The book is well written and very well illustrated not only with photographs, but also with plans and maps of the area. It also brings the story of Ancoats up to the present day with former mills being converted for residential use. This book is a 'must read' for all those interested in the history of Ancoats and the way in which some of the most important industrial buildings in Manchester and the area where those who worked there lived have been preserved for the future.

Friends of Platt Fields Park, *A centenary of Platt Fields Park, Manchester 1910–2010* (Manchester, 2010). 78pp. Illus. £5.

In May 1910 the opening of Platt Fields Park provided the residents of Rusholme and Fallowfield with a large public park where they could walk, relax and engage in sporting activities. The layout of the new park reflected that changes in the way parks were regarded that had taken place in the closing years of the nineteenth century, namely less formal layouts. This well illustrated book was published to mark the centenary of the opening and as well as tracing the history of the site and the fight to prevent the park being developed for residential purposes includes reminiscences of those who used its facilities over the years. This book will be of value to those interested in the history of Rusholme, how people spent their leisure time and in the history and developments of Manchester's parks.

D. Brumhead, *Coal mining in Marple and Mellor* (Marple, 2012). 42pp. Illus. Maps. ISBN 9780954058234.

This new publication outlines the history of coal mining in Marple and Mellor, an industry that has tended to be overlooked in the past although coal mining has been known about on Ludworth Moor, in New Mills and Disley. This well illustrated and very informative book gives details of the various locations where mining has taken place, a grid reference for those who want to try and find the site as well as a summary of the site's history as far as it is available. It is an important addition to the information on the history of Marple and Mellor and should be of interest both to local people and industrial archaeologists.

D. Leitch, *Looking back with Diana Leitch: glimpses of people and places in South Manchester* (6 vols, Didsbury, 2011–12). 32pp per volume. Illus. £2 each vol.

These six slim volumes bring together 65 articles Diana Leitch has written for the *South Manchester Reporter* on a wide range of topics relating to Didsbury and various parts of south Manchester. For example, volume 1 includes articles on Parrs Wood, Warburton Street and the Simons whilst the latest volume includes articles on the Old Parsonage in Didsbury, Didsbury Cricket Club, Longford Park and tithe maps. The articles are slightly longer than those which actually appeared in the paper, full of interesting facts and information, and are written in a very readable manner. Their publication in this format means that they are more widely available than other would have been the case when they appeared in the press. The range of subjects covered should ensure that they have a wide appeal not only in Didsbury, but throughout the whole south Manchester area.

D. Leitch and S. Good, *Didsbury's heritage 3: a self-guided family walking trail around some of East Didsbury's historic places of interest* (Didsbury, n.d.). 16pp. Illus. £1.

This self-guided walk covers East Didsbury, starting at the corner of Didsbury Park and Wilmslow Road and makes it way towards Parrs Wood and Cheadle Bridge. The route is easy to follow and the text is well written and well researched with a lot of interesting information on the area, including an extract of the 1845 tithe map that shows the area as it was 150 years ago. The walk is aimed at both the individual walker and at families and encourages the user

to be observant by looking for specific sites en route. This is a booklet that all residents of the district should have on their shelves and a walk that all should undertake so that they are aware of the history of the village.

P. Giles (comp.), *Celebrating Didsbury: stories and pictures of Didsbury* (Didsbury, 2010). 37pp. Illus. Map. £1.50.

P. Giles (comp.), *Celebrating Didsbury: more stories and pictures of Didsbury* (Didsbury, 2010). 37pp. Illus. Map. £1.50.

These two small booklets contain many interesting short items about different aspects of Didsbury and its history and include a number of personal recollections about life in the area in the twentieth century. The topics covered range from information gleaned from the census, brief histories of buildings and personalities as well as extracts from existing publications. There are photographs and illustrations on most of the pages relating to the subject matter, a feature that enhances the interest of these two publications that brings together information that might otherwise have been lost or be difficult for the average person to discover.

P. Siddons (comp.), *West Didsbury: A walk on the west side* (Didsbury, rev. ed., 2010/11). 32pp. Illus. Map.

Although it is easy to discover information about the centres of towns and villages, it is less easy to do so for areas that lie outside the central core. There are two walks in this publication that takes the reader around West Didsbury, an area that developed in the latter half of the nineteenth century when Palatine Road was constructed and a railway station opened at its junction with Lapwing Lane. Attention is drawn to prominent buildings and houses as well as small details that might easily be overlooked by a visitor wandering around the area without the aid of this publication. The book is well illustrated and there is a clear map showing the route the compiler has followed.

B. Hayes, *Two hundred years of stationary engines in Stockport* (Stoneclough, 2011). 71pp. Illus. Diags. £6. ISBN 9781852161699.

When steam power began to take over from water power as a means of driving machinery, the resultant steam engines were far more complex than the waterwheels that had previously been used. New factories were established to build and maintain these stationary steam engines and later machines powered by gas and electricity. In this book, Bernard Hayes outlines the development of the stationary engines and traces their use by various firms in Stockport. He also traces the history of some of the firms, like Mirrless, who were responsible for the construction of these engines that provided power to drive machines used for manufacturing goods. This book contains a lot of useful and interesting information and is well illustrated with both photographs and diagrams of the steam engines referred to as well as a list of some of the mills and their engines and a helpful glossary that will help those unfamiliar with the vocabulary. This publication will be a useful addition to the material available on the industrial archaeology of Stockport as well as the history of some of the local Stockport firms engaged in manufacturing stationary steam engines.

G. Atkinson (comp.), *Building the Big Ditch: a photographic record of the construction of the Manchester Ship Canal* (Radcliffe, 2012). 48pp. Illus. £4.50. ISBN 9781852161505.

This collection of photographs of the construction of the Manchester Ship Canal were taken by Edward Ward for the Manchester Ship Canal Company and now form part of the Frank Mullineux collection. Around 59 photographs have been selected to show construction at different points a long the canal between Manchester and Eastham and show all aspects of the work ranging from cuttings to machinery. Each photograph is accompanied by an informative and interesting caption that provides much useful information written by Glen Atkinson whose detailed research on the canal has brought each picture alive. This is an important addition to the material that is available on the Ship Canal as these illustrations do not appear to have been reproduced before and throws additional light onto the conditions under which the navvies worked at the time.

S. Richardson and R. Weston, *Sarah Newton 1787–1850: a Stockport girl makes good* (New Mills, 2009). 36pp. Illus.

This booklet traces the history of the life of the daughter of a Stockport family who were involved with the development of textile machinery at the end of the eighteenth century and who were persuaded to travel to France to establish a factory manufacturing carding machinery. It traces the history of the family in France and in particular the life of Sarah who was married to a leading French general who was killed just before Waterloo. After her remarriage, she became accepted as a member of French society in the first half of the nineteenth century. Her story provides an interesting sidelight on French society at the time whilst at the same time indicating that there were those who were prepared to work abroad, even in a country undergoing dramatic changes and at war with their country of birth.

R.M. Bryant, *Some deeds of Bugsworth and Furness Vale* (New Mills, 2012). 52pp. Illus. Maps.

This latest volume in the New Mills History Society series consists of summaries of documents purchased by the Society in 1983 relating to Bugsworth and Furness Vale although there are references to other places in the New Mills area. This publication makes it possible for those researching the area and who are not skilled in deciphering such documents to discover whether there is anything of relevance in these important records. This publication is an important addition to the printed material available on this part of north Derbyshire and should be of interest to those interested not only in the history of the area, but also some of those who lived there.

S. Good and D. Leitch, *Didsbury Church of England Primary School 1612–2012* (Didsbury, 2nd ed., 2011). 29pp. Biblog. Illus.

This booklet traces the history of the school from the foundation of the first place of education in the village by Sir Nicholas Mosley to the present day. Drawing on school log books as well as memories of former pupils, this book provides an interesting insight into primary education in Didsbury from the middle of the nineteenth century to the present day. It gives the reader an insight not only into the history of primary education in the district, especially in the days before council schools were established, but also into the history of Didsbury itself, supplementing that which is available in existing publications on the area. It should also provide encouragement for other schools to think of marking significant dates in their history in a similar way, thus preserving local information and experiences that would otherwise be lost.

T. Hurley, *Beggars and builders: my story of Gorton Monastery* (Manchester, n.d.). 165pp. Illus. £6.99. ISBN: 9780957148406.

This book combines the history of this iconic building in Gorton with an account of its rescue from oblivion and subsequent restoration from the point of view of the author who was closely involved with its rescue and restoration. Although a history of the church was published in 1961 to mark its centenary, this book brings the story up to date by focusing on what happened after its closure, vandalism and the attempts to find a suitable new use for the building which culminated in the building's restoration as a focal point of the community. The story that Hurley relates should be inspirational to all those seeking to save important buildings from destruction and a reminder to Mancunians and residents of Gorton of the architectural gem in their midst.

J. Crummett, *Abel Buckley Wimpenny: the life and times of a nineteenth-century Hayfield mill manager, political activist and social reformer 1844–1905* (Hayfield, rev. ed., 2010). 99pp. Illus. Bibliog. £5+p&p.

This biographical account of the life of Abel Wimpenny not only traces the life of this prominent resident of Hayfield, but also throws light on a wide range of matters relating to the events and life in the village itself. This is an interesting and informative publication that is more than just a biography, it is a history of aspects of life in Hayfield in the latter half of the nineteenth century that will probably not be covered in the more traditional histories of the community.

D. Brumhead, *The Ollerset Waterworks 1831–1907* (New Mills, 2011). 28pp. Illus. Maps. Diags. Bibliog.

Fresh, clean water is essential for the health of any community, but in the first half of the nineteenth century, few communities had such a luxury. Many of the expanding towns relied on wells, water butts and drawing water from heavily polluted rivers and streams. In New Mills, a local estate owner obtained permission to build a reservoir to supply his properties and part of the town with water. This book is the story of this water supply and the problems encountered by the local sanitary authority in trying to ensure its quality and eventually take it over as a local government enterprise. The book is well researched and makes interesting reading about the problems faced by small authorities in trying to ensure that there residents had the best supplies possible.

M. Nevell and T. Wyke (eds), *Bridgewater 250: the archaeology of the world's first industrial canal* (Manchester, 2012). 128pp. Illus. Diags. Maps. Bibliog. £10. ISBN: 9780956594716.

2011 saw the 250th anniversary of the opening of the first section of the Bridgewater Canal as far as Stretford. It was to be three years later before it reached its ultimate destination, Manchester. Over the years, there have been a number of publications that trace the history of this important waterway and those involved with its construction. However, until the publication of this book, there had been no studies of the archaeology of the canal and its remains.

The anniversary was marked by a conference in Worsley that included contributions from those who have contributed articles to this well-illustrated publication. Amongst the topics covered by this book are the underground canals at Worsley, the archaeology of the canal at Castlefield and at Worsley, the aqueducts at Barton, the Grocer's Warehouse as well as articles on researching the archaeology of the canal and its beginning. There is also an article that includes a trail around Worsley pointing out areas of interest.

This publication is an important addition to the history of the canal and the information that is available on it. It should appeal to those who cruise the canal who want to be aware of what they are seeing as they travel along it as well as industrial archaeologists and local historians for whom the canal was an important step in the development of bulk transport and eventually industry in Manchester and the surrounding area.

D. Vale, D. George and T. Wright (eds), *The Mersey & Irwell Navigation* (Manchester, rev. ed., 2012). 119pp. Map. Illus. Bibliog. £5.

The Mersey & Irwell Navigation resulted from improvements made to the rivers Mersey and Irwell in the early eighteenth century in order to try and improve the transport of goods between Manchester and Liverpool. During the next 50 years, further improvements were made and implemented whilst other ideas failed to win support and were abandoned. David Vale's book on the Mersey Irwell Navigation is the first publication on this subject since Hayman's book in 1981, during which time research has resulted in additional information being discovered and existing material re-interpreted in the light of these finds. Vale traces the history of the waterway and places it into its historical context with other transport developments in the eighteenth and nineteenth centuries. This revised edition will be of interest to all those interested in transport between Manchester and Liverpool at this critical time in the growth of industry in the region.

R.A. Wright, *Aspects of the Manchester and Salford Junction Canal* (Manchester, 2012). 17pp. Illus.

This publication outlines the history of this canal that was constructed in the mid 1830s in an attempt to reduce the road traffic crossing Manchester between the canal networks separated by the River Irwell. As a functioning canal, it had a short life with a section of it being abandoned in the early 1870s when Central Station was built. Although there have been other publications that refer to this canal, this booklet adds additional information about the canal and its operation during its short history.

A. Simpson, *The history of Chorlton-cum-Hardy* (Stroud, 2012). 288pp. Illus. Maps. Plans. Bibliog. £18.99. ISBN 9780752489667.

Chorlton-cum-Hardy lies on the south-west side of Manchester and was originally a separate township until it became part of Withington Local Board of Health, later Withington Urban District Council, finally being incorporated into Manchester in 1904. Although there have been several books on the history of Chorlton in the past, this is the first detailed history of the district to be written.

Simpson takes as his starting point the tithe map of 1847 using the map as the basis for his history of Chorlton. This is a very interesting way of looking at the history of the community as the information contained in the tithe map provides a very useful starting point for his examination of the many and varied aspects of the area's history. Amongst the topics Simpson examines are subjects such as religion, children, work, crime as well as parliamentary and local politics as well as a walk around Chorlton using the tithe map as a starting point. There are, however, areas that appear to have been overlooked such as the arrival of the railway and its effect on the growth of Chorlton in the last quarter of the nineteenth century. Likewise, there is little or no reference to Chorlton as part of the Withington Local Board or UDC and the more recent history of the district which detracts somewhat from the usefulness of the book.

It would have been helpful to have included a map of the district, say around 1900, so that the places referred to could be places in their geographical context. Although some readers may be able to locate some of the placed, there will be those who might find it difficult to place some of the locations mentioned in the book. These are minor criticisms of a book that does much to provide a detailed and well illustrated history of Chorlton-cum-Hardy and may well provide a template for other histories of Manchester's districts and in complete contrast to the usual approach of pictures with captions of a limited size. Unfortunately, the only maps in the book are of the tithe map. It would have been useful to have had a more recent map showing such things as the railway.

# Article abstracts and keywords

## John Gardner
### *William Hone's Peterloo*

William Hone, a London-based reforming pamphleteer who worked in collaboration with the illustrator George Cruikshank, produced four main publications that relate to the government-sanctioned killings at St. Peter's Field on 16 August 1819. His three best-selling and most influential responses to Peterloo: *The Political House that Jack Built*, *The Man in the Moon* and *A Slap at Slop*, had combined sales of around 250,000 copies, and were read by the full spectrum of society, from Cabinet ministers to soldiers. However he also produced another less well-known poem that purports to be by Lord Byron, *Don Juan Canto the Third*. A function of Hone's verse squibs and Cruikshank's cuts was to educate the public. The poetry and the illustration could exist independently, but together each enhanced the significance of the other, and as a young William Makepeace Thackeray noted, helped to educate the 'grinning, good-natured mechanics, who spelt the songs, and spoke them out for the benefit of the company'. Hone's style of pamphlet was so successful that it encouraged his political opponents to ape his productions. Opposing publications, with names such as *The Christian House*, and *The Real or Constitutional House that Jack Built*, attempted to challenge Hone by producing similar pamphlets that also synthesize woodcuts and doggerel, but on the whole they were miserable, humourless failures that attempted to justify the current Tory government. This article will examine Hone's four Peterloo publications in the order that they were released, and in particular how they tried to shape the representation of that event in the minds of the public in the face of opposing publications.

**Keywords:** *Peterloo; William Hone; George Cruikshank; political pamphlets; romantic period radical culture*

## Ruth Mather
### *'These Lancashire women are witches in politics': Female reform societies and the theatre of radicalism, 1819–1820*

This article re-examines the emergence of female reform societies in north-west England in 1819, looking in particular at their use of domestic imagery in addresses and speeches. While this has tended to be dismissed by historians as an attempt to neutralize criticism, I argue that the situation was rather more complicated than this. The words and actions of the women involved should be read in terms of an ongoing contest over language and symbolism with the opposing forces of loyalism, in which the ability to inhabit multiple personas enabled women to play an important role in a carnivalesque subversion of power.

**Keywords:** *gender; domesticity; radicalism; political culture; Peterloo*

## Alison Morgan
### *Starving mothers and murdered children in cultural representations of Peterloo*

Of the fifteen people killed at Peterloo, four were women; of the 654 recorded casualties, 168 were women. These statistics reveal that more than a quarter of all casualties at Peterloo were women, even though they comprised only 12 per cent of those present. This apparent targeting of women by the yeomanry resulted in the widespread use of the motif of mother and child across a range of print media and other cultural artefacts produced in response to Peterloo. Through the exploration of this significant trope, this essay demonstrates how a range of texts and artefacts including ceramics, textiles, songs, poems and prints are inter-related. This connection between texts and artefacts creates a powerful discourse with the repeated use of the trope resulting in a sense of a collective response to these terrible events. This essay begins by outlining the scale and variety of responses to Peterloo that employ the trope of mother and child, firstly in newspaper articles followed by satirical prints and other cultural artefacts and, finally, poetry. It can be shown that this trope, shared across many genres, is crucial to the creation of a shared radical discourse following Peterloo.

**Keywords:** *Peterloo; women; caricature; poetry; radicalism*

## Katrina Navickas
*Lancashire Britishness: Patriotism in the Manchester region during the Napoleonic Wars*

Historians have argued that the Napoleonic Wars were a key period in the formation of British identity. Manchester and its region responded to the threat of French invasion in a distinctive way. This article examines the volunteer regiments and the 1809 jubilee celebrations to argue that the region developed its own sense of Britishness during this period: a Lancashire Britishness. Patriotism was not a simple response to national propaganda. Rather, it was shaped by its particular social, economic and political structures. In the Manchester region, patriotism was composed of three elements: an inchoate mix of civic pride in the textile industry; Church-and-King loyalism and reaction against popular radicalism; and the sectarian Orange movement.

**Keywords:** *patriotism; Napoleonic Wars; loyalism; radicalism; Britishness*

## Frank O'Gorman
*Manchester loyalism in the 1790s*

Manchester has often appeared in historical narratives of the later eighteenth century as a progressive and reformist city, and this is indeed true. Yet we should also consider the strength of more conservative opinion, opposing reform, committed to positive support of the wars against revolutionary France and Napoleon and defending Anglican attitudes and institutions. The conflict between these two political forces dominated Manchester in the 1790s. To investigate the 'loyalist' section of opinion demonstrates a different type of popular politics from that usually depicted, more violent, more traditional and more aggressive. Consideration of the street politics of Manchester during the 1790s reveals much about contemporary political attitudes and methods.

**Keywords:** *loyalism; patriotism; urban history; Manchester*

## Robert Poole
*What don't we know about Peterloo?*

The article offers a survey and analysis of the main evidence for the Peterloo massacre of 1819 in Manchester, focusing on the 300 or so eye-witness accounts collected by the Peterloo Witness Project. The main outlines of Peterloo, once the subject of controversy, are not in doubt: a peaceful rally was attacked without provocation by troops under the command of the magistrates. Accounts by victims and reformers correlate well with those of independent eye-witnesses, while accounts by the agents of the authorities correlate mainly with each other, and have a formulaic quality dictated by Home Office criteria for the evidence needed in court. The article concludes by setting out aspects of Peterloo which remain unexplained, including the high-risk strategy of confrontation adopted by the authorities, the character and consequences of female involvement, and the wider strategy of the reformers: had the rally not been attacked, what would have happened next?

**Keywords:** *Peterloo; radicalism; Manchester; Shelley; Chartism*

## Matthew Roberts
*Radical banners from Peterloo to Chartism*

This article explores why banners were used much more heavily by Chartists in the Manchester region than anywhere else in Britain. Two databases have been constructed, which detail inscriptions and images on over 500 banners (the most comprehensive study of its kind to date), the findings of which suggest that the symbolic stakes were higher in the Manchester region there than was the case elsewhere. The article suggests that one of the main reasons why the stakes were higher was the enduring legacy of the Peterloo massacre, a legacy that shaped both Chartist understandings about the public sphere and the way in which the state responded to Chartism. Yet, as the article goes on to show, neither Chartism nor the state's response to it was static. While early Chartism was much more of an outdoors and festive movement, from

1842 Chartism moved indoors and sought to distance itself from the effusive but transient political culture of the mass platform, a move that fuelled and was fuelled by the resurgence of a long-standing iconophobic current within radicalism. The result was that banners were much less prominent, and their use much more circumscribed, in late Chartism.

**Keywords:** *radicalism; visual and material culture; mass platform*

## Terry Wyke
*Remembering the Manchester Massacre*

The article discusses the commemoration and memorialization of the Peterloo massacre from 1819 to the present day. Its focus is principally on Manchester and on particular moments in the diverse and disparate processes of commemoration. It draws attention to the changing perception and contested nature of the massacre over time, helping to account for the absence of any significant memorial on the massacre site. It raises questions of the processes through which memories are transformed into memorials at a time when there is an campaign to erect an appropriate and publicly accessible monument, close to the site of the massacre. Attention is drawn to the more successful commemoration of events such as the Tolpuddle Martyrs and the Scottish rising of 1820. It concludes that more attention needs to be paid by historians of Peterloo to the politics of the culture of commemoration, especially in understanding the meaning of the massacre in the formation of political identities since 1819.

**Keywords:** *Peterloo massacre; commemoration; collective memory; political identities; memorialization; Manchester; Henry Hunt*

# Contributors' notes

**Chris Burgess** is the Collections Access Officer at Salford's Working Class Movement Library, and Manchester's People's History Museum. He works on the 'Unlocking Ideas' project, which promotes access to the collections of both institutions.

**Paul Fitzgerald,** aka 'Polyp' the political cartoonist, is author of two graphic novels *Speechless: world history without words* (New Internationalist, 2009) and *The co-operative revolution* (New Internationalist, 2013). He is chair of the Peterloo Memorial Campaign.

**John Gardner** is a principal lecturer in English literature at Anglia Ruskin University. He is author of *Poetry and popular protest: Peterloo, Cato Street, and the Queen Caroline Controversy* (Palgrave, 2011).

**Ruth Mather** is a PhD student in the History Department and the Centre for Studies of Home at Queen Mary, University of London. Her research explores the roles of home and family in radical political culture in late Georgian England.

**Alison Morgan** is a visiting lecturer at the University of Salford where, in 2012, she completed her PhD, 'Shelley and Peterloo: radical, nationalist and balladeer'.

**Frank O'Gorman** taught for thirty-six years at the University of Manchester. He is the author of a number of works on British history in the eighteenth century and is at present working on a second edition of one of them, *The Long Eighteenth Century*, originally published in 1997.

**Robert Poole** is Guild Fellow in History at UCLan. He has written several articles on Peterloo and Samuel Bamford, and his most recent book is *The Wonderful Discovery of Witches in the County of Lancaster* (Carnegie, 2011). See also http://uclan.academia.edu/RobertPoole.

**Matthew Roberts** is a senior lecturer in Modern British History at Sheffield Hallam University. He works on popular politics, protest, and the visual and material culture of politics in nineteenth-century Britain.

**Terry Wyke** teaches social and economic history at Manchester Metropolitan University.

# Manchester Region History Review

### Editors
Melanie Tebbutt     Craig Horner     John F. Wilson

### Editorial board
Morris Garratt (Libraries)    John V. Pickstone
Clare Hartwell                Paula Moorhouse
Karen Hunt                    Catharine Rew (Museums)
Alan Kidd                     Mike Rose
Neville Kirk                  Bill Williams
Brian Maidment                Terry Wyke
Chris Makepeace (Short Reviews)

### Book Reviews editor
Fiona Cosson (f.cosson@mmu.ac.uk)

## Corresponding members
Robert Glen, University of New Haven, US
Kazuhiko Kondo, University of Tokyo, Japan

## Correspondence
The Editors
Manchester Region History Review
Manchester Centre for Regional History
Manchester Metropolitan University
Geoffrey Manton Building
Rosamond Street West
Manchester M15 6LL
United Kingdom
http://www.mcrh.mmu.ac.uk

For full details of individual and institutional
subscription rates for the UK and overseas,
refer to:
http://www.hssr.mmu.ac.uk/mcrh/mrhr/

## Illustrations
We are grateful to the British Museum;
Manchester Archives and Local Studies;
Chetham's Library; Manchester City Art
Gallery; Kirklees Museums and Galleries; John
Ryland's Library; Textile Conservation Studio
at the People's History Museum, Manchester;
Oldham Local Studies; Local Studies, Arts
& Heritage Service, Link4Life; Bill Johnson;
Terry Wyke; Jeff Cowton/Wordsworth Trust;
Dave McGealy; Nick Mansfield; Manchester
International Festival; and Paul Fitzgerald for
permission in reproducing illustrations.
Every effort has been made to contact the
copyright holders but if any have been
inadvertently overlooked, the editors will be
pleased to make the necessary arrangements at
the first opportunity.

## Notes for contributors
If you would like to contribute to this journal,
please contact the editors before submitting
copy. Authors should consult: http://www.hssr.
mmu.ac.uk/mcrh/mrhr/
Conventional articles should not exceed 8,000
words including footnotes, although they can
be much shorter. We encourage a variety of
contributions and are willing to discuss ideas
and draft articles at an early stage. Intending
contributors to the Libraries, Museums and
Societies sections should consult the editors in
the first instance. Book reviews should be sent
to the Book Reviews editor. All submitted work
should be in Word format.

## Advertisements
For details of advertising rates, please contact
the editors.

## Indexing
Articles appearing in this journal are
abstracted and indexed in: HISTORICAL
ABSTRACTS and AMERICA: HISTORY
AND LIFE.